AF847831

Fiscal Policies in High Debt Euro-Area Countries

Antonella Cavallo · Pietro Dallari
Antonio Ribba

Fiscal Policies in High Debt Euro-Area Countries

Springer

Antonella Cavallo
Department of Economics
University of Modena and Reggio Emilia
Modena
Italy

Antonio Ribba
Department of Economics
University of Modena and Reggio Emilia
Modena
Italy

Pietro Dallari
Fiscal Affairs Department
International Monetary Fund
Washington, DC
USA

ISBN 978-3-319-70268-1 ISBN 978-3-319-70269-8 (eBook)
https://doi.org/10.1007/978-3-319-70269-8

Library of Congress Control Number: 2017957207

© Springer International Publishing AG 2018
This work is subject to copyright. All rights are reserved by the Publisher, whether the whole or part of the material is concerned, specifically the rights of translation, reprinting, reuse of illustrations, recitation, broadcasting, reproduction on microfilms or in any other physical way, and transmission or information storage and retrieval, electronic adaptation, computer software, or by similar or dissimilar methodology now known or hereafter developed.
The use of general descriptive names, registered names, trademarks, service marks, etc. in this publication does not imply, even in the absence of a specific statement, that such names are exempt from the relevant protective laws and regulations and therefore free for general use.
The publisher, the authors and the editors are safe to assume that the advice and information in this book are believed to be true and accurate at the date of publication. Neither the publisher nor the authors or the editors give a warranty, express or implied, with respect to the material contained herein or for any errors or omissions that may have been made. The publisher remains neutral with regard to jurisdictional claims in published maps and institutional affiliations.

Printed on acid-free paper

This Springer imprint is published by Springer Nature
The registered company is Springer International Publishing AG
The registered company address is: Gewerbestrasse 11, 6330 Cham, Switzerland

Preface

Disclaimer: The ideas and positions expressed by the authors of the book are exclusively personal and do not in any way represent the positions of the IMF and its policies.

This book deals with the effects produced on the macroeconomic variables by exogenous changes in fiscal policy. The focus is on the Euro Area, both as a whole and on a group of member countries affected by high levels of public and/or private indebtedness. We also examine the spillover effects exerted on the other member countries by expansionary fiscal policies pursued by the leading country of the Euro Area, i.e. Germany. These topics are of the greatest relevance, and in recent years, marked by the so-called Great Recession, they have consequently received much attention from scholars and policymakers. The methods of our approach are mainly based on the VAR (Vector Autoregression) and VAR panel models.

Inasmuch as the authors belong to three distinct generations of researchers, a selective list of acknowledgements must include, first and foremost, our teachers/supervisors (and subsequently friends) Graziella Bertocchi, Fabio Canova, Mario Forni and Marco Lippi. Our interest in topics of applied macroeconomics owes much to their teaching. Needless to say, we remain in their debt for whatever merit this book may have, while any shortcomings or errors are ours alone. We have received useful comments and suggestions regarding parts of the research on the occasion of seminars held in recent years at the IMF, the Banque de France, DIW Berlin, IMT School of Advanced Studies, Lucca, and in presentations at the International Conference of Economic Modelling, Lisbon 2016, and the VIII Economics and Finance Conference, London 2017. Special thanks are also due to our family members and partners for their patience and support.

The research has benefited from a grant from the University of Modena and Reggio Emilia, FAR2016DIP.

While the book is the result of collective planning, working out and writing, Chap. 2 is mainly to be ascribed to Antonella Cavallo; Chaps. 3, 4 and 5 to Antonio Ribba; Chaps. 6 and 7 to Pietro Dallari. Chapter 6 has also benefited from research on fiscal spillovers in the Euro Area conducted by Pietro Dallari jointly with Era Dabla-Norris and Tigran Poghosyan. Chapter 7 represents a reworking of a chapter of Pietro Dallari doctoral thesis, presented at the Pompeu Fabra University of Barcelona.

Modena, Italy
Washington, DC, USA
Modena, Italy
September 2017

Antonella Cavallo
Pietro Dallari
Antonio Ribba

Contents

Chapter 1
Introduction

Abstract In this book we aim to measure fiscal policy in the Euro Area by using structural VAR (Vector Autoregression) and Panel VAR methodologies. In particular, we focus on a group of Euro-area countries affected by high public and/or high private debt. We show that the fiscal austerity has exerted significant recessionary effects in Greece, Italy and Portugal, i.e. high public debt countries but, instead, has had expansionary effects on aggregate output in high private debt economies like Ireland, the Netherlands and Spain. In this book we also motivate the importance for the Euro Area of a fiscal union for purposes of macroeconomic stabilization and, moreover, study spillovers from German fiscal expansions to the other Eurozone economies. We investigate the effects of fiscal shocks on a wide set of macroeconomic variables and also consider the labour market outcomes of fiscal austerity in a set of Euro-area Member States. In this introductory chapter we highlight the content of the book and briefly present and discuss the most relevant topics dealt with.

1.1 The Controversial Macroeconomic Outcomes of Fiscal Policy

The main aim of the investigations conducted in this book is to measure fiscal policy in the Euro Area. We focus on the Economic and Monetary Union (EMU) period and pay particular attention to a selected group of Euro-area countries affected by high public and/or private debt. We also aim to document the important role that a centralized responsibility and conduct of fiscal policy at the Euro-area level, endowed with a sizeable fiscal capacity, might play in order to achieve the goal of macroeconomic stabilization. Another notable subject investigated in this research concerns the ability of expansionary fiscal policy in the core country of the Area, i.e. Germany, to stimulate economic growth in the other countries. We study the effects of exogenous changes in fiscal policy on a broad set of macroeconomic variables by also investigating the response of labor market variables to fiscal austerity in Euro-area countries.

In order to accomplish the task we use structural VAR (Vector Autoregression) and panel VAR models.

© Springer International Publishing AG 2018

A. Cavallo et al., *Fiscal Policies in High Debt Euro-Area Countries*,
https://doi.org/10.1007/978-3-319-70269-8_1

For at least 20 years following the second World War, full employment was a major target for governments of industrialized countries and, in pursuing this goal, a primary role was attributed to fiscal policy. The consensus was that, in line with Keynesian precepts, fiscal policy is a powerful macroeconomic stabilization tool. An important corollary of the traditional Keynesian view concerned the ancillary role played by monetary policy. For example, in Italy, the central bank ensured the full absorption of government bonds, while in the United Kingdom the government retained the formal responsibility for the setting of interest rates.

However, both fact and theories determined in the 1970s a radical rethink of the role of monetary policy (see e.g. Friedman 1968) and, conversely, of fiscal policy. In particular, the oil shocks caused a strong increase in inflation in all oil-importing industrialized countries and the related monetary disorder paved the way for new central bank legislation aiming to strengthen central bank independence and for the definition of macroeconomic targets more skewed towards price stability. These economic and political processes were common to the majority of industrialized Western Countries. The new consensus on the role of monetary policy was well expressed in a letter of 1997 from the Chancellor, Gordon Brown, to the Bank of England Governor, Eddie George, in which new arrangements for monetary policy-making in the United Kingdom were proposed: "Price stability is a precondition for high and stable levels of growth and employment" (Brown 1997).

The Maastricht Treaty of 1992 (Treaty on European Union), in the parts concerning functions and objectives of the European Central Bank (ECB), fully incorporates these views on central bank independence and pre-eminence of the target of price stability.

Although it may sound quite paradoxical to devote a notable space to monetary policy when dealing with fiscal policy, let us note that recent research has confirmed the importance of taking into account that fiscal and monetary policy operate in tango (see, among others, Davig and Leeper 2011).

As far as the goal of full employment is concerned, it would be misleading to believe that central bankers and policy makers may never have neglected the economic and social importance of keeping the unemployment rate at moderate levels. However, the conceptual separation between structural (or "natural" in Friedman's terminology) and cyclical unemployment, which became the dominant view starting from the 1970s - with the related emphasis on structural reforms in labor markets - weakened the importance of a proper management of aggregate demand, and hence the macroeconomic role of fiscal policy.

On the other hand, a group of scholars led by Barro (1981) were critical with regard to the traditional estimation of fiscal multipliers. Barro argued that the size of output fiscal multipliers might have been largely oversized in the Keynesian approach and that only in time of war, in the presence of exogenous military build-ups in government expenditures, were sizeable fiscal multipliers detected. Nonetheless, at the end of the 1980s, some new empirical evidence showed that not only the size but, at a pinch, also the sign of fiscal multipliers may not exhibit Keynesian features since, under certain conditions, credible fiscal contractions may generate expansionary effects on the economy (see Giavazzi and Pagano 1990), through the improvement of expectations of consumers and businesses.

In short, gradually the time-honoured Keynesian view on fiscal policy, together with its use for purpose of stabilization of business cycle fluctuations, became a matter of modern antiques.

In the 1980s and in the 1990s the empirical research based on multivariate time series techniques, aiming to investigate the sources of business cycle fluctuations and the related role of macroeconomic policies, saw the dominance of studies on measuring monetary policy (see Bernanke and Mihov 1998), and the review presented in Christiano et al. (1999), while empirical studies on fiscal policy seemed to be consigned to oblivion. However, and maybe not surprisingly, a rather significant revival of fiscal policy has characterized the last decade, with the economies plagued by the so-called Great Recession. For, large fiscal packages were deployed by a number of countries in response to the severe downturn that had hit the economies following the financial crisis of 2008. For example, one of the largest one, the American Recovery and Reinvestment Act, implied a combination of increase in government expenditures and decrease in government revenues of around 5% of GDP over the period 2008–2010. Of course, this revival of fiscal policy, starting with the influential work by Blanchard and Perotti (2002), has also concerned research on the macroeconomic outcomes of changes in government spending and taxes. In fact, as we try to document in the review presented in Chap. 3, fairly heterogeneous results are found in the most recent literature.

Nonetheless, it seems possible to draw from the bulk of the research an emerging consensus based on the conclusion that the macroeconomic outcomes of fiscal policy are conditioned by a selected set of key macroeconomic factors. Among these, a pre-eminent role is played by: (a) the monetary policy stance; (b) exchange rate regime; (c) degree of openness to trade; (d) country financial conditions. (See, among others, Canova and Pappa 2011, Ilzetzki et al. 2013). In particular, as far as country financial conditions are concerned, in the present research we show that for a proper understanding of the mixed effects of fiscal shocks on macrovariables, often detected in the various economies, it is crucial to take into account both public and private debt.

1.2 Does the Euro Area Needs a Fiscal Union?

Starting with the world economic and financial crisis of 2008, the European economy has experienced a deep recession and an associated strong increase in unemployment to levels never seen in more than two decades. In some Euro-area countries, like Greece and the other southern economies, the recession has shown particular virulence and persistence. In the view of a number of scholars and policymakers, the Great Recession has highlighted various structural weaknesses affecting the Eurozone (see, among others, Pissarides 2016 and De Grauwe and Ji 2016) among which, at least in our opinion, a pre-eminent one is represented by the absence of a Fiscal

Union, i.e. a centralized fiscal capacity and conduct of fiscal policy with the main goal of macroeconomic stabilization in response to large adverse shocks hitting the currency union. Indeed, the Euro Area is a unique historical example of interaction between a centralized conduct of monetary policy and a domestic responsibility of fiscal policy, though this last one is tempered by a common set of European rules.

Thus, in Chap. 2 our answer to the title of this section will turn out to be a qualified yes. "Qualified" in the twofold sense of being based on the empirical study undertaken in the chapter, showing that a centralized fiscal policy in the Euro Area may reach the goal of macroeconomic stabilization, and of being supported by a growing number of scholars and institutions (see e.g. Tabellini 2016 and European Commission 2017).

A quick comparison between the response of fiscal policy to the Great Recession, respectively, in the US and in the Euro Area may help to focus the question. In the late 2008, President Obama had become convinced that a sizeable fiscal stimulus was needed for the US economy, hit by the deepest economic and financial crisis since the Great Depression. This also in light of the difficulties experienced by monetary policy in providing further stimuli to aggregate demand in the presence of interest rates quickly approaching the zero lower bound. Thus, Obama decided to call Christina Romer, the Chair of the Council of Economic Advisers, in order to discuss and design the fiscal package. In fact, a quite aggressive fiscal stimulus plan, of around 5% of GDP, was then approved by Congress in February 2009. The stimulus package, denominated American Recovery and Reinvestment Act consisted in a combination of tax cuts, reinforcement of transfers for unemployment insurance and increase in infrastructure investment (see Romer and Bernstein 2009).

Turning to the Euro Area, who has called (and still calls) who in the case of large adverse shocks hitting the economy, as in the severe economic and financial crisis begun in 2008? Given the lack of a centralized responsibility of fiscal policy and the related absence of a Euro-area fiscal capacity, a strong coordination of national fiscal policies would have been required. Nevertheless, the effective effort made to stabilize the Euro-area economy through the European Recovery Plan turned out to be quite far from that of US, and barely around 2% of GDP.

Another important problem was represented by high public debt levels affecting a group of Euro-area countries, in primis Greece and Italy, that amid growing fears of sustainability in public finances after 2011 led to the implementation in these countries, in compliance with the European common framework for fiscal policy, of severe fiscal consolidation plans. The evidence presented in Chaps. 4, 5 and 7 shows that fiscal austerity in countries like Greece, Italy and Portugal has caused a significant (both economically and statistically) worsening of the recessionary conditions. Clearly, in the presence of a full working fiscal union, an expansionary fiscal policy at the Euro-area level might have contributed to stabilizing the currency area and, at the same time, to making the required macroeconomic adjustment in Greece and in some other Euro-area countries less costly. After all, it may be worth recalling that in the last decade the Euro Area and the World Economy have experienced the worst economic and social crisis since the Great Depression.

In Chap. 2 we find that output fiscal multipliers in the Euro Area are sizeable and well above one. Moreover, we find that in the presence of monetary policy accommodation fiscal multipliers show a substantial increase. A strand of the literature has explored the role of monetary policy accommodation (see e.g. Canova and Pappa 2011, Christiano et al. 2011) and the shared conclusion is that fiscal stimuli have larger effects on aggregate output under an accommodative monetary policy pursued by the central bank.

In Chap. 2 we also provide an outline of the evolution of the common European framework for national fiscal policies, from the Maastricht Treaty of 1992 to the Treaty on Stability Coordination and Governance signed in 2012. As discussed in the chapter, the Euro Area is currently characterized by the presence of a plethora of rules and regulations driving national fiscal policies under the surveillance of European authorities - rules accumulated over two decades and mainly reflecting a paternalistic approach towards national governments and parliaments.

The evolution of the Euro Area towards a full Economic and Fiscal Union, that will likely proceed side by side with the evolution of the Euro Area towards a Political Union and hence a Federal State, will of course require the existence of strict rules governing the national fiscal policies, i.e. it should be clear that the fiscal union is no free lunch. However, also in light of the historical experience of other currency unions and Federal States, rather than a long list of rules, procedures and definitions, what is required is a binding rule on medium term budget balance for member states and a credible no-bailout rule.

An example of credible no-bailout rule comes from the USA where, as stressed by Henning and Kessler (2012), the rule is not written in the Constitution or in laws at the State levels. Yet, since the 1840s, when Congress rejected the bailout of a number of highly indebted states, a no-bailout norm has effectively been in operation in the US fiscal union.[1]

1.3 The Macroeconomic Outcomes of Fiscal Policy in High Debt Euro Area Countries

In Chap. 4 we show that in a group of Euro-area countries affected by high public debt, i.e. Greece, Italy and Portugal, fiscal policy shocks have generated Keynesian effects in the economy under the EMU. In other words, aggregate output has moved in the same direction as exogenous changes in government expenditures. Nonetheless, in another group of Euro-area countries characterized by high private debt, i.e. Ireland, Spain and the Netherlands, the conclusion is opposite: exogenous changes in fiscal variables have produced non-Keynesian effects on the economy in the EMU period. In other words, in this second group of countries we find evidence of expansionary effects exerted by fiscal consolidations.

In the empirical investigation conducted in Chap. 4, we estimate and identify a structural near-VAR model. We take the national countries as small open economies

[1]The implementation of a credible rule may be consistent with isolated exceptions. In fact, the federal government promoted the bailout of the District of Columbia in the 1990s.

operating within a monetary union and thus separate a first block of exogenous Euro-area variables from a second one, which includes an endogenous set of domestic variables. "Near-VAR" since the variables included in the first block are not influenced by the variables of the second block. In other words, the macroeconomic variables selected at the Euro-area level are assumed to unidirectionally cause the domestic variables at all horizons. Thus, although we estimate separate VAR models, one for each country, the adopted specification allows an invariant set of structural shocks at the Euro-area level to be recovered. This methodology was adopted by Cushman and Zha (1997) in order to identify monetary policy shocks in a small open economy, represented by Canada. A recent application of the near-VAR approach, for studying the effects of common monetary policy shocks in a group of Euro-area countries, is provided in Cavallo and Ribba (2015).

Government spending shocks and government revenues shocks are identified by imposing a set of contemporaneous restrictions essentially based on the idea, first suggested by Blanchard and Perotti (2002), that fiscal variables react with lags to changes in macroeconomic conditions.

In Chap. 5 we undertake a robustness analysis by using a VAR model in which full interaction among variables is allowed and by focusing on the reaction of domestic variables to fiscal contractions. In this context the negative government spending shock is identified by imposing sign restrictions (see Uhlig 2005). The results obtained in the previous chapter are substantially confirmed, implying that fiscal consolidations implemented in these countries in the last decade have been rather costly in terms of output losses and worsening of labour market conditions. Another interesting finding shown in Chap. 5 concerns the size of government spending multipliers, well above one at selected horizons both in Greece and Italy.

Recent literature has raised the problem of fiscal foresight, i.e. the ability of households and entrepreneurs to anticipate future tax or government spending obligations. In the presence of fiscal foresight the information set of agents is larger than the econometrician's one, posing the risk of uncorrect identification of fiscal shocks by using the structural VAR methodology, and hence producing unreliable estimations of fiscal multipliers (see e.g. Leeper et al. 2013).

In order to tackle this problem of "information deficiency" (Forni and Gambetti 2014) we enrich the VAR specification by including a set of variables useful to predict fiscal series and other macrovariables, such as the Economic Sentiment Indicator and stock market indexes.

Let us note that the finding that the government spending multiplier has a positive, Keynesian sign in some southern Euro-area economies notoriously affected by high public debt is an important result that contrasts with the results recently presented in Ilzetzki et al. (2013). The authors investigate the macroeconomic outcomes of fiscal expansions in a large set of OECD countries and give a notable contribution to this area of research by showing that the sign of fiscal multipliers is closely related to some relevant country macroeconomic factors. However, their conclusion that government spending multipliers are negative in countries affected by high public debt, in light of our results, seems to be not robust. Instead, the results of our research suggest that for a proper understanding of the dynamic effects of fiscal shocks on aggregate output and consumption, separation of countries on the basis of the nature of high indebtedness is crucial, i.e. it matters if high indebtedness characterizes the public or, alternatively, the private sector.

In Chap. 5 we pay particular attention to the reaction of private consumption to unexpected cuts in government spending. Clearly, the response of consumption to fiscal shocks is of great importance in determining the overall response of aggregate output. Indeed, as argued by Giavazzi and Pagano (1990) and Alesina and Ardagna (2010), in the presence of credible fiscal adjustments, expectations over future income may improve and cause an increase in current consumption. At a pinch, the increase in private consumption might offset the decrease in aggregate demand associated with the fiscal contraction, thus determining an overall expansionary effect in the economy.

While in Chaps. 4 and 5 the focus is mainly on the responses of aggregate output and consumption, in Chap. 7 we complement the analysis by characterizing the dynamic responses of unemployment and other labour market variables to fiscal austerity in a set of Euro-area Member States. Indeed, the study of the link between fiscal policy and the labor markets has received less attention with respect to investigations on the dynamic effects of fiscal shocks on output and aggregate demand. Nonetheless, the results presented in the chapter show that important insights may come from studying the effects exerted by changes in government spending on other indicators of real activity, such as labor market variables.

In this chapter, we use a panel VAR model and identify government spending shocks by imposing sign restrictions on the response of output on impact. The restrictions are consistent with the effects of fiscal policy predicted by a class of New Keynesian Models (see Canova and Pappa 2011). We also present calculations of the unemployment fiscal multipliers. Interesting findings are that unemployment multipliers are heterogeneous across countries and, moreover, the size is related to the specific government spending tool selected.

Fatas and Summers (2016) have recently maintained that fiscal austerity in Europe may have produced long-run negative effects on aggregate output. Nevertheless, according to the main findings of our research, the Euro Area offers a more articulated, and mixed, picture. For, we find the macroeconomic outcomes of fiscal shocks in countries like Greece and Italy might be consistent with the hypothesis of hysteretical effects on output of Keynesian sign but, conversely, for other countries like Ireland and Spain, although persistent effects of contractionary fiscal policies are detected, the response of output exhibits non-Keynesian sign. Thus, it does not seem possible to draw one single conclusion that fits well with all Euro-area countries.

1.4 Spillovers of German Fiscal Policies in the Euro Area

The results presented in Chap. 2 support the idea that fiscal stimuli at the Euro-area level may contribute to the macroeconomic stabilization of the Economic and Monetary Union. We believe that this finding represents a further argument in favor of the evolution of the Euro Area towards a fiscal union. Yet, it is apparent that it will require many years (or, less optimistically, some decades) to equip the currency area with a centralized fiscal capacity. This leads to the conclusion that currently, in practise, only Germany, the largest Euro-area economy, might implement a robust fiscal stimulus package.

In general, measuring the effects of government spending shocks in the national economy and the spillovers in foreign economies is important both for academic economists and policymakers. To this end, in Chap. 6 we measure fiscal policy in Germany and spillover effects in other Euro-area countries. We consider a sample of eleven Euro-area countries over the EMU period.

Two macroeconomic facts, among others, have characterized the German economy in the last decade: Its conspicuous current account surplus, with the current account-to-GDP ratio persistently above 6%, and the substantially government-balanced budget. Both facts have conspired in recent years for repeated calls to the German government for expansionary fiscal policies to be implemented. Indeed, an expansionary fiscal policy in Germany would make much macroeconomic sense,[2] given the fiscal space disposable in Germany, by contributing to cushion the severe recessions in southern countries which exhibit, symmetrically, deficit in their current account. It is also worth recalling that a threshold of 6% has been established by the European Commission (2012) for the surplus in the current account as an indicator of potential macroeconomic imbalances.

Abstracting from the rather limited success that these calls for expansionary fiscal policies have so far achieved, at this stage there is still little evidence on the macroeconomic effects of German fiscal shocks on other countries. Thus in Chap. 6 we try to fill this gap and undertake an empirical investigation on the spillover effects exerted by positive spending shocks in Germany on the other Euro-area countries. We model cross-country interdependences and dynamic linkages by adopting a panel VAR methodology. The identification strategy adopted to recover the domestic government spending shock consists in imposing a set of sign restrictions on impact to the responses of aggregate output and public deficit (see Canova and Pappa 2007).

The main findings shown in Chap. 6 are: (i) The domestic government spending multiplier is positive and large (around 1.5); (ii) spillover effects in the other Euro-area economies are significant, both economically and statistically. In particular, spillovers turn out to be sizeable in the case of countries with strong trade flows and of small countries characterized by less economic diversification. We also show that another important channel of transmissions of the effects of German fiscal policy is represented by the strength of financial flows.

On the whole, since Germany is a large open economy, with a high degree of trade and financial integration with the other Eurozone economies, these results are far from surprising.

---

[2]Or, even better, a strong fiscal expansion in Germany would have made much sense in response to the second European recession of 2012–2013, after the financial crisis of 2008. In particular, a number of Euro-area countries, starting from 2011, faced a severe sovereign debt crisis, being forced as a consequence to implement large fiscal adjustments that, also in light of the results presented in this book, contributed to worsen the economic crisis.

Thus, our main conclusion is that not only can Germany do it but that, probably, it should do it. Of course, one might legitimately wonder if it is reasonable to expect Germany to shoulder (part) of the burden of the macroeconomic adjustment required in the Euro Area. In order to give a balanced response to this doubt, one should also consider that a very large current account surplus, like the one that has characterized German economy for many years, is an indicator of both high competitiveness of the export sector and of shortage of public and/or private investments. Therefore, by looking at this question from the point of view of the shortage of investments, it becomes more clear that the German authorities may risk underestimating the long-term problems that arise from neglecting the quality and quantity of public infrastructures, both material and non-material.

References

Alesina A, Ardagna S (2010) Large changes in fiscal policy: taxes versus spending. Tax policy and the economy, vol 24. NBER, Cambridge, pp 35–68
Barro RJ (1981) Output effects of government purchases. J Polit Econ 89:1086–1121
Bernanke BS, Mihov I (1998) Measuring the monetary policy. Q J Econ 113:869–902
Blanchard OJ, Perotti R (2002) An empirical characterization of the dynamic effects of changes in government spending and taxes on output. Q J Econ 117:1329–1368
Brown G (1997) The new monetary policy framework. Letter from the Chancellor, Gordon Brown, to the Bank of England Governor, May 1997
Canova F, Pappa E (2007) Price differentials in monetary unions: the role of fiscal shocks. Econ J 117:713–737
Canova F, Pappa E (2011) Fiscal policy, pricing frictions and monetary accommodation. Econ Polit 26(68):555–598
Cavallo A, Ribba A (2015) Common macroeconomic shocks and business cycle fluctuations in Euro area countries. Int Rev Econ Financ 38:377–392
Christiano L, Eichenbaum M, Evans CL (1999) Monetary policy shocks: what have we learned and to what end? In: Taylor JB, Woodford M (eds) Handbook of macroeconomics, vol 1. North Holland, Amsterdam, pp 65–148
Christiano L, Eichenbaum M, Rebelo S (2011) When is the government spending multiplier large? J Polit Econ 119:78–121
Cushman D, Zha T (1997) Identifying monetary policy in a small open economy under flexible exchange rates. J Monet Econ 39:433448
Davig T, Leeper EM (2011) Monetary-fiscal policy interactions and fiscal stimulus. Eur Econ Rev 55(2):211–227
De Grauwe P, Ji Y (2016) How to reboot the Eurozone and ensure its long-term survival. In: Baldwin R, Giavazzi F (eds) How to fix Europe's monetary union: views of leading economists. CEPR Press, London (VoxEU.org eBook)
European Commission (2012) First alert mechanism report on macroeconomic imbalances in member states. MEMO/12/104
European Commission (2017) Reflection paper on the deepening of the Economic and Monetary Union
Fatas A, Summers LH (2016) The permanent effects of fiscal consolidations. NBER Working Paper No. 22374
Forni M, Gambetti L (2014) Sufficient information in structural VARs. J Monet Econ 66:124–136
Friedman M (1968) The role of monetary policy. Am Econ Rev 58:1–17

Giavazzi F, Pagano M (1990) Can severe fiscal contactions be expansionary? Tales of two small European countries, NBER Chapters. NBER Macroecon Annu 5:75–122
Henning CR, Kessler M (2012) Fiscal federalism: US history for architects of Europe's fiscal union. Bruegel Essay and Lecture Series
Ilzetzki E, Mendoza EG, Végh CA (2013) How big (small?) are fiscal multipliers? J Monet Econ 60:239–254
Leeper EM, Walker TB, Yang S-CS (2013) Fiscal foresight and information flows. Econometrica 81:1115–1145
Pissarides C (2016) Rebooting Europe: closer fiscal cooperation needed. In: Baldwin R, Giavazzi F (eds) How to fix Europe's monetary union: views of leading economists. CEPR Press, London (VoxEU.org eBook)
Romer C, Bernstein J (2009) The job impact of the American recovery and reinvestment plan. 8 January 2009
Tabellini G (2016) Building common fiscal policy in the Eurozone. In: Baldwin R, Giavazzi F (eds) How to fix Europe's monetary union: views of leading economists. CEPR Press, London (VoxEU.org eBook)
Uhlig H (2005) What are the effects of monetary policy on output? Results from an agnostic identification procedure. J Monet Econ 52:381–419

Chapter 2
The Common Framework for National Fiscal Policies and the Euro Area Fiscal Union

Abstract The aims of this chapter are threefold. First, we provide an outline of the existing European regulatory framework for national fiscal policies. Second, we present and discuss some existing proposals of Fiscal Union for the Euro Area. Third, in the perspective of the evolution of Euro Area towards a full Monetary and Fiscal Union, we estimate and identify a structural VAR in order to study the effects of area-wide government spending shocks on aggregate output and other macroeconomic variables during the EMU period. We find that the government spending multiplier is above one, i.e. there are positive and sizeable effects exerted on output by increases in government expenditures. We also find that when fiscal stimuli are accommodated by monetary policy, spending multipliers have a notable increase. This overall picture is reinforced by analyzing the effects of government investment on macrovariables. Our main conclusion is that a centralized fiscal policy might successfully pursue the goal of macroeconomic stabilization in the Euro Area.

2.1 Introduction

The Economic and Financial Crisis has signaled some important limitations of Economic and Monetary Union (EMU) in its current framework. Among the various shortcomings stressed by scholars and institutions, in our opinion a very important weakness lies in the peculiar interaction between a single monetary policy, conducted at the Euro-area level, and fiscal policies, conducted at the country level, though within a set of shared rules. This architecture, which uniquely characterizes the Euro Area with respect to other currency areas, makes difficult - if not impossible - the unavoidable coordination of monetary and fiscal policy that is required in the presence of strong adverse shocks hitting the economic system. Another relevant problem signaled by the last crisis, is given by the absence of a central bank able to guarantee and provide liquidity to the government bond markets, since this may constrain the liquidity availability of the governments and therefore degenerate into a sovereignty and domestic bank crisis.

© Springer International Publishing AG 2018

A. Cavallo et al., *Fiscal Policies in High Debt Euro-Area Countries*,
https://doi.org/10.1007/978-3-319-70269-8_2

Thus, it seems that in order to sustain integration and stability, the Euro Area needs to evolve towards a monetary and fiscal union, with a sizeable common budget managed at the centralized level. To put it another way, the Euro Area needs a further macroeconomic stabilization tool, besides monetary policy.

The necessity for the Euro Area to create a fiscal tool with a stabilization purpose and able to sustain the aggregate demand was institutionally stressed in the EMU for the first time by the President of the European Council Herman Van Rompuy in 2012.[1] He suggested that strengthening the discipline was not enough and proposed the adoption of fiscal tools at the Euro-area level. Some years later, this point was also emphasized in the Five Presidents' Report (see European Commission 2015). However, proposals for the Euro-area budget for stabilization purposes were suggested even before the start of EMU in two Reports, MacDougall (1977) and Delors (1989), but since then they have been abandoned in favor of a strategy based on higher surveillance and rules imposed on national fiscal policies.

Currently, fiscal policy in the Euro Area is carried out at national levels under a set of rules defined by European Treaties signed over the years by member countries.[2] Since the Maastricht Treaty of 1992, fiscal rules have been reinforced through a growing surveillance at both national and central level, respectively by Fiscal Councils and the European Fiscal Board,[3] and by putting in place corrective measures to ensure that countries comply with fiscal discipline. Clearly, the Euro-area fiscal union even before being a governance matter - i.e. a set of rules, institutions and organizations - is a cultural and political issue. In particular and preliminarily, it requires a broad consensus among member states on the goal of a closer political integration. As stressed by Bordo et al. (2011) the process toward the Euro-area fiscal union is even more complicated because there are no other historical cases to use as guidance. Indeed, the Euro Area is a unique example of Currency Union in which monetary and fiscal policies are carried out at two different levels. Despite this lack, Bordo et al. (2011), by using the experiences of some existing Federal States (Argentina, Brazil, Canada, Germany and United States), identify the necessary conditions for a fiscal union to work efficiently.

It is worth pointing out that although we attribute primary importance to a centralized fiscal capacity for purpose of macroeconomic stabilizations, a fiscal union may also facilitate stabilization targets through temporary transfers among member States. As maintained by some scholars (e.g. Pissarides 2016, De Grauwe and Ji 2016), since the Economic and Monetary Union is notoriously far from being a optimal currency area, and hence is unable to deal with asymmetric shocks, fiscal union could be an important, alternative corrective mechanism.

---

[1] See European Commission (2017a).

[2] The main EU Treaties and Regulations concerning fiscal policies are chronologically summarized in Fig. 2.1.

[3] The former are independent public institutions at national level, established by the so-called Two-Pack, introduced in 2011, in charge of monitoring the compliance of the country with fiscal rules. The latter is an independent advisory board on fiscal matters, which provides the Commission with an evaluation of the implementation of the EU fiscal rules.

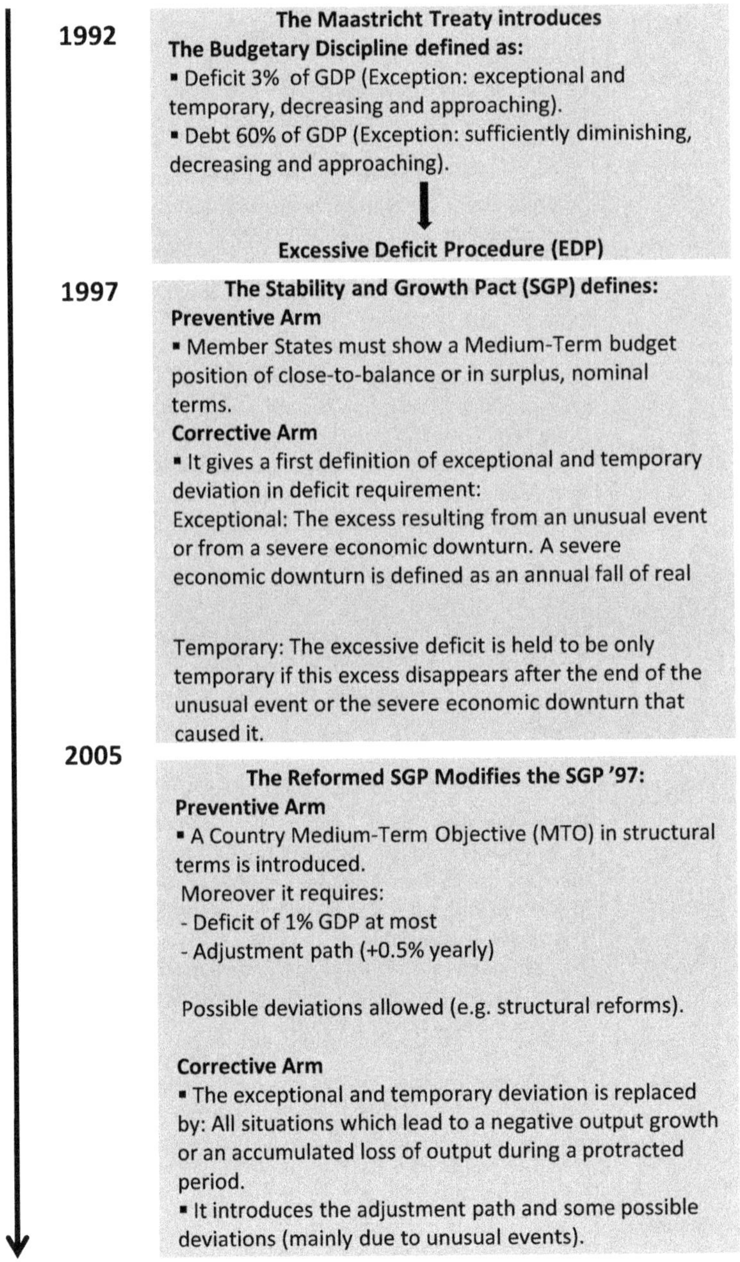

Fig. 2.1 From the Maastricht treaty to the treaty on stability coordination and governance in the economic and monetary union

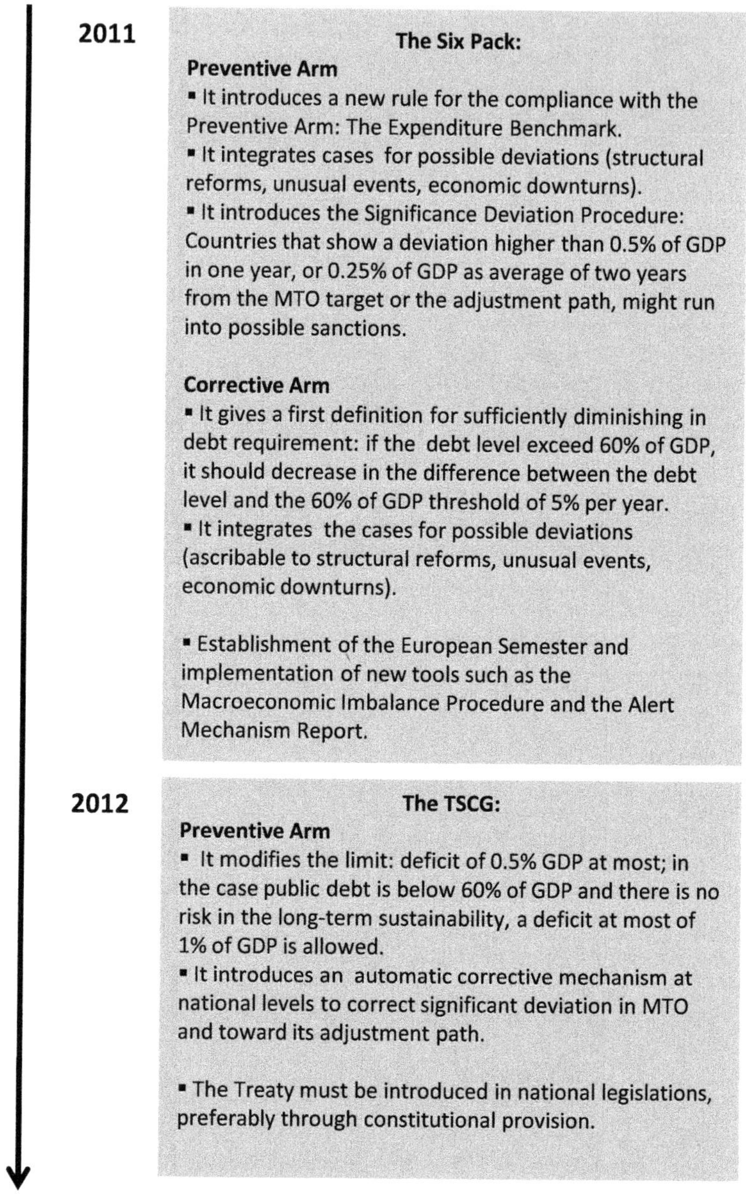

Fig. 2.1 (continued)

However, in recent decades the role of fiscal policy as an important stabilization mechanism has been questioned, both on the theoretical and the empirical side. Starting with the study of Barro (1981), some researchers have supported the conclusion that fiscal multipliers are quite small in normal times and that sizeable exogenous effects of government expenditures are detected for the US economy only during war periods, as a consequence of the associated military build-ups. Other researchers, instead, reach more Keynesian conclusions on the effectiveness of fiscal policy in the postwar US economy. Blanchard and Perotti (2002), using a structural VAR approach, find that the government expenditures multiplier is around one over the period 1960–1997. Similar qualitative results are obtained by Mountford and Uhlig (2009) who adopt a structural VAR in which fiscal shocks are recovered by imposing sign restrictions.

In the light of the uncertainty on the ability of fiscal policy to significantly influence aggregate output, in this chapter we also aim to investigate the macroeconomic outcomes of fiscal shocks during the EMU period. More precisely, we will study whether a Euro-area government spending shock may exert a stabilization effect on the currency area through the management of aggregate demand. An important objection to this strategy might be that a centralized budget did not exist in the first two decades of EMU and hence this could be a rather artificial exercise. In our opinion, there are at least two possible answers to this concern: (i) Given the common fiscal rules characterizing Euro-area countries and the single monetary policy regime under which national fiscal policies work, it seems possible to attribute a sensitive economic interpretation to area-wide fiscal shocks; (ii) Moreover, the economic interpretation of the spending shocks recovered at the Euro-area level may also lie in a counterfactual assumption of strong coordination of fiscal policies across countries over the EMU period.

In recent years, the Euro-area fiscal union has been a widely debated issue among scholars, who have looked at the topic from several perspectives - a reason why different meanings have been attributed to the term fiscal union. In this chapter we mainly focus on the macroeconomic stabilization role of fiscal union using a centralized Euro-area budget, being aware that the redistribution function may also have an important role.[4]

Maybe not surprisingly, there is a still limited number of empirical studies on the effects of fiscal policies on macroeconomic variables at the Euro-area level. The relative scarcity of results is mainly due to the lack of official quarterly general government data. For, although Eurostat has published yearly government data since 1999, the quarterly statistics are only available from February 2012. Starting from Blanchard and Perotti (2002), the importance of quarterly data for purposes of measuring fiscal policy has been repeatedly stressed in the literature.

[4]A heterogeneity of opinions exists both on the priority for the Euro Area to be embedded in a fiscal union and on how the fiscal union should be put in place, i.e. by creating a Euro-area budget for conducting a discretionary fiscal policy or, alternatively, by using automatic stabilizers (see inter alios De Grauwe and Ji 2016, Tabellini 2016, Ubide 2015, Sapir and Wolff 2015, Gros and Belke 2015 and Wyplosz 2005). Nonetheless, in the historical experience of currency unions and national states these two functions are indeed seen as complimentary.

Burriel et al. (2010) and Canova and Pappa (2011) have analyzed the effects of fiscal policy shocks in the Euro Area by using databases compiled by private researchers (see Paredes et al. 2009, Forni et al. 2009 and Fagan et al. 2005).

As far as the Euro-area output fiscal multipliers are concerned, there is lack of consensus on the estimated size. Instead, scholars widely agree about the larger efficiency of fiscal stimuli when nominal interest rates are around the zero lower bound and/or when monetary policy accommodates fiscal expansions (see, among others, Canova and Pappa 2011, Christiano et al. 2011 and Coenen et al. 2013).

This paper contributes to the existing literature in at least two ways: First, it is one of the first papers which use quarterly official statistics, thus providing additional results on fiscal shocks at the Euro-area level based on updated statistics. Second, we use a sample period consistent with the start of the European Monetary Union (EMU). Thus, by using a homogeneous period with a single monetary policy regime, we may be more confident in the reliability of results concerning the macroeconomic effects of both fiscal and the other identified Euro-area shocks.

We set up an ad-hoc database for the Euro Area as a whole in which Euro-area government expenditures are obtained as aggregation of national government expenditures. Data go from 2002:Q1 to 2016:Q3. Then, by using the structural VAR model and a recursive identification, we analyze the effects of a Euro-area government spending shock on Euro-area prices and aggregate output. Moreover, given the potential importance of public investments, we also separate the government spending variable into its components of consumption and investments and analyze the effects of a Euro-area investment shock on the selected macrovariables.

The second step consists in studying the dynamic effects of an increase in government spending under an accommodative monetary policy. In this case the fiscal shock is recovered by imposing sign restrictions. As emphasized in recent literature, the possible presence of fiscal foresight poses some difficulties in the identification of fiscal shocks in classical VARs. In order to tackle this issue we add in the VAR specification a number of leading indicators (see e.g. Forni and Gambetti 2014), and specifically the Economic Sentiment Indicator for the Euro Area and S & P Euro stock market index.

Our main results can be summarized as follows: (a) A positive government spending shock has an expansionary effect on Euro-area output and, moreover, the spending multiplier is well above one and statically-significant on impact; (b) Similar conclusions hold when the government investment shock is considered; (c) Under an accommodative monetary policy, an increase in government spending has a notable expansionary effect on Euro-area output but more persistent; (d) The cumulative fiscal multipliers are much larger compared to those calculated without accommodative monetary policy.

Therefore, we are led to conclude that a centralized budget and an associated discretionary fiscal policy conducted at the Euro-area level may strongly contribute to the macroeconomic stabilization of the currency area.

The rest of the paper is organized as follows. In Sect. 2.2 we present and discuss the common fiscal policy framework in the Euro Area, mainly looking at rules defined in the signed Treaties since the start of the Economic and Monetary Union. In Sect. 2.3

we discuss some proposals for the Euro-area budget architecture by even considering the experience of the existing Federal States. Section 2.4 is devoted to brief survey of the literature dealing with the dynamic effects of government spending shocks in the Euro Area. In Sect. 2.5 we present the strategy of identification of the VAR model together with the dynamic responses of the Euro-area variables to government spending shocks and then to government investment shocks. In Sect. 2.6 we undertake a sensitivity analysis to analyze the robustness of our results. In Sect. 2.7, by using a sign restrictions approach, we identify the government spending shock under an accommodative monetary policy and we show its effect on the Euro-area variables. In Sect. 2.8 we compare the fiscal multipliers obtained with and without monetary policy accommodation. Section 2.9 concludes.

2.2 The Common European Framework for National Fiscal Policies

The fiscal policy framework in the Euro Area is based on a set of EU legislations. Since the Maastricht Treaty public finances of the European Member States have been subjected to fiscal rules. However, important changes were introduced by the Stability and Growth Pact (SGP) adopted in 1997, later amended in 2005 and in 2011, and by the Treaty on Stability Coordination and Governance in the Economic and Monetary Union (TSCG) signed in 2012.[5]

Although over the years there has been a strengthening of fiscal policy rules that Member States have to respect, there is some degree of flexibility characterizing the interpretation of those rules, in particular in carrying out the obligations regarding the process of deficit and debt reduction.

The Maastricht Treaty specified for the first time Member States' budgetary policy based on the principle of avoidance of excessive deficits and debt, defined respectively as 3 and 60% of GDP.

It is worth noting that over the years changes in the fiscal rules have never concerned variations in the reference values for deficit and debt but rather have referred to clarifications of the budgetary discipline and, more in general, to the reinforcement of monitoring and correcting phases.

Defining a clear limit to Member State deficit and debt was necessary for a Monetary Union where fiscal policies were the only available tool for countries to face out asymmetric shocks. At the same time, high debt increases the risk for national governments to default and the spillover effects of unsustainable national debt and deficit in some countries can put the European Central Bank (ECB) under pressure. Therefore, the Maastricht Treaty tried to reduce such risks defining a

[5]Other legislations also contribute to define the current framework. We have summarized the main changes of fiscal rules over the years in Fig. 2.1. For additional details see European Commission (2017a).

specific limit for deficit to be at most 3% of GDP and requiring debt to sufficiently decrease towards 60% of GDP.

As far as the specific numeric limits are concerned, De Grauwe (2016) argues that they are quite arbitrary and they were set based on the average values that Member States experienced in the early 1990s.

The actual framework lays the foundations around these rules and is the result of a long process of amending the European Treaties. It is organized around two arms, a preventive and a corrective one.[6] The former aims to ensure sound budgetary policies over the medium term and hence the underlying logic is that the compliance with the preventive arm should avoid excessive deficit and debt. The latter aims to correct budgetary position and includes all the required steps to reduce excesses in deficit or in debt.

2.2.1 *Preventive Arm*

The core element of the preventive arm is the country-specific Medium Term Objectives (MTO), introduced by the reformed Stability and Growth Pact in 2005. Before that date, Member States were committed to achieve a budget position of "close-to-balance or in surplus" in nominal term. After the reform of 2005 each Member State can achieve a Medium Term Budgetary Objective in structural terms and based on the country specific characteristics. The MTO corresponds to the structural budgetary position that Member States should reach, and maintain, over the cycle.

In order to monitor budgetary positions, each year Member States submit the Stability and Convergence Programmes (SCPs) which include the country specific MTO that can be calculated by themselves or defined as the minimum MTO computed by the Commission. More specifically, the MTO should take into account three requirements:

- Provide a safety margin with respect to the 3%. This margin is computed by adjusting the 3% of GDP deficit threshold for the effects of normal cyclical fluctuations.
- Ensure sustainability or rapid progress to sustainability, by defining a lower limit which considers the budgetary impact of aging populations and a supplementary debt-reduction effort for countries with a debt higher than 60%.
- Consider that their maximum level of structural deficit is set to at most 1% of GDP. The signatories of the TSCG have committed themselves to an MTO of at least −0.5% of GDP. However, their limit remains at −1% of GDP, only if their debt ratio is significantly below 60% of GDP and the risks of sustainability of their public finances are low.

[6]These arms were initially introduced by the Stability and Growth Pact in 1997, which aimed to improve the budgetary discipline defined by the Maastricht Treaty but has been amended and then implemented by a set of subsequent rules. The more recent changes have been introduced by the TSCG and by the so-called Two-Pack.

The Commission has the task both to assess if the MTOs defined by the Member States are set to appropriate levels or aligned to the minimum MTO, and to verify if Member States reach their specific MTO. Compliance with the preventive arm is evaluated based on two criteria: the structural balance and the expenditure benchmark.

The structural balance is defined as the cyclically-adjusted general government balance net of one-off and other temporary measures, and is compared with the MTO to see whether the country is at its MTO and, if this is not the case, it should be on an appropriate adjustment path to reach it.

The main concern regarding the structural balance is that it is not directly observable, like the closely related concept of output gap. Thus, they need to be estimated, and many alternative techniques can be used to compute those variables. An important consequence is that measures of output gap and structural balance are subject to considerable uncertainty. This raises notable concerns, given the implications for the fiscal adjustment requirements. In this regard, the European Commission widely discuss the adopted approach based on Production Function, considering pros and cons that can lead to biased estimations.[7]

In regard to the expenditure benchmark, introduced by the Six-Pack, it is computed by the Commission and provides guidance for the Member States on how net expenditure should be set to maintain the structural balance at its MTO, or how to fulfill the adjustment path. The Commission has the task to evaluate if net expenditures of each country are in line with the expenditure benchmark.

Countries that do not reach their MTO or do not respect the expenditure benchmark must show a yearly adjustment path of 0.5% of GDP in structural term, as a benchmark, but the required effort should be higher in good times and more limited in bad times. This means that countries can have also a yearly adjustment path below the 0.5%.[8] Flexibility in term of possible temporary deviations from their MTO and adjustment paths is granted: (i) When Member States adopt structural reforms that impact on the long-term sustainability of public finance; (ii) when Member States finance specific investments that have an effect on the budgetary position; (iii) when events outside of Member States control occur; (iv) in periods of economic downturn (this set of conditions has been last updated by the Six-Pack).

However, when there are no conditions to justify temporary deviations and the country shows a significant deviation, measured as a deviation of 0.5% of GDP in one single year or 0.25% of GDP in two consecutive years, from the MTO or from the adjustment path toward it, the Significant Deviation Procedure (SDP) is launched. This procedure implies possible sanctions for countries that continue not to make enough efforts to correct the structural balance and the expenditure benchmark.[9] Moreover, the TSCG states that only signatories of the treaty must implement an automatic correction mechanism at national level which will operate in the event of

---

[7] See European Commission (2014).

[8] The Commission defines a matrix that specifies the fiscal adjustment requirements under the preventive arm of the Pact. For additional details see European Commission (2017a).

[9] Sanctions in the preventive arm have been introduced by the Six-Pack.

significant observed deviations. This mechanism can be activated by an independent body, as for example the Fiscal Council.

Member States are evaluated by the Commission through an ex-ante, in year and an ex-post analysis. While the ex-ante and in year analysis, are mainly used to help countries in programming their MTO, the ex-post analysis is used to express a final assessment on the compliance to the preventive arm and to activate the Significant Deviation Procedure. For example, if the Commission identifies a significant deviation for a specific country in an ex-ante and in year analysis, can only send a recommendation and it cannot activate a Significant Deviation Procedure, which should instead be launched only when a significant deviation is confirmed in the ex-post analysis. Based on Vade Mecum 2017, only Hungary and Malta showed a significant deviation in 2015.

Given the importance of this arm, the Euro-area signatories of the TSCG have committed themselves to integrate the preventive process into their national legal framework, using preferably constitutional law, to ensure a respect for all procedures. Moreover, since 2011 with the Six Pack, the preventive arm has been part of the European Semester which consists in an annual scheduling of the surveillance activities, and aims to ensure that both budgetary and economic policies monitoring take place in parallel and in time in all the EU countries.

2.2.2 *Corrective Arm*

The corrective arm aims to solve the excessive deficit and debt positions. Indeed, it implements a step by step procedure, known as the Excessive Deficit Procedure (EDP), to reduce deficit and debt below the allowed limit. The EDP starts when the Commission identifies a violation of either the deficit or debt criterion in a Member State. Specifically, the corrective arm calls for:

- a Member State is non-compliant with the deficit requirement if its general government deficit is greater than 3% of GDP, unless the excess is exceptional, meaning that it depends on: (i) a unusual event outside of the Member States control; (ii) a severe economic downturn which lead to a negative real growth of GDP or to an accumulated loss of output during a protracted period (defined by Stability Growth Pact in 2005).
- A Member State is non-compliant with the debt requirement if the government debt is greater than 60% of GDP and the difference between the debt level and the 60% of GDP threshold does not decrease by 5% per year and over 3 years (This is the definition for "sufficiently diminishing" which has been specified in the Six-Pack).

When either deficit or debt violates the budgetary discipline, the Commission should prepare a report which expresses an overall assessment for launching the Excessive Deficit Procedure. The evaluation should be done by considering a list of other relevant factors that can impact deficit and debt as, for example, structural reforms, contributions from the Member States to the European Fund for Strategic Investments etc. If the Commission concludes that an excessive deficit exists and the Council votes in favor of the EDP activation, the Member States will receive a recommendation containing, among other information, time-frame to correct the error and annual target to be achieved. Moreover, from 2013, countries under the EDP must present an Economic Partnership Program (EPP), which sets out the fiscal structural reforms and all the other effective measures able to correct their EDP.

Countries in the EDP are committed to achieving an annual minimum fiscal adjustment of at least 0.5% of GDP in structural term. Even in this case, as for the preventive arm, possible deadline extensions are allowed when structural reforms are implemented or, alternatively, effective actions have been taken but periods of economic downturn and events out of the control of Member States impact on government finances. When not enough effort have been made to implement effective action a stepping up of the procedure will be applied. Finally, the EDP is abrogated when the excessive deficit is corrected.[10]

It is worth recalling that following the European financial crisis of 2011, 24 countries have entered the Excessive Deficit Procedure. Nonetheless, currently only three European Countries are monitored under the Excessive Deficit Procedure: France, Spain and UK.[11] As far as a big "sick man of Europe" is concerned, i.e. Greece, the European Commission announced on July 12, 2017 that it recommended the end of the Excessive Deficit Procedure against Greece.

To sum up, Member States must respect fiscal rules in term of both deficit and debt. However, these rules are defined and measured with mechanisms such that in their practical implementation they become relatively flexible, so that they do not always require strong interventions to reduce deficits.

In Fig. 2.1 we summarize the evolution of European fiscal rules from the Maastricht Treaty of 1992 to the TSCG of 2012.

2.3 Towards a Euro-Area Budget for the Fiscal Union?

The Great Recession has highlighted a number of problems affecting the Euro Area which lie at the root of the weaknesses revealed during the crisis. These problems mainly derive from an incomplete financial and fiscal architecture characterizing the currency area. Of course, the strong adverse shocks which have affected the global economy in the last decade have amplified these weaknesses.

Indeed, over the last few years efforts have been made to stabilize the Euro Area through: (a) Financial solidarity mechanisms; (b) steps towards the implementation of a Banking Union; (c) new fiscal commitments for countries, with the entry into force of the TSCG and the Six and Two-Pack. Yet, one may have doubts on the

[10]For more details see European Commission (2017a).

[11]Information Updated to August 1st 2017.

fact that EMU would have survived the Great Recession without the extraordinary efforts, at the limits of its mandate, put in place by the European Central Bank.

Thus, still new challenges for the Euro Area remain. Based on the ideas suggested by the Five Presidents Report, the European Commission, in 2017, published the Third Reflection Paper titled: "Reflection paper on the deepening of the Economic and Monetary Union" and re-opened a debate on the future of the European Union. The proposals concern gradual steps towards the completion of the Economic and Monetary Union by 2025. The main idea is to create a more integrated Economic and Fiscal Union, as well as a well-functioning Financial Union and, closely related, to strength Euro-area institutions. The Commission's Proposal envisages the implementation in two phases. The first one, from 2017 to the end of 2019, should complete the Banking and Capital Markets Union through several measures, notable among which an agreement on a European Deposit Insurance Scheme and the (controversial) establishment of the Sovereign Bond-Backed Securities for the Euro Area. At the same time some reflections should be initiated about the fiscal stabilization function for the Euro Area. The second phases, from 2020 to 2025, should implement the Fiscal Union, besides completing the Financial Union. During both phases, the EMU governance should be reinforced by creating a more formalized dialogue with the European Parliament and building a Euro-area Treasury for the management of fiscal policy and a European Monetary Fund. Therefore, creating a fiscal tool able to provide a macroeconomic stabilization role for the EMU, through a centralized Euro-area budget, is a priority for the European Commission.

Moreover, European Commission (2017b) defines the necessary conditions that member states should meet in order to move toward the fiscal union and, in particular, the convergence of the amplitudes of business cycles among member states, as well as, quite obviously, a broad political consensus. Both are essential requirements for the future of fiscal union as emphasized by some scholars (see e.g. De Grauwe and Ji 2016). Tackling economic and social divergences is a fairly important issue because in the long-run they can lead to persistent disparities and to a loss of competitiveness of member states. Instead, as far as the political consensus is concerned, the Third Reflection Paper invites member states and stakeholders to discuss the best and efficient solutions to create a fiscal union.

According to traditional theory of fiscal federalism (e.g. Musgrave 1959 and Oates 1972) the stabilization function should be task of central governments, which will be able to respond to different political preferences across countries, could take into account the externalities of regional fiscal policies and improve the fiscal responsibilities of national government. In addition, the classical theory of Optimum Currency Areas (OCA) (e.g. Mundell 1961; McKinnon 1963; Kenen 1969), argues in favor of a macroeconomic stabilization tool, seen as necessary in absence of exchange rate flexibility and when national instruments are not able to deal with idiosyncratic shocks.

Currently, the European Union already has a common budget which stands at about 157.9 billion, in 2017. The budget is yearly, is used within a multi-annual financial framework (MFF) of 7 years and has some principles to which it must adhere. For example, it cannot exceed 1% of the 28 EU countries' gross domestic product (GDP), and it is not allowed to be unbalanced. The budget is financed for 98% by European revenues based on Value Added Tax (VAT), Gross National Income (GNI), customs duties on imports from outside the EU and sugar levies; the remaining 2% is financed by other sources of revenues. Moreover, a correction mechanism is in place to rebalance excessive contribution paid by certain member states. The EU Budget is mainly addressed to enrich competitiveness for growth and jobs, but also to increase the economic, social as well as territorial cohesion among European countries.[12] Specifically almost 85% of the EU Budget, in 2017, goes to create growth and jobs, economic and social cohesion policies and to natural resources as agriculture, rural development, fisheries and environmental protection (respectively around 14, 34 and 37%).[13] In other words, the centralized budget is very small in relation to the Euro-area GDP and is not designed to pursue stabilization purposes. In fact, it has more a redistribution function, by supporting European policies across countries and helping them in the convergence path.

The creation of a large common Euro-area budget might have several advantages. First, a major macroeconomic stabilization role by allowing the management of aggregate demand for the currency union as a whole. It is worth recalling that fiscal policy is an important alternative tool when monetary policy has no more arrows in its quiver once in the neighborhood of the zero lower bound. Indeed, fiscal policy does not work only as an alternative to monetary policy but, not rarely, they are coordinated to achieve macroeconomic stabilization. Recent research has extensively studied the interaction between fiscal and monetary policy and both theoretical and empirical results converge to the conclusion that fiscal multipliers are larger in the presence of accommodative monetary policies (see, among others, Canova and Pappa 2011, Christiano et al. 2011).

The coordination of monetary and fiscal policy appears to be unavoidable in the presence of large negative shocks hitting the economic system. The last deep economic and financial crisis represents, unfortunately, a clear example of the importance of this coordination and, conversely, of the problems that may arise when the coordination is lacking.

An example of (at least implicit) coordination between fiscal and monetary policies is represented by the response of US policymakers during the Great Recession. In 2009 Obama's Administration promoted the American Recovery and Reinvestment Act, known as the Recovery Act (ARRA). It was based on the idea that, during recessions, the government should offset the decrease in private spending with an increase in public spending in order to stimulate a recovery of the economy. The fiscal stimulus package was signed by President Barack Obama in February 2009. The main declared aim of the Recovery Act was to save the existing jobs and create new ones, but also to invest in infrastructure, education, health, and renewable energy. The Stimulus Package was financed by the US Federal Budget for a total of US $787 billion (around 5% of US GDP) and hence it was a quite sizeable fiscal stimulus.

[12]Part of the EU Budget is addressed to security, justice, foreign policy and for administrative issues.

[13]Data on European Budget come from the Section Budget on the European Commission web page.

On the European side, the European Commission responded to the economic and financial crisis with the European Economic Recovery Plan (EERP) aiming to stimulate investments in key sectors such as cars, construction, and green technologies, and to create jobs. More generally, one goal was to sustain labor markets in EU countries. This plan, announced at the end of 2008, was financed with different sources: EU and national budgets and by the European Investment Bank (EIB) for a total of 1.5% of EU's GDP (the total package amounted to around €200 billion) to be used in two years. Although at that time a stimulus of 1.5% across member states was thought to be sufficient, there is clearly a notable difference in the size of the two fiscal packages.

Nonetheless, both packages have been evaluated by scholars. For example, Coenen et al. (2013) have studied the impact of the European Economic Recovery Plan on Euro-area GDP and have found that expenditure stimuli have a multiplier larger than 1. In regard to the assessment of the American Recovery and Reinvestment Act, Drautzburg and Uhlig (2015), by using a New Keynesian model, find a positive short-run multiplier around 0.53 and a negative long-run multiplier around −0.36. This result is in sharp contrast with the conclusion of Romer and Bernstein (2009) who estimated a government spending multiplier well above one and hence argued that ARRA produced a significant increase in the US GDP. These results were confirmed by Blinder and Zandi (2010).

Looking at the US fiscal experiment during the Great Recession, it seems that a centralized budget of 5–7% of GDP is the minimum required for the Euro Area to pursue stabilization goals. However, a Euro-area budget implies that countries should be willing to transfer part of sovereignty over taxation and spending to European Institutions. This process is not without political difficulties mainly due to moral hazard or free rider issues which may prevent a broad political consensus (see Rubio 2015). In order to overcome these difficulties, it is widely accepted by scholars and institutions that a stabilization function should not lead to permanent transfers among member states. Given the heterogeneity of countries and the risk of durable transfer that may arise, it is essential to avoid free rider behavior of member states. Thus, an important conclusion is that a larger Euro-area budget and a fiscal policy conducted at central level for macroeconomic stabilization purposes should be accompanied by even stricter fiscal policy rules at national level. To borrow an expression used by Conservatives, the Fiscal Union is no free lunch!

Thus, it could be useful to continue to monitor national budgets and ensure the compliance of each member state with the Common European Fiscal Policies Framework. Moreover, a credible commitment to a no-bailout rule should be one important pillar of the fiscal union.

In line with this interpretation, Bordo et al. (2011) have analyzed the evolution of five fiscal federalism (Argentina, Brazil, Canada, Germany and United States) from both a political and a historical point of view. The authors argue that the elements which make a well functioning federal state and limit moral hazard and free rider issues is mainly the existence of strict fiscal rules at the decentralized levels. They also stress that the compliance with fiscal rules at national level depends on the presence of a credible no-bailout rule, constitutional restrictions and with clear disciplines for financial markets concerning government debt.

2.3.1 Some Comparison with Existing Federal States

The Euro Area is a unique example of currency union where monetary and fiscal policies are set at two different levels of responsibility, the first centralized, the second at country level. It also lacks any historical guidance. However, the set-up of the Euro-area budget requires important points to be considered for which it could be useful to look at the existing Federal States.

Table 2.1 shows some characteristics of the most successful fiscal federations, such as US, Canada, Germany, and Switzerland. As far as the budget size is concerned, column (3) shows that Germany has the highest size of the budget at central level, over 28% of GDP, followed by the US which shows a size close to 20% and then by Canada and Switzerland which show values around 15%. In regard to the allocation of expenditures and revenues, column (4) shows that expenditures are highly decentralized in Canada and Switzerland with values, respectively, of close to 65 and 56%. The US is characterized by a more balanced allocation between the State and the Local Level. Germany, instead, allocates only 38% of the total

Table 2.1 Fiscal federation features

Country	Level	Budget Size (%)	Expendit. (%)	Reven. (%)	Transfer Reven. (%)	No-bailout Rule
(1)	(2)	(3)	(4)	(5)	(6)	(7)
CA	Central	14.79	35.01	45.70	0.14	Yes
	State/Local	27.30	64.99	54.30	14.85	
DE	Central	28.82	62.03	65.25	0.52	Yes
	State/Local	17.59	37.97	34.75	9.24	
SW	Central	15.00	44.42	52.02	0.95	Yes
	State/Local	18.85	55.58	47.89	11.37	
US	Central	19.12	50.95	56.7	0.00	Yes
	State/Local	18.34	49.05	43.26	8.45	

Note Country: includes Canada (CA), Germany (DE), Switzerland (SW), United States (US); *Level*: includes Central and State/Local levels. *Size Budget*: the share of Total Expenditures relative to Gross Domestic Product. *Expendit.*: the expenditures of each level expressed as percentage of Total General Government Expenditures. *Reven.*: the revenues of each level expressed as percentage of Total General Government Revenues. *Transfer Reven.*: intergovernmental transfer revenues defined as transfers payable to each level by other levels. *No-bailout Rule*: indicates the presence of a rule for which local governments are responsible for their debts, i.e. Central level shall not assume the commitments of State/Local level

Source OECD Fiscal Decentralisation Database. Average sample period from 1995 to 2015

government expenditures to the decentralized level. Revenues, in column (5), are collected mainly at the central level in Germany, Switzerland and US, where the central share is above 50%, reaching 65% in Germany. Canada, instead, exhibits a substantial degree of decentralization, since around 54% of revenues are collected at local level. Looking at data on received transfers in column (6), these do not exceed 15% and, more specifically, Canada shows that the decentralized levels are those that receive the highest transfer revenues from central government (14.85%), so their revenues are the most dependent, while, on the contrary, the decentralized level of the United States shows the lowest dependence on central transfers.

It is important to point out that all the analyzed federations have a formal no-bailout rule. However, some differences can be detected. Indeed, while the United States, Canada, and Switzerland in their federal history have refused to bailout indebted states, it is not the same for Germany where in 1987, respectively, the Bremen and Saarland Landers received supplementary transfers from the central government to tackle their high debt. It is well-known that the German Government and the German Central Bank (Bundesbank) are famous for their prudent policies and full respect of rules; however at least at the fiscal decentralized level they do not seem to have been so performing and successful.[14] Rubio (2015) argues that a no-bailout clause in the US as well as in Canada mainly works because there are other fiscal risk-sharing tools which offer guarantees for regions or states so that even in bankruptcy they will not be without minimum government services and financial stability.

Two relevant lessons seem to come for the Euro Area from the most important existing Federal States: (i) The existence of a sizeable central budget, which ranges from a minimum of 15% of GDP in Canada to a maximum of 29% in Germany; (ii) the existence of a no-bailout rule. The conclusion is that these two components are both essential in a well functioning currency area and hence *aut simul stabunt aut simul cadent*.

As far as fiscal regulations are concerned, it should be clear from the survey that we have conducted in Sect. 2.2 that the Euro Area is affected by a plethora of rules and, not less important, these rules are also subject to continual changes. Yet, following the interesting analysis by Henning and Kessler (2012), it is possible to draw another very important lesson from the more than bicentenary history of the United States.

Although in the US a no-bailout norm is not written in the Constitution nor included in state laws, this norm has been effectively in force since 1940. During the 1820s and 1830s, there was an increase in expenditure devoted to infrastructures and, as a consequence, several states became more indebted. Ultimately they demanded bailout from the federal government, i.e. they implicitly assumed a commitment by the federal government. Nonetheless, Congress refused the bailouts and eight of them defaulted. In response to this decision by the federal government, in the subsequent decades many states autonomously adopted balanced budget amendments and rules.

[14]For more details see Bordo et al. (2011).

Thus, it may be beneficial for the Euro Area to simplify the set of rules adopted for the conduct of national fiscal policies and at the same time to strengthen their degree of credibility.

2.3.2 The Euro-Area Budget Architecture: Some Proposals From the Literature

In regard to the dimension of the common Euro-area budget as a stabilization tool, for business cycle fluctuations, the basic idea is that the greater the dimension, the greater will be the stabilization effect. However, a group of scholars argue that a budget size close to 2% of EU GDP would be sufficient to ensure a stabilization effect (see Pisani-Ferry et al. 2013, Delors 1989). Some others suggest that the Euro Area does not need to build a large tax capacity, but rather collect revenues for a very long time, and that the fiscal capacity should be organized by combining some joint issuance of bonds with national fiscal discipline and surveillance (see Tabellini 2016; Ubide 2015; Corsetti et al. 2015). Differently, another group of scholars stresses that all the proposals based on small amounts would not be able to address stabilization policies in very open economies such as those of members of EMU. This position has been largely supported since the Mac Dougall Report (1977) which proposed a European budget comprised between 7.5 and 10%.

In the previous section we have argued that by also looking at the recent US experience, where a fiscal stimulus plan of quite sizeable amount has been implemented to contrast a deep recession, the Euro-area budget should rapidly approach 5% of Euro-area GDP, with if possible a steady increase over the years in order to reach 10%.

Clearly, in the absence of a full Political Union, with legislative and executive powers as expression of popular vote, a Euro-area fiscal capacity could be obtained only by collecting revenues from national government levels.

Moreover, a Euro-area budget with stabilization purpose would require a Euro-area executive board and a strong discretionary power, which could be addressed by the creation of an EMU finance minister or by a fiscal authority. In this regard Tabellini (2016) proposes the creation of a European Fiscal Institute (EFI). According to this idea, the institute would have a governing body similar to the ECB, of course exercising quite different functions. Decisions should be taken with a simple or qualified majority, depending on the subject, but the EFI should have a power of veto on national budgets. Similarly, Sapir and Wolff (2015) propose the creation of a Eurosystem of Fiscal Policy (EFP) that should work to ensure fiscal debt sustainability and an adequate area-wide fiscal position. The EFP should be composed of Euro-area finance ministers. This institute would take fiscal decisions by qualified majority and should have the power to impose specific targets to all member states to achieve an appropriate fiscal stance in the Eurozone at a whole. The institute should work jointly with ESM and would have the power to activate loan facilities only for special purposes.

Widely discussed is the issue of how the EU budget should be used, if only in exceptional or even in normal times. Over the years there has been an increase in consensus around the possibility to use the EU budget only for very large shocks and to face up to new crises (Tabellini 2016; Wolff 2012). However, Rubio (2015) argues that the actual identification of exceptional circumstances as in the SGP is so wide-ranging in practice and should eventually be reviewed.

In our opinion, the centralized fiscal capacity should be thought of primarily as an instrument to tackle large adverse shocks and thus to help the stabilization of the macroeconomic system. This is one of the main and clearer lessons from the current crisis. On the other hand, the uncertainty surrounding the macroeconomic outcomes of fiscal shocks should discourage a fine tuning approach to fiscal policy.

To maximize the stabilizing effect, the EU budget could be composed of the most cyclical revenues and expenditures, meaning those that have a stronger correlation with economic activity. On the revenues side, a notable part of the literature focuses on VAT and corporate income taxes (see, e.g. Corsetti et al. 2015 and Mauro 2014). These could be initially supported by a national tax, but over the years they should be replaced by Euro-area revenues i.e. EU-wide value-added tax (VAT) or by introducing a European corporate tax (see Mauro 2014 and Dullien and Schwarzer 2009). However, as we have already stressed, although taxes imposed at the Euro-area level seem a logical consequence of the establishment of a centralized fiscal capacity, it is difficult to apply this solution without a full political union which, to date, appears still far from feasible either at short or medium horizons.

From the expenditure side, using the EU budget has several advantages in terms of economies of scale capable of reducing costs as well as in terms of possibility to coordinate and afford issues of common concern. Indeed, EU expenditures could be addressed to items that are currently not at all centralized at the European level, but generally have to do with the central level, i.e. energy, IT, transport, human capital, R & D, justice, security, and in the form of public investment strategy arranged both at national and European levels. Another important advantage is that although public investments would be implemented at the national level, they can have positive spillover effects across the Euro-area economies. The spillovers may be even higher when investments are addressed to the most productive projects and sectors. In this regard, Veld (2016) shows that a debt-financed increase in government investment for countries in surplus can have positive GDP spillovers to the rest of Euro Area. These effects will be higher when monetary policy accommodates public investments and when these are addressed to the most productive projects. Moreover, the author finds that due to the low borrowing costs the increase in government debt for surplus countries would be modest, while government debt ratios in the rest of the Euro Area could fall, even if to a small extent.

In Chap. 6 we will present a study on the spillover effects exerted by German government spending shocks on the other Euro-area countries. As we will see, there are sizeable effects, since an increase of German government expenditures generates a significant increase in aggregate output for Germany and for the other Euro-area economies.

Finally, as already stressed before, the Euro-area budget should be accompanied by a credible no-bailout rule and by a full respect of common European Fiscal discipline by each country.

2.3.3 *Other Proposals for Fiscal Union: Automatic Fiscal Stabilizers*

Among the various proposals advanced for the fiscal union, notable support has enjoyed the approach based on the so-called automatic fiscal stabilizers. As against a Euro-area budget designed for discretionary fiscal policies, the automatic stabilizers do not require subjective choices aiming to achieve the goal of macroeconomic stabilization, since they are based on the specific design of the shock-absorption function. In other words, contributions and disbursements among member states are decided a priori, based on a pre-specified common policy.

The automatic rule has the advantage that national governments, as well as the European one, would have no formal way of exerting influence on decisions and, also for this reason, are often preferred to discretionary tools. Another important advantage is that automatic stabilizers require less lags in terms of the decisions to take and to put into practice (see e.g. Dullien and Schwarzer 2009).

However, automatic stabilizers also show weak points. For example, they might not be a sufficient fiscal policy tool in the case of large cyclical asymmetries in the Euro Area, mainly due to the nature of automatic stabilizers which can only cushion macroeconomic shocks but cannot fully offset them. Moreover, in the presence of permanent supply shocks, the automatic stabilizers tend to prolong the adjustment process which could become unsustainable in the long run. Another important limitation is that they can induce people and businesses to delay their adjustment to shocks. In these cases, policy makers may face a crucial trade off between stabilization and efficiency - even more considering that automatic stabilizers are triggered by indicators. Consequently, even in the presence of indicators and well designed policies, it is likely that they will not fit well with all the possible shocks.

Consistently with the view expressed in this chapter (and throughout the book), we believe that another relevant shortcoming of fiscal stabilizers is that they are largely insufficient when big, adverse shocks hit the economic system. In these cases, infrequent but clearly of paramount importance, the problem is not represented by asymmetries, since all countries suffer from the same exogenous events, but by the common destabilizing effects played by such shocks. In similar situations, it seems essential to dispose of a discretionary fiscal policy, and hence of an adequate fiscal capacity, to sustain aggregate demand.

Different proposals about automatic stabilizers have been advanced in the fiscal literature and they are mainly based on unemployment and output gap measures. We summarize the main underlying idea, while for a more complete overview see European Commission (2013).

In regard to output gap measures, for example Enderlein et al. (2012) propose a mechanism where countries experiencing an output gap larger (smaller) than the Euro-area average pay into the fund (receive payments from the fund). Furceri and Zdzienicka (2013) suggest a mechanism which collects contributions as a share of the Gross National Product of each member state and pays transfers proportional to the impact on the output gap.

A more widespread approach is based on unemployment measures, for which two main alternatives have been discussed in the literature: the re-insurance national unemployment scheme and the European unemployment insurance scheme. The main difference between the two schemes is that while in the first one EU transfers are collected and distributed by and to member states, which will use the money for areas with high unemployment, in the second one transfers will be directly collected from employers and/or employees and distributed to unemployed persons.

An example of re-insurance national unemployment scheme is proposed by Italianer and Vanheukelen (1992). The authors suggest two options. A first one, in which a member state should receive transfers proportional to the difference between the Eurozone average unemployment rate and country-specific unemployment rate. A second one, in which countries will receive transfers only if the differences between the two yearly changes in the unemployment rates will be above a minimum threshold. The idea of setting a threshold which activates automatic stabilizers has also been suggested by Gros (2014), which argues that the Eurozone needs a system which protects against rare and potentially catastrophic events.

As far as a European Unemployment Benefit Scheme is concerned one of the most famous proposals is that of Dullien and Fichtner (2013). The authors suggest a scheme where employees would pay a part of their wages into a European unemployment insurance scheme for a limited period and would receive transfers from this fund when they become unemployed and for a maximum period of time. According to this proposal, the European insurance should be combined with a national insurance scheme, and while the former should offer a basic level of protection for unemployed (i.e. in terms of eligibility criteria, a limited duration for receiving transfer, etc.) the latter should extend this level allowing more guarantees. Moreover, the authors argue that in order to avoid permanent transfers and moral hazard, it could be useful to introduce a condition to limit draw benefits and guarantee the insurance only for those who have been continuously paying contribution for a long period (i.e. 2 years). However, it cannot be ruled out that even with the imposition of these limits, structural characteristics of the economies may lead to transfers going in one sole direction for extended periods.

Finally, it is worth pointing out that, in principle, discretionary fiscal policies and automatic fiscal stabilizers are not mutually exclusive. Rather, in modern economies both tools are usually at the disposal of governments. Maybe, the greatest difficulty in applying a European Unemployment Scheme in the short term lies in the very different macroeconomic conditions characterizing labor markets in Euro-area countries. In other words, the ideal starting point of a European Scheme should be when a reasonable convergence of business cycle conditions among countries has been achieved.

2.4 The Effects of Government Spending Shocks in the Euro Area. Selected Literature

In Sect. 2.2 we have provided a description of the common regulatory framework for national fiscal policies, while in Sect. 2.3 we have highlighted the most important elements, at least in our opinion, regarding the proposal of a Euro-area budget for the evolution of the currency area towards a monetary and fiscal union.

In the second part of this chapter we aim to empirically investigate if a Euro-area fiscal stimulus, interpretable as originating from an artificial Euro-area budget or from a coordination among Euro-area countries fiscal policies, has the capability of exerting a stabilization effect on the aggregate Euro-area output. In particular, we will first study the impact of a Euro-area government spending shock and then investigate the effects of an exogenous change in the investments component of government expenditures.

It is worth stressing that studying the effect of fiscal stimuli at the Euro-area level is not an easy task, mainly because we are simulating the existence of a fiscal policy conducted at Euro-area level. Further, as already remarked, there is still only a small number of empirical studies concerning the Euro Area and, not less important, they do not reach a consensus on the effects that government spending shocks have on the Euro-area output.

Indeed, the traditional Keynesian view argues that fiscal stimuli have an expansionary effect on aggregate output and that, they are particularly effective when, after a large negative shock, nominal interest rates are not able to react significantly because they are close to the zero lower bound. Nonetheless, some New Keynesian models lead to the conclusion that government spending multipliers are quite smaller compared to the one postulated by more traditional Keynesian models (see e.g. Cogan et al. 2010). Yet, some studies show that at the zero lower bound of interest rates, government spending multipliers can be very large and welfare-improving (see, among others, Christiano et al. 2011 and Eggertsson 2011).

Of course, a historically very low level of interest rates could also be the consequence of an aggressive monetary policy pursued by the central bank. For, some investigations converge to the conclusion that an accommodative monetary policy strengthens the expansionary effects on output of fiscal stimuli (see Canova and Pappa 2011). However this result is rejected, on a theoretical ground by neoclassical models since the real interest rate is predicted to be independent by monetary policy. Not surprisingly, authors supporting this model usually reach the conclusion that the government spending multiplier is low, and more precisely near zero, in normal times (see, for example, Barro and Redlick 2011).

Empirical studies for the Euro Area do not reach consensus on the effect exerted by fiscal stimuli on output, showing quite heterogeneous fiscal multipliers. Among the more recent papers, Burriel et al. (2010), using a quarterly data set for the period 1981–2007 and a SVAR methodology, analyze the impact of fiscal policy shocks in the Euro Area as a whole and in the US. Their results show that expansionary fiscal shocks have a short-term positive impact on GDP, and the (cumulative) spending multiplier is around 1 at peak.

Another study is Canova and Pappa (2011) who, by using quarterly data and SVAR models, investigate the effects of government spending shocks at the aggregated level for Euro Area, US and UK.[15] The authors conclude that coordination between fiscal policy and monetary policy is quite important in determining the macroeconomic outcomes of fiscal packages. Specifically, results concerning the Euro-area show that under an accommodative monetary policy an increase in government consumption expenditure has expansionary effects on the Euro-area economy and that in this case the estimated fiscal multiplier, at impact, is around 2. These empirical results seem to support the idea that in the presence of an expansionary fiscal policy, if the central bank in turn adopts an accommodative monetary policy stance, in order to prevent the increase in the interest rate, it encourages spending by consumers and businesses, thus avoiding a crowding out effect on the economy.

These two studies obtain quite different results on fiscal multipliers. These dissimilarities can be, at least in part, ascribable to the different identification strategies adopted, the Cholesky decomposition in Burriel et al. (2010) and the sign restrictions approach in Canova and Pappa (2011). There are also some differences in the selected sample periods.

A recent strand of research has focused on spillover effects in the Euro Area. Gallio and Gambetti (2016) use a time-varying coefficients VAR model and study fiscal policy coordination and spillovers over the period 1995–2014. Government spending shocks are identified by adopting a Cholesky orthogonalization of the structural disturbances. The two main findings are that: (i) fiscal shocks originating in the largest Euro-area countries propagate notable effects on the other countries; (ii) there is little evidence of fiscal coordination among countries over the selected sample period.

Other recent studies exploring spillovers from fiscal policy shocks include Georgiadis and Hollmayr (2016) and Eller et al. (2017). In both investigation, Global-VAR (G-VAR) models are used. These studies, too, find that fiscal expansions generate positive cross-border output spillovers.

2.5 Measuring Fiscal Policy at the Euro Area Level

In this section we study the effects exerted by a Euro-area government spending shock on the Euro-area's GDP and on other macrovariables. By using quarterly data from 2002:Q1 to 2016:Q3, we estimate and identify a structural VAR in order to model dynamic interactions among the aggregated Euro-area variables.

We start our analysis by estimating the following reduced form VAR model:

$$X_t = A(L)X_{t-1} + e_t \tag{2.1}$$

[15]Data sample depends on the country. For the Euro Area it starts from 1993:Q1 to 2008:Q4.

where X_t is a 8 × 1 vector of macroeconomic variables; e_t is the vector of error terms, such that $E(e_t) = 0$ and $E(e_t e_t') = \Sigma_e$; A(L) is the 8 × 8 matrix polynomial in the lag operator L.
More precisely we have:

$$X_t^{'} = \left(g_t\ t_t\ p_t\ y_t\ i_t - i_t^*\ \varepsilon_t\ esi_t\ s\&p\right)$$

which includes the following variables for the Euro Area at time t: government spending, g_t; government revenues, t_t; the HICP, p_t; the real gross domestic product, y_t; the differential between the European overnight interest rate (Eonia), i_t, and the US federal funds rate, i_t^*; the nominal exchange rate, ε_t, defined as US dollars per currency unit; the economic sentiment indicator, esi_t; the stock market index, $s\&p$, is the Standard and Poor's euro price index. The model specification also includes a constant. The list of variables and their sources are detailed in the Data Appendix.

Government spending is constructed as the sum of government consumption and government investment, whereas government revenues are obtained by subtracting transfers and interest expenses from the total revenue stream (see Blanchard and Perotti 2002). The main idea underlying these definitions of the two variables is that public spending on goods and services impacts aggregate demand directly, while transfers and taxes change the amount of disposable income, and therefore the savings-investment decisions of households. In this model the Euro Area is treated as a large open economy that has important interactions with the US economy - the reason why we take into account potential influences from the US Federal Funds rate and exchange rate (see e.g. Scotti 2011).

Since fiscal policies are widely debated in the parliamentary process, rational economic agents can anticipate future tax or government spending decisions. This ability known as Fiscal Foresight can lead to an uncorrected identification of fiscal shocks in the structural VAR approach, because the information set of agents is larger than the econometricians' one. In order to tackle this "information deficiency" problem affecting fiscal VARs, Forni and Gambetti (2014) suggest enriching the VAR specification by including leading indicators, i.e. series that Granger-cause fiscal variables. Canova and Sahneh (2016) argue that including the growth rate of consumers' confidence to a bivariate VAR helps to recover shocks. Other contributions also introduce leading indicators in their VAR specification (see Cavallo and Ribba 2017 and Dallari and Ribba 2015).

Thus we also include economic sentiment indicators and a stock market index in our VAR specification. In order to easily calculate the shock effects on variables in percentage, the variables included in the model, with the exception of interest rates differential, are log-transformed and then multiplied by 100. As for lag length selection, we follow the Schwartz criterion and estimate the model by applying 1 lag.

Given the small sample considered, we test neither for possible cointegration relations among variables nor do we apply any transformation eventually needed to obtain stationary series. Thus, we include variables in levels in the VAR model, since in the presence of long-run equilibrium relations this represents a correct specification of the VAR model.

We can write the following reduced-form moving average representation of the VAR model:

$$X_t = C(L)e_t \tag{2.2}$$

where $C(0) = I$.

We recover the structural shocks by imposing a contemporaneous recursive structure to the estimated VAR model. The structural moving-average representation is given by:

$$X_t = B(L)\eta_t \tag{2.3}$$

in which $B(L) = C(L)B$, and $\eta_t = B^{-1}e_t$. B is the matrix of contemporaneous coefficients that measure the impact of structural shocks on variables. More precisely, B is the Cholesky factor of Σ_e, i.e. the unique lower triangular matrix such that $BB' = \Sigma_e$.

Thus we are imposing the following restriction: As in Blanchard and Perotti (2002), fiscal variables do not respond within the quarter to changes in macroeconomic conditions. This restriction is quite reasonable, considering that we are using quarterly data, and that policymakers require time both to learn about a macroeconomic shock and to plan effective fiscal measures. Moreover, we are imposing that the demand shock also exerts a delayed effect on prices, while the monetary policy shock does not influence either prices or aggregate output within the quarter (as well as fiscal variables). The exchange rate does not exert a contemporaneous effect on fiscal variables and, moreover, on prices and aggregate output. Finally, the changes in the economic sentiment indicator and in the stock market index do not affect all the other macrovariables within the quarter.

2.5.1 *The Response of Variables to a Euro-Area Government Spending Shock*

Figure 2.2 reports Euro-area responses to a Euro-area government spending shock for a group of variables included in the VAR model, i.e. Gross Domestic Product, Consumer Price Index, Interest rate differential, Economic Sentiment Indicator (ESI) and Stock market index.

An increase in the Euro-area government spending variable has an expansionary effect on Euro-area output for around two years and it also leads to an increase in the economic sentiment indicator, i.e. there is a higher consumer and business confidence following the increase in government expenditures, which is statistically significant from the second to the fourth quarter after the shock. It is worth stressing that both variables show a negative impact in the first quarter. However, these negative effects turn out to be not statistically significant.

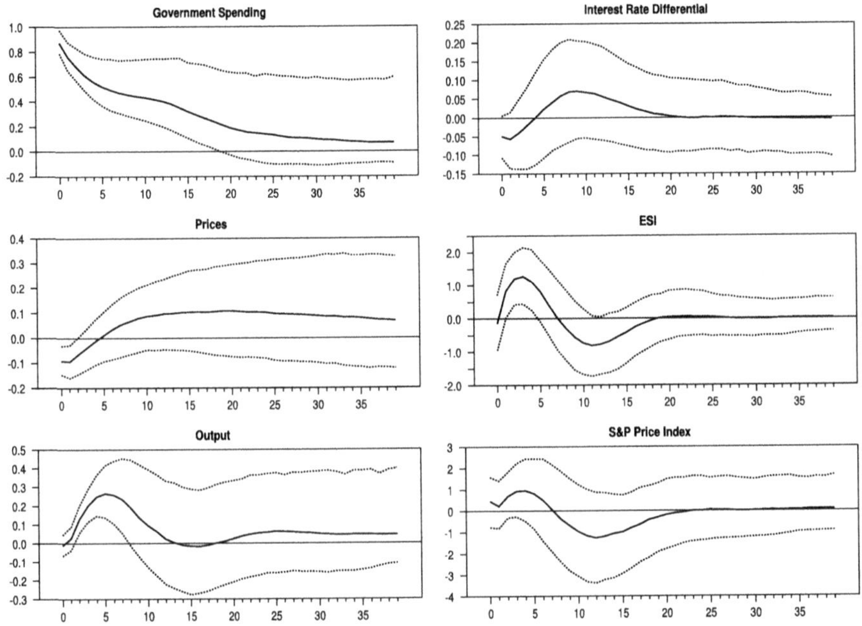

Fig. 2.2 Responses of Euro-area variables to a Euro-area government spending shock. *Note* Solid line: median estimate; dashed lines: 68% confidence interval

The increase in government spending is quite persistent, since it vanishes (becomes statistically non-significant) only after around 4 years. In regard to the response of Euro-area prices, there is a significant negative response, i.e. prices decrease, that is difficult to reconcile with the expansionary effects generated by the fiscal expansion. Nonetheless, apart from the first two quarters the response of prices is non-significant at all horizons.

Given the estimated confidence error bands, the interest rate differential shows a statistically non-significant response at all horizons.

Comparison with other studies requires caution because they use different sets of variables, alternative identification strategies and, above all, different sample periods. Nevertheless, an important difference with respect to Burriel et al. (2010) is that our results show that the effect of a government spending shock on output requires more time to disappear, i.e. we detect more persistent effects of fiscal shocks.

2.5.2 *The Response of Variables to a Euro-Area Government Investments Shock*

In the previous section we have analyzed the dynamic effects of Euro-area government spending shocks. Let us recall that government spending includes both

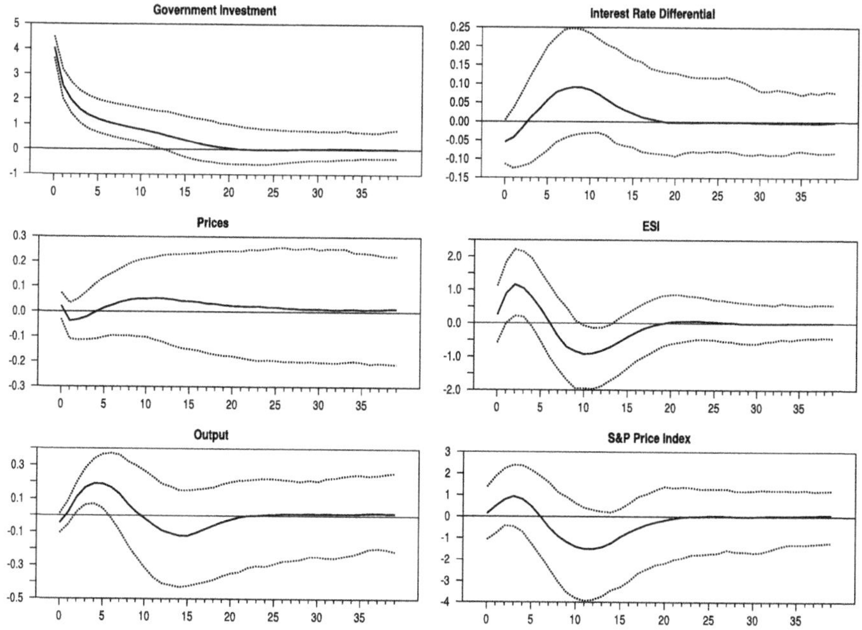

Fig. 2.3 Responses of Euro-area variables to a Euro-area government investment shock. *Note* Solid line: median estimate; dashed lines: 68% confidence interval

government investment and consumption. In this section we investigate the effects exerted on macrovariables by the investment component of government expenditures.

In order to recover the government investment shock we follow the same methodology, but now our VAR model includes Euro-area government investments, $ginv_t$, instead of Euro-area government spending g_t and hence X_t is given by:

$$X_t' = \left(ginv_t \; t_t \; p_t \; y_t \; i_t - i_t^* \; \varepsilon_t \; esi_t \; s\&p\right) \tag{2.4}$$

Thus, as in the previous section, first we estimate the reduced form, then we recover the structural shocks by imposing a Choleski decomposition.

Figure 2.3 shows the responses of Euro-area variables to a Euro-area government investments shock. Results show that an increase in Euro-area government investment has a positive effect on output. Nonetheless, this effect is statistically significant only for a few quarters and, more specifically, for around 1 year. We detect an increase even in the economic sentiment indicator, which reaches its peak after 3 quarters. The positive effect disappears 1 year after the shock.

As far as the other variables are concerned, they show statistically non-significant responses at every horizon. By comparing results in Figs. 2.2 and 2.3 it is clear that the qualitative conclusions are the same. In particular, the expansionary effects on the economy of public spending shocks are confirmed. However, we find that the effects exerted by government investment shocks on aggregate Euro-area output are less persistent with respect to unexpected changes in total government expenditures.

2.6 An Alternative Identification Strategy of Government Spending Shocks

In this section we present a sensitivity analysis in order to check the robustness of our results on the dynamic effects of Euro-area government spending shocks. We identify fiscal shocks by adopting an alternative identification strategy based on sign restrictions. More specifically, we impose a positive sign on impact to Euro-area government spending and aggregate output. Then, we follow the same strategy to study the effects of Euro-area government investment shocks.

In the next section we will use sign restrictions on the responses of some macrovariables to investigate the macroeconomic outcomes of government spending shocks in the presence of monetary accommodation.

Theoretical models do not give great support to restrictions on the response of output to fiscal shocks at short and medium horizons. Instead, the restrictions on impact adopted in this section are consistent with a class of New Keynesian Models (see Canova and Pappa 2011). However, it is worth noting that studies converging to the conclusion of a possible existence of non-Keynesian effects of fiscal policy, emphasize the importance of credible, persistent fiscal consolidations in order to generate a positive reaction of private spending and hence of aggregate output (see e.g. Giavazzi and Pagano 1990, Alesina and Ardagna 2010). Thus, in the appendix to this chapter we will try to take into account this possibility and will restrict the response of government spending to be negative for four periods. On the other hand, in that case we will leave free the response of output. As we will see, the qualitative conclusions previously obtained, i.e. Keynesian effects of fiscal policy in the Euro Area, are largely confirmed.

2.6.1 Recovering Government Spending Shocks by Sign Restrictions

In order to identify a Euro-area government spending shock we proceed as follows. First we estimate the following reduced form for a VAR model of order 1:

$$X_t = A_1 X_{t-1} + e_t \tag{2.5}$$

where the vector X_t includes the set of variables as in the previous section. e_t is the 8×1 vector of error terms, such that $E(e_t) = 0$ and $E(e_t e_t{}') = \Sigma_e$.

Second, given the relation between the error terms, e_t, and the exogenous macroeconomic shocks ε_t, $e_t = F\varepsilon_t$, the matrix Σ_e is randomly drawn from the posterior distribution of the matrix of the VAR coefficients. Moreover, since $E(\varepsilon_t \varepsilon_t{}') = I$ and given that $FF' = \Sigma_e$, by imposing sign restrictions on the responses of some variables to selected shocks, we aim to identify an impulse vector f, such that $f = F\alpha$,

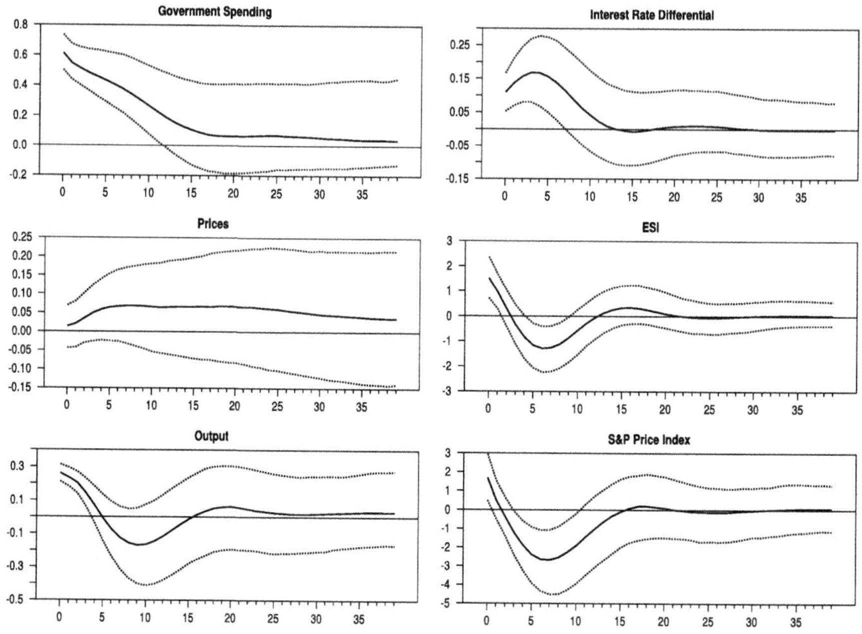

Fig. 2.4 Responses of Euro-area variables to a Euro-area government spending shock identified by sign restrictions. *Note* Solid line: median estimate; dashed lines: 68% confidence interval

where $||\alpha|| = 1$. In order to have a unique set of impulse responses to the identified shock we introduce a penalty function as in Uhlig (2005).

The confidence bands are built by using the Bayesian approach proposed by Sims and Zha (1999), where it is assumed that VAR errors are normal and that both prior and posterior density belong to the Normal-Wishart family. Moreover, we take 5000 draws from the posterior.

The sign restrictions imposed on impact are the following: (i) Government spending increase; (ii) Output increase. The responses of the other Euro-area variables entering the model are instead left completely free.

In Fig. 2.4 the responses of Euro-area variables to a government spending shock are reported.

Following the fiscal expansion, there is a statistically significant increase in output which lasts for around one year. Hence, the expansionary effects exerted by the positive government spending shock turns out to be not particularly persistent. An interesting difference with respect to the results obtained by imposing a recursive structure concerns the interest rate, which now exhibits a (expected) significant increase over a horizon of two years. Clearly, the positive response of interest rates helps to explain the smaller persistent effects of fiscal shocks on output obtained with respect to the recursive identification strategy.

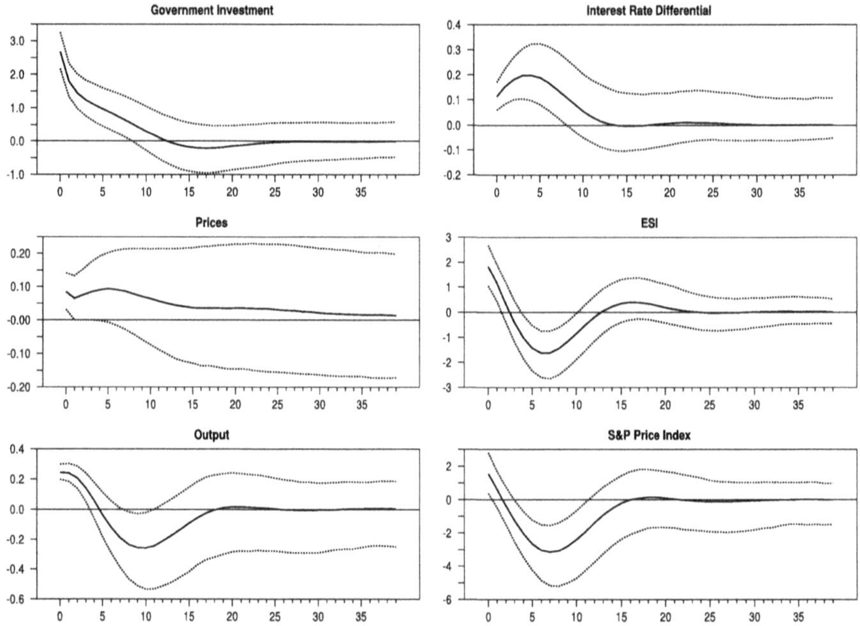

Fig. 2.5 Responses of Euro-area variables to a Euro-area government investment shock identified by sign restrictions. *Note* Solid line: median estimate; dashed lines: 68% confidence interval

Both the ESI index and the stock price index show a positive response on impact. Nonetheless, after around two years both the indexes show a negative sign. As for prices, the results substantially confirm a quite mute response at all horizons.

On the whole, however, this result confirms the conclusion reached in the previous section concerning the ability of fiscal policy at the Euro-area level to achieve the goal of macroeconomic stabilization.

2.6.2 Government Investment Shocks

In this section we report the responses of variables to a positive Euro-area government investment shock. The sign restrictions are the same as adopted to recover the government spending shock.

Figure 2.5 shows a picture that is very similar to the one previously obtained for the effects of government spending shocks (see graph in Fig. 2.4). Briefly, an exogenous increase in the Euro-area government investment, recovered by imposing sign restrictions, shows a positive effect on output for around 4 quarters. The responses of the other variables are very similar to those obtained in the previous section, since the interest rate increases for around eight quarters and both the ESI and the stock price index have a significant increase on impact. Nonetheless, there is an important difference which regards the response of the Consumer Price Index: on impact, prices increase in response to the positive government investment shock; then, from the second quarter on, the response of prices becomes statistically non-significant.

To summarize, the two alternative identification strategies, sign restrictions and the recursive one, show behavioral responses for Euro-area variables that are very similar, both in analyzing a Euro-area government spending shock and a Euro-area government investment shock. Therefore we can conclude that the results obtained are robust to the selection of (some) alternative identification strategies.

Now there is another question we wish to investigate: Have government spending shocks larger expansionary effects under an accommodative monetary policy? In other words, can a coordination of fiscal and monetary policies be more powerful in stabilizing the Euro-area economy on the whole? In the next session, we will try to answer this important question.

2.7 The Effects of Government Spending Shocks Under an Accommodative Monetary Policy

In the previous sections we have seen that a government spending shock has an expansionary effect on the Euro-area output and that this positive effects vanishes after around one year. In this section, we study if a coordination of monetary and fiscal policies leads to stronger expansionary and persistent effects on the economy.

The new set of sign restrictions, imposed on impact, is the following: (i) Euro-area government expenditures increase; (ii) aggregate output increases; (iii) interest rates decrease.

Figures 2.6 and 2.7 show the responses to Euro-area fiscal policy shocks under an accommodative monetary policy, in which the solid line indicates median estimate and dashed lines correspond to the 68th percent confidence interval.

An increase in government spending under an accommodative monetary policy still has, of course, an expansionary effect on the Euro-area output. However, by comparing this result to the one without accommodation (Fig. 2.2), it clearly appears that the effects on output are larger and more persistent since in this case the expansionary effects on the economy last for around three years.

The overall picture is quite similar when we consider a government investment shock under monetary accommodation and in this case, too, we find more significant effects (both economically and statistically) on output and, not less important, more persistent effects.

As for the other macrovariables, the picture is largely consistent with an expansionary economic environment. The confidence index (ESI) shows a significant increase for one year, from the second to the fifth quarter after the shock and a similar behaviour characterizes the response of the stock market index.

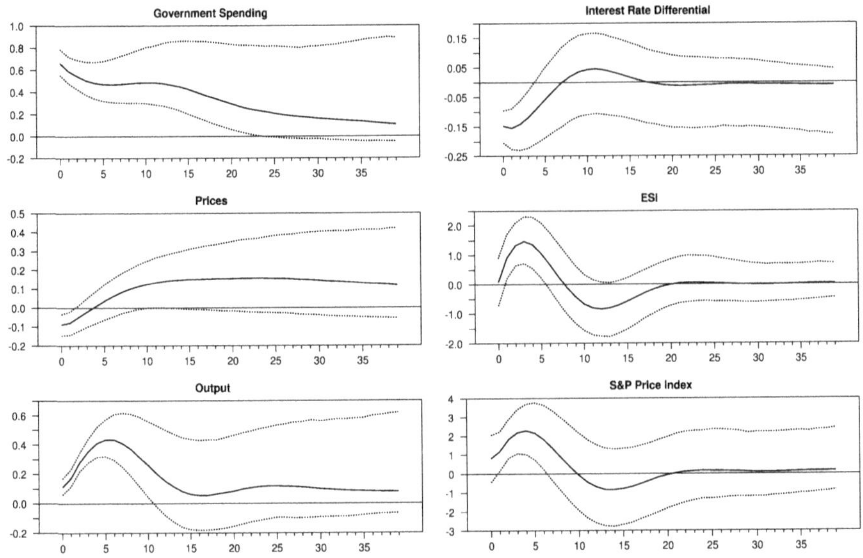

Fig. 2.6 Responses to a government spending shock under an accommodative monetary policy. *Note* Solid line: median estimate; dashed lines: 68% confidence interval

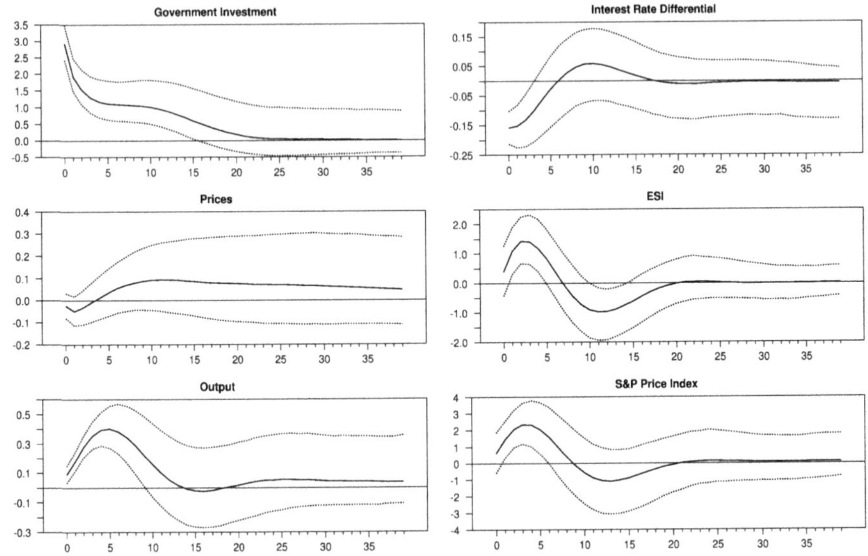

Fig. 2.7 Responses to a government investment shock under an accommodative monetary policy. *Note* Solid line: median estimate; dashed lines: 68% confidence interval

Somewhat enigmatic remains the dynamic response of the CPI, which shows non statistically significant effects at almost all horizons.

In the next section we will present some calculations concerning the government spending multipliers that confirm the role played by accommodative monetary policies in magnifying (at least at some horizons) the expansionary effects generated by fiscal expansion. We also point out that our findings on the interaction between fiscal and monetary policy in the Euro Area are, on the whole, in line with previous results obtained by Canova and Pappa (2011). Nonetheless, Canova and Pappa (2011) investigated a rather heterogeneous sample period, covering from 1993 to 2008, whereas our investigation focuses on the EMU period.

2.8 Fiscal Multipliers: Results

In this section we show the main results concerning the fiscal multipliers obtained by identifying Euro-area government spending shocks by imposing sign restrictions, with and without monetary policy accommodation (Table. 2.2).

The literature contains alternative definitions of fiscal multipliers[16] and in this chapter we will compute two alternative measures of multipliers. The first is the impact multiplier, given by:

$$Impact\ Fiscal\ Multiplier = \frac{\Delta Y_t}{\Delta G_t} \tag{2.6}$$

The second is the cumulative multiplier at horizon j, which is given by the ratio of the cumulated response of output and the cumulated response of government spending at the selected horizons (see e.g. IMF 2009). It can be written as:

$$Cumulative\ Fiscal\ Multiplier = \frac{\Sigma_{j=0}^{k} \Delta Y_{t+j}}{\Sigma_{j=0}^{k} \Delta G_{t+j}} \tag{2.7}$$

Table 2.2 reports Euro-area output multipliers computed at different horizons and separating the multipliers obtained, respectively, in the presence of and without monetary policy accommodation.

Looking at the table above we can highlight two main aspects concerning the estimated fiscal multipliers. First, in the absence of monetary accommodation, multipliers are significant only on impact or, more precisely, given the estimated confidence intervals a value of zero cannot be ruled out at horizons of one and two years. This reflects the less persistent effects exerted by fiscal expansions in this context. Nevertheless, the size of the multipliers on impact is notable, since they show values well above 1.

[16]For a more extensive discussion on fiscal multipliers, see Chap. 3.

Table 2.2 Fiscal multipliers

Horizons	Government spending multipliers		Government investment multipliers	
	no accommodation	mp accommodation	no accommodation	mp accommodation
Impact	1.7*	0.7*	2.8*	1*
1 year	1.6	1.6*	2.9	3.9*
2 years	0.8	2.6*	4.4	6.7*

Note The table reports government spending and investment multipliers at various horizons for the Euro Area. The first column reports the government spending multiplier with no monetary accommodation. The second column reports calculation of multipliers in the presence of monetary accommodation, i.e. in this case the sign of the response of interest rates is restricted to be negative on impact. Government expenditures is defined as the sum of government consumption and investment. The third and fourth column reports, respectively, government investment multipliers with no monetary accommodation and government investment multipliers in the presence of monetary accommodation

*Indicates statistically significant estimates at 68% confidence interval

In the presence of monetary accommodation, the multipliers are smaller on impact while their values are somewhat larger, and not less important statistically significant, at horizons of one and two years. In particular, both the government spending multiplier and the government investment multiplier reach their peak after two years when monetary policy has an accommodative stance.

Thus, on the whole, our results seem to be in line with Canova and Pappa (2011), who underlined the importance of monetary accommodation. Instead, with respect to the results presented in Burriel et al. (2010), who find that fiscal shocks exert significant effects for three years (without monetary accommodation), we find rather less persistent effects.

Of course, it is worth recalling that both these studies consider quite different sample periods, covering both pre - and post - EMU periods.

2.9 Conclusions

In the first part of this chapter we have provided an outline of the Euro Area's regulatory framework for national fiscal policies and have presented and discussed some proposals for evolution of the Euro Area towards a complete monetary and fiscal union. Instead, in the second part of the chapter, we have investigated the dynamic effects of government spending shocks on aggregate output and other relevant Euro-area macrovariables.

The main conclusions concerning the Euro-area common framework for national fiscal policies and the establishment of a fiscal capacity at the centralized level are that a simplification of rules and regulations would be highly desirable, in the light of the plethora of legal rules introduced by the Maastricht Treaty of 1992 up to the TSCG of 2012. However, it needs to be as clear as possible that the creation of a Euro-area fiscal union will unavoidably be associated with stricter rules on national deficit and public debts. In particular, a credible no-bailout rule is at the core of almost all the functioning monetary and fiscal unions in the world.

If one of the main goals of a Euro-area fiscal union should be, as we believe, macroeconomic stabilization in response to strong adverse shocks, then a quantitative evaluation of the ability of fiscal policy to achieve this goal clearly becomes of great importance.

In this chapter we have accomplished this task, by estimating and identifying a variety of SVAR models. In the first empirical exercise we have identified a government spending shock in the spirit of the approach suggested by Blanchard and Perotti (2002). In a second exercise, we have identified the fiscal shock by imposing sign restrictions, on impact, on the responses of some variables. The main findings are that a government spending shock has an expansionary role on the Euro-area output, i.e. Keynesian results emerge from this investigation. Moreover, in the presence of monetary accommodation by the central bank there is a sizeable increase in the response of output, i.e. the government spending multiplier is somewhat larger with monetary accommodation.

Similar macroeconomic results are found when we separately investigate the effects exerted by the investment component of government spending.

Finally, we have conducted a further empirical experiment: is it possible that by imposing a more persistent action in fiscal consolidations the sign of fiscal multipliers are reversed? (see, among others, Alesina and Ardagna 2010). The results concerning this further robustness analysis are presented in the appendix and indeed they confirm the qualitative conclusions on the Keynesian signs characterizing fiscal policy at the aggregate Euro-area level.

We have stressed throughout the chapter that the empirical experiment conducted could be seen as quite artificial, given the non-existence of a centralized budget for stabilization purposes in the Euro Area. However, the experiment can be alternatively interpreted in terms of a (counterfactual) strong fiscal coordination among member countries during the EMU period.

Appendix 1. Some Further Robustness Analysis

In this appendix we present some further robustness analysis on the dynamic effects of government spending and investment shocks on a selected set of Euro-area macrovariables. We recover the spending shocks by imposing sign restrictions on the responses of some variables and adopt the following strategy: with respect to the identification strategy of Sect. 2.6, we leave completely free the response of aggregate output and of the other variables entering the VAR model; instead, as far as the restrictions on government spending and investments are concerned, we impose a negative sign over four periods, i.e. four quarters. The logic behind this choice is that we now aim to investigate if a persistent fiscal contraction may generate non-Keynesian responses of aggregate output. In other words, we explore the possibility, stressed by an important strand of the literature (e.g. Giavazzi and Pagano

1990, Alesina and Ardagna 2010), that in the presence of more persistent (and thus more credible) fiscal consolidation, improved expectations may induce an increase in private spending such as to offset the decrease of aggregate demand caused by the government spending cut. This may happen if consumers are confident that fiscal consolidations will cause an increase in their future income and this confidence generates an increase in current consumption.

Results are reported in Figs. 2.8 and 2.9. The conclusions reached in Sect. 2.6 on the Keynesian effects of government spending shocks in the Euro Area are substantially confirmed: the response of aggregate output is statistically non-significant on impact but from the second quarter it begins to decrease. Moreover, the contractionary effects of the negative fiscal shock are more persistent with respect to those detected in Sect. 2.6, when the restriction imposed on the sign of the fiscal variable had been only on impact.

As for the responses of the other variables, they are largely statistically non-significant at almost all horizons.

Turning to the macroeconomic outcomes produced by a government investment shock, the results are similar but it is worth pointing out a difference with respect to the previous finding: the reaction of the Euro-area output is statistically significant only at a horizon of one year and it appears weaker than that detected in Sect. 2.6.

On the whole, it seems that we can conclude that a fiscal capacity at the Euro-area level, i.e. a discretionary fiscal policy conducted at the centralized level may contribute to reach the goal of macroeconomic stabilization in the EMU.

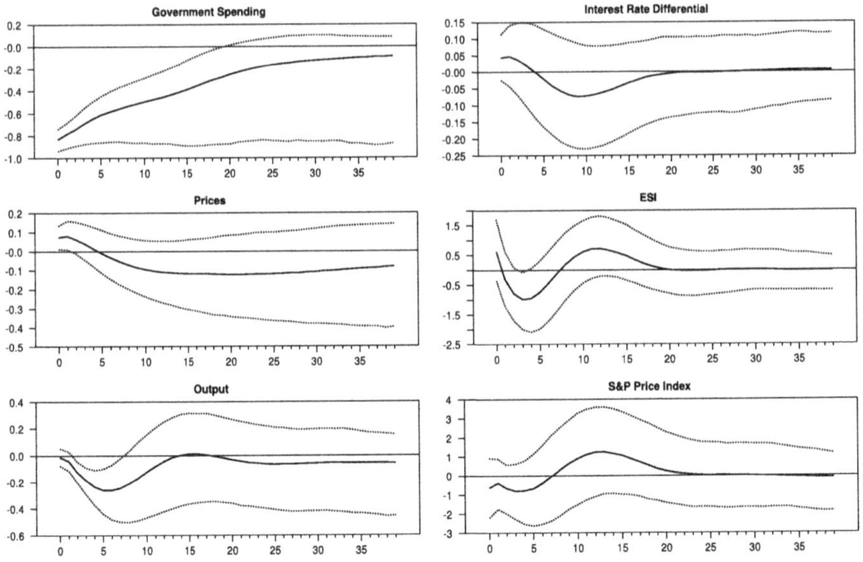

Fig. 2.8 Responses to a Euro-area government spending shock identified by sign restrictions. Signs restricted for four periods. *Note* Solid line: median estimate; dashed lines: 68% confidence interval

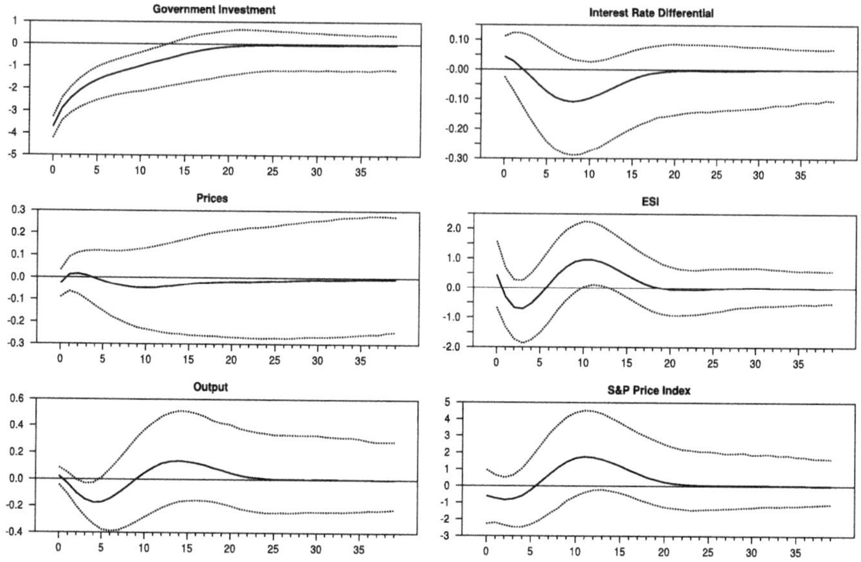

Fig. 2.9 Responses to a Euro-area government investment shock identified by sign restrictions. Signs restricted for four periods. *Note* Solid line: median estimate; dashed lines: 68% confidence interval

Data Appendix

- **Government Spending**: Data are collected from Eurostat, using the Quarterly non-financial account for general government. Government spending for the Euro Area (19 Countries) is the sum of Euro-area government consumption and Euro-area government investment. Once collected, Euro-area data from Eurostat are seasonally adjusted and transformed in real terms using GDP Deflator.
- **Government Revenues**: Data are collected from Eurostat, using the Quarterly non-financial account for general government. Government revenues for the Euro Area (19 Countries) are obtained by subtracting transfers (transfers are the sum of subsidies, other current expenditure, social benefits and social transfers in kind) and interest expenses from the Euro-area total revenue stream. Once collected, Euro-area data from Eurostat are seasonally adjusted and transformed in real terms using GDP Deflator.
- **Government Investment**: Data are taken from Eurostat, using the Quarterly non-financial account for general government (Euro Area 19 Countries). Once collected, Euro-area government investment data from Eurostat are seasonally adjusted and transformed in real terms using GDP Deflator.
- **Prices**: Euro Area (19 Countries) HICP is collected from European Central Bank with quarterly frequency. Data are seasonally adjusted by using the moving average technique. The reference year is 2015.

- **Output**: The real Gross Domestic Product for the Euro Area (19 Countries), Chain linked volumes (2010) is collected from Eurostat by using the GDP and main components database. Data are already available adjusted for seasonality.
- **Interest rate differential**: The variable is the difference between the European overnight interest rate (Eonia) and the US Federal Funds rate. The former is collected from Eurostat. The latter is retrieved from FRED, Federal Reserve Bank of St. Louis.
- **Exchange rate**: Euro/ECU exchange rates collected from Eurostat. Data are quarterly and expressed as US dollars per currency unit.
- **Economic Sentiment Indicator**: The Euro Area (19 Countries) Economic Sentiment Indicator comes from the European Commission - Directorate general for economic and financial affairs (DG ECFIN). It is already adjusted for seasonality. The monthly values have been aggregated to quarters through simple average.
- **S&P Euro Stock Market Index**: The variable is collected from Datastream with a quarterly frequency. It is adjusted for seasonality by using the moving average technique.

References

Alesina A, Ardagna S (2010) Large changes in fiscal policy: taxes versus spending. Tax policy and the economy, NBER 24:35–68

Barro RJ (1981) Output effects of government purchases. J Polit Econ 89:1086–1121

Barro RJ, Redlick CJ (2011) Macroeconomic effects from government purchases and taxes. Q J Econ 126(1):51–102

Blanchard O, Perotti R (2002) An empirical characterization of the dynamic effects of changes in government spending and taxes on output. Q J Econ 117:1329–1368

Blinder AS, Zandi M (2010) Stimulus worked. Finance and Development, December 2010

Bordo MD, Jonung L, Markiewicz A (2011) A fiscal union for the Euro: some lessons from history. NBER Working Paper No. 17380

Burriel P, De Castro F, Garrote D, Gordo E, Paredes D, Perez JJ (2010) Fiscal policy shocks in the Euro area and the US: an empirical assessment. Fisc Stud 31(2):251–285

Canova F, Pappa E (2011) Fiscal policy, pricing frictions and monetary accommodation. Econ Policy 26:555–598

Canova F, Sahneh MH (2016) Are small-scale SVARs useful for business cycle analysis? Revisiting non-fundamentalness. Working Papers 2/2016, BI Norvegian Business School

Cavallo A, Ribba A (2017) Measuring the effects of oil price and Euro-area shocks on CEECs business cycles. Department of Economics 0111, University of Modena and Reggio Emilia

Coenen G, Straub R, Trabandt M (2013) Gauging the effects of fiscal stimulus packages in the Euro area. J Econ Dyn Control 37(2):367–386

Cogan JF, Cwik T, Taylor JB, Wieland V (2010) New Keynesians versus old Keynesians government spending multipliers. J Econ Dyn Control 34(3):281–295

Corsetti G, Feld L, Lane P, Reichlin L, Rey H et al (2015) A new start for the Eurozone: dealing with debt: monitoring the Eurozone 1. CEPR Press

Christiano L, Eichenbaum M, Rebelo S (2011) When is the government spending multiplier large? J Polit Econ 119:78–121

Dallari P, Ribba A (2015) Economic shocks and their effects on unemployment in the Euro area periphery under the EMU. Department of Economics No. 114, University of Modena and Reggio Emilia
De Grauwe P (2016) Economics of monetary union, 11th edn. Oxford Press, Oxford
De Grauwe P, Ji Y (2016) How to reboot the Eurozone and ensure its long-term survival. In: Baldwin R, Giavazzi F (eds) How to fix Europe's monetary union: views of leading economists. CEPR Press, London (VoxEU.org eBook)
Delors J (1989) Report on Economic and Monetary Union in the European Community
Drautzburg T, Uhlig H (2015) Fiscal stimulus and distortionary taxation. Rev Econ Dyn 18(4):894–920
Dullien S, Schwarzer D (2009) Bringing macroeconomics into the EU budget debate: why and how? J Common Mark Stud 47(1):153–174
Dullien S, Fichtner F (2013) A common unemployment insurance system for the Euro area. DIW Econ Bull 3(1):9–14
Eggertsson G (2011) What fiscal policy is effective at zero interest rates? NBER Macroecon Annu 25(1):59–112
Eller M, Feldkirchner M, Huber F (2017) How would a fiscal shock in Germany affect other European countries? evidence from a Bayesian GVAR model with sign restrictions. Austrian central bank. Focus on Eur Econ Integr 1:54–57
Enderlein H, Delors J, Schmidt H, Bofinger P, Boone L, De Grauwe P, Piris J, Pisani-Ferry J, Rodrigues M, Sapir A, Vitorino A, Fernandes S, Rubio E (2012) Completing the Euro: a road map towards fiscal union in Europe. Report of the Tommaso Padoa-Schioppa Group
European Commission (2013) Paper on automatic stabilizers
European Commission (2014) The production function methodology for calculating potential growth rates and output gaps
European Commission (2015) Completing Europe's economic and monetary union
European Commission (2017a) Vade mecum on the stability and growth pact
European Commission (2017b) Reflection paper on the deepening of the economic and monetary union
Fagan G, Henry J, Mestre R (2005) An area-wide model (AWM) for the Euro area. Econ Model 22(1):39–59
Forni L, Monteforte L, Sessa L (2009) The general equilibrium effects of fiscal policy: estimates for the Euro area. J Public Econ 93(3):559–85
Forni M, Gambetti L (2014) Sufficient information in structural VARs. J Monet Econ 66:124–136
Furceri D, Zdzienicka A (2013) The Euro area crisis: need for a supranational fiscal risk sharing mechanism? IMF Working Paper 13(198)
Gambetti L, Gallio F (2016) Measuring fiscal policy spillovers in the Euro area. ADEMU WP 2016/044
Georgiadis G, Hollmayr J (2016) Fiscal spillovers in the Euro area: sign, size and determinants. Mimeo
Giavazzi F, Pagano M (1990) Can severe fiscal contractions be expansionary? tales of two small European countries. NBER chapters. NBER Macroecon Annu 1990:75–122
Gros D (2014) A fiscal shock absorber for the Eurozone? insurance with deductible. Int Econ 49(4):199–203
Gros D, Belke A (2015) Banking union as a shock absorber: lessons for the Eurozone from the US. CEPS, Bruxelles
Henning CR, Kessler M (2012) Fiscal federalism: US history for architects of Europe's fiscal union
IMF (2009) Fiscal multipliers. IMF Staff Position Note No. 09/11
Italianer A, Vanheukelen M (1992) Proposals for community stabilization mechanisms: some historical applications. Eur Econ 5(93):493–510
Kenen P (1969) The theory of optimum currency areas: an eclectic view. In: Mundell R, Swoboda A (eds) Monetary problems of the international economy. University of Chicago Press, Chicago
MacDougall D (1977) Report of the study group on the role of public finance in European integration

Mauro P (2014) Role of fiscal policy to spur growth in Europe. In: Posen A, Ubide A (eds) PIIE briefing 14–5: rebuilding Europes common future. Peterson Institute for International Economics, Washington
McKinnon R (1963) Optimum currency areas. Am Econ Rev 717–724
Mountford A, Uhlig H (2009) What are the effects of fiscal policy shocks? J Appl Econom 24:960–992
Mundell R (1961) A theory of optimum currency areas. Am Econ Rev 51:509–517
Musgrave RA (1959) The theory of public finance. McGraw Hill, New York
Oates W (1972) Fiscal federalism. Harcourt Brace Jovanovich, New York
Paredes J, Pedregal D, Pérez J (2009) A quarterly fiscal database for the Euro area based on intra-annual fiscal information. ECB Working Paper 1132
Pisani-Ferry J, Vihriala E, Wolff G (2013) Options for a Euro-area fiscal capacity. Bruegel Policy Contribution 01, Bruegel, Brussels
Pissarides C (2016) Rebooting Europe: closer fiscal cooperation needed. In: Baldwin R, Giavazzi F (eds) How to fix Europe's monetary union: views of leading economists. CEPR Press, London (VoxEU.org eBook)
Romer C, Bernstein J (2009) The job impact of the American recovery and reinvestment plan
Rubio E (2015) Federalising the Eurozone: towards a true European budget? IAI Working Papers 15
Sapir A, Wolff G (2015) Euro area governance: what to reform and how to do it. Bruegel Policy Briefs
Scotti C (2011) A bivariate model of federal reserve and ECM main policy rates. Int J Cent Bank 7:37–78
Sims CA, Zha T (1999) Error bands for impulse responses. Econometrica 67:1113–1156
Tabellini G (2016) Building common fiscal policy in the Eurozone. In: Baldwin R, Giavazzi F (eds) How to fix Europe's monetary union: views of leading economists. CEPR Press, London (VoxEU.org eBook)
Ubide A (2015) Stability bonds for the Euro area. Peterson International Institute for International, Economics No, pp 15–19
Uhlig H (2005) What are the effects of monetary policy on output? results from an agnostic identification procedure. J Monetary Econ 52(2):381–419
Veld J (2016) Public investment stimulus in surplus countries and their Euro area spillovers. European Commission Economic Brief, No, p 016
Wolff GB (2012) A budget for Europe's monetary union. Bruegel Policy Contribution 22
Wyplosz C (2005) Fiscal policy: institutions versus rules. Natl Inst Econ Rev 191(1):64–78

Chapter 3
The Macroeconomic Effects of Fiscal Policy Shocks: A Review of the Literature

Abstract In this chapter we provide a review of the literature using multivariate time series techniques, and in particular structural VARs and panel VARs, to study the effects of fiscal policy shocks on macroeconomic variables. In the last decades the traditional Keynesian view on fiscal policy as a useful tool for macroeconomic stabilization has been challenged on the ground of possible expansionary effects associated with fiscal consolidations. However, as will be seen, recent research shows heterogeneous results. It seems possible at this stage to identify an emerging consensus, related to the conclusion that the size of fiscal multipliers, i.e. the size of the response of output to exogenous changes in government expenditures or revenues, is significantly affected by some selected macroeconomic factors. Among these factors, country financial conditions are particularly relevant in the context of the present research, since they are closely related to the levels of public and private indebtedness as measured by debt-to-GDP ratios.

3.1 Introduction

In recent years the research on the macroeconomics outcome of fiscal policies has experienced renewed interest after some decades of relative quiet, in which a greater attention had been paid to studies aiming to measure the effects of monetary policy. Clearly the recent boost to fiscal studies is closely related to the bitter fruit of the "Great Recession", with the associated debate, characterizing in particular the Euro Area, on fiscal stimulus versus austerity policies as the more proper way to face the economic and financial crisis which began in late 2007.

Indeed, the traditional Keynesian view makes a clear prediction of the expansionary effects exerted by increases in government spending on aggregate output and, in consequence, attributes an important, stabilizing role to fiscal policy. Thus, according to the Keynesian view, *a fortiori* in the context of deep recession affecting the world economy during 2008, a strong expansionary fiscal policy would be required in order more rapidly to achieve economic growth and jobs. In fact, looking at the United States and consistently with this view, the Obama Administration was confident that the aggressive fiscal stimulus approved by Congress in February 2009 would be very

© Springer International Publishing AG 2018
A. Cavallo et al., *Fiscal Policies in High Debt Euro-Area Countries*,
https://doi.org/10.1007/978-3-319-70269-8_3

effective since the so-called government spending multiplier had a positive sign and was greater than one (see e.g. Romer and Bernstein 2009).[1]

In line with this interpretation, Blinder and Zandi (2010) concluded their analysis maintaining that the fiscal stimulus caused a significant increase of GDP during 2010 and that it was an appropriate policy response to an extraordinarily huge recession.[2]

However, both in the public debate and in the literature, the traditional Keynesian view of fiscal policy has often been criticized and put into question in recent decades. According to Cogan et al. (2010) a New Keynesian model incorporating rational expectations would predict a much smaller government spending multiplier with respect to the estimation of Obama's Council of Economic Advisers.[3]

In a more neoclassical key, Robert Barro in an editorial published on the Wall Street Journal accused the Team Obama of being affected by "extreme demand-side view", claiming that the multiplier effect of government spending on economic output is likely to be zero in peacetime (cf. Barro 2009).

As for the European economy, the sequence of strong adverse economic shocks which, starting with the world financial crisis of 2007, hit the European countries in the last decade, caused a deep recession and an associated increase in unemployment to the highest levels in 20 years and, also as a consequence of the social and economic difficulties experienced by a large number of Euro-area countries, posed doubts on the viability of the Economic and Monetary Union (EMU). In fact, the deep and persistent economic crisis has raised important questions regarding the effective policy tools available to Euro-area economies to contrast strong adverse shocks. These questions are closely related to the peculiar architecture of the Currency Union, with the quite singular interaction between the centralized responsibility of monetary policy and the domestic conduct of fiscal policy, though within a set of supra-national rules. The current crisis has shown, among various structural weaknesses, that the absence of the second leg in the Currency Union, i.e. a Fiscal Union with a centralized budget and a management of aggregate demand capable to tackle adverse shocks of particular virulence, may threaten the survival of EMU.

An increasing number of scholars has supported in more recent years the evolution of EMU towards a European Fiscal Union and has proposed developments in terms of a centralized Euro-Area Budget with purpose of macroeconomic stabilization. This might take the form of active fiscal policies aiming to influence the aggregate demand and/or temporary transfers towards member countries experiencing a contractionary phase of business cycle, for example in the form of a European Unemployment Scheme (see e.g. Pissarides 2016; De Grauwe and Ji 2016; Tabellini 2016; Sapir and Wolff 2015). Yet (Gros and Belke 2015) maintain that a Fiscal Union is not a priority for the Euro Area, since an efficient banking union might well accomplish

[1]The United States launched a large fiscal stimulus package over the period 2008–2010 of about 5 percent of domestic GDP (cf. OECD 2009).

[2]In order to estimate the impact of the fiscal stimulus, Blinder and Zandi used Moody's Analytics model.

[3]Cogan et al. (2010) base their estimations of fiscal multipliers on the New Keynesian model developed for the US economy by Smets and Wouters (2007).

the task to tackle new crises. A similar position was expressed by Wyplosz (2005) a few years after the onset of the euro. Wyplosz argued that strengthening fiscal rules and improving the quality of institutions would have helped to stabilize public debts and hence to achieve macroeconomic stability.

On the political and institutional front, the European Commission published on May 2017 an important reflection paper on the future of the Economic and Monetary Union. The Commission's Proposals concerns the completion of the Financial Union by the end of 2019 and the creation of a centralized fiscal capacity finalized to Area-wide macroeconomic stabilization by the end of 2025 (see European Commission 2017).

It is worth recalling that, under the European common rules for national fiscal policies, severe consolidations of public finance have been imposed on some member-countries, like Greece, in recent years. One important motivation invoked by European authorities and national governments for these contractionary fiscal policies adopted in economies suffering from both a deep recession and a high level of public debt, was that a primary goal for these countries should be to recover the confidence in the sustainability of public finances. In turn, this confidence was (and is still) seen as a necessary condition for regaining stable growth.

However, in a recent paper, Fatas and Summers (2016) have argued that fiscal consolidations have caused a permanent decrease in aggregate output in the European economies. The authors conclude that fiscal consolidations, also as a consequence of the recessionary effects exerted, paradoxically are likely to have missed the goal of reducing the public debt-to-GDP ratio.

Looking at this global debate, one is quite naturally led to wonder if, after all, it is only a question of empirical measuring of the effects of fiscal policy on output and other macroeconomic variables in order to discriminate between these alternative views. Surprisingly, after two decades of extensive empirical research on the subject of fiscal shocks there is more, and not less, uncertainty on the macroeconomics outcomes associated with fiscal policies.

In this survey of the literature we will mainly refer to study on the effects of fiscal shocks based on multivariate time series techniques and, in particular, on the structural VAR approach. As will be seen, a large body of research based on this approach has tried to measure the fiscal policy in the U.S. economy and in other OECD countries in the last decade but less attention has been devoted to Euro-area member countries.

As far as the United States is concerned, although heterogeneous results characterize the estimated size of fiscal multipliers, there is a large consensus on the Keynesian effects exerted on aggregate output by fiscal policies. For example, estimations of the spending multipliers range from a minimum of 0.64 by Mountford and Uhlig (2009) to a maximum of 1.57 by Romer and Bernstein (2009).[4]

---

[4]By also including studies that produce separate estimations of fiscal multipliers in recessions and espansions, the variability increases. For example, in Auerbach and Gorodnichenko (2012) the spending multipliers may vary from (around) zero to 3.6.

More uncertainty arises from estimations concerning unemployment fiscal multipliers where, on the one side, we find the results by Monacelli et al. (2010) of a negative multiplier around 1 at peak (an increase in government spending causes a reduction of unemployment of 1 percent) and, on the other, the conclusions of Brückner and Pappa (2012) of a positive unemployment fiscal multiplier for the US and the majority of OECD countries in the postwar period (i.e. a fiscal expansion produces an increase in unemployment).

Instead, looking at the European economies, we find heterogeneity of results often concerning both signs and sizes of fiscal multipliers. In their interesting investigation on the effects of fiscal stimuli in 44 countries, which also includes many European countries, (Ilzetzki et al. 2013) found negative multipliers for the group of European countries affected by high public debt. The implication would be that a fiscal expansion might cause an economic recession in countries like Italy and Greece. However, in the study presented in this book, we find that a positive government spending shock has an expansionary effect on aggregate output and hence, according to our results, the presence of public debt does not necessarily prevent a Keynesian effect associated with government spending.

Of course, the first study to suggest the possible existence of negative output spending multipliers is due to Giavazzi and Pagano (1990). They found that fiscal consolidations produced expansionary effects in two small European economies, i.e. Denmark and Ireland, in the 80s, the main underlying idea being that credible fiscal consolidations may cause an increase in private demand through the improvement of expectations.

More recently, Alesina and Ardagna (2010) examined evidence on large fiscal consolidations and fiscal expansions in OECD countries over the period 1970–2007. One of their main findings is that credible fiscal consolidations, i.e. fiscal tightenings implemented through permanent contractions of government spending or increases in taxes, are more likely to produce expansionary effects on output. In line with (Giavazzi and Pagano 1990) expansionary effects on aggregate output may be generated if agents' expectations improve. More precisely, this happens if consumers believe that fiscal consolidations will permanently increase their future income, thus causing an expansion of current private consumption able to offset the decrease in public demand.

In an article aiming to characterize the dynamic effects of fiscal shocks on unemployment in the Euro-area periphery under EMU, (Dallari and Ribba 2015) find that a negative government spending multiplier characterizes a group of countries including Ireland, Portugal and Spain. The authors stress that all the countries exhibiting a negative spending multiplier have been affected in the last 16 years by remarkable private debt-to-GDP ratios rather than high public debt-to-GDP ratios. The authors conclude that this empirical evidence challenges macroeconomic models to take into account the role played by private debt in shaping the dynamic effects of fiscal policy. In particular, it seems that in the presence of high private debt there is a reduction in the size of fiscal multipliers and, at a pinch, a switching of signs as financial conditions worsen.

Indeed, one of the aims of this critical literature review is to shed some light on these heterogeneous findings concerning the European countries.

One strand of the research has recently investigated the relation between the state of the economy and the size of fiscal multipliers. Canzoneri et al. (2016) have argued that fiscal multipliers can be state-dependent. They develop a theoretical model of the business cycle which includes costly financial intermediation and conclude that fiscal multipliers are much larger in recessions. Auerbach and Gorodnichenko 2012 use alternative methodologies to estimate the size of spending multipliers and find that for the postwar US economy the multiplier is much larger in recessions. An interesting finding by Auerbach and Gorodnichenko regards the largest estimated spending multiplier associated with military spending.

Another important research topic developed in recent years concerns fiscal spillovers, i.e. the effects exerted by domestic fiscal policy shocks on output of other countries. Clearly, this subject is of particular relevance for the Euro Area. Researches on spillovers in EMU countries include, among others, Beetsma et al. (2006), Belke and Osowski (2016); Georgiadis and Hollmayr (2016), Gallio and Gambetti (2016), Eller et al. (2017). On the whole, these studies find that there are significant spillovers, both statistically and economically. From the largest Euro-area economies and that there is heterogeneity in the effects exerted on other countries. This heterogeneity is mainly explained by the intensity of trade ties since these studies identify the trade flows between countries as the most relevant channel for the international transmission of fiscal shocks.

Auerbach and Gorodnichenko (2013) stress the importance of business cycle as another factor able to explain heterogeneity of spillovers. In particular, investigating a group of OECD countries, they find that spillovers are higher in recessions and lower when the economies experience expansionary phases.

To sum up, the main conclusion we draw from this survey of the literature is that there is no reason to expect the same responses of macroeconomic variables to fiscal policy for every country and for every time. The motivation is that the effects of fiscal shocks are strongly associated with peculiar macroeconomic factors affecting the various economies. As shown in the empirical investigations by Ilzetzki et al. (2013) and Dallari and Ribba (2015), among others, the monetary policy stance, the degree of openness and the level of national debt (both public and private) with respect to GDP, are all relevant factors capable of explaining the different macroeconomic outcomes of fiscal shocks.

The structure of this chapter is organized as follows. Following the introduction, Sect. 3.2 discusses the main competing approaches to fiscal shocks identification. In Sect. 3.3 we focus on the strategy of identification of fiscal shocks mainly followed in the structural VAR approach, while in Sect. 3.4 we briefly present and discuss some alternative definitions of fiscal multipliers widely adopted in the literature. Sections 3.5 and 3.6 present the main results obtained, respectively, for the US and Euro-area economies in a selected group of empirical studies. In Sect. 3.7 we review some studies investigating the spillover effects from fiscal shocks. In Sect. 3.8 we discuss the role of a set of macroeconomic factors exerting a significant influence on the responses of macrovariables to fiscal shocks. In particular, we concentrate attention on degree of openness and exchange rate regime, monetary policy stance and role of public and private debt. Section 3.9 is devoted to discussion of fiscal foresight, a phenomenon associated with the ability of economic agents to anticipate future fiscal obligations which might produce unreliable estimations of fiscal multipliers using the structural VAR approach. Section 3.10 concludes the chapter.

3.2 Alternative Methodologies for the Identification of Fiscal Shocks

In general, measuring the effects of fiscal policy is a not so easy task, due to a classic Achilles heel affecting much applied macroeconomics investigating causal nexus among variables. In the case of fiscal policy it is represented by the bidirectional causality characterizing the relation between output and government expenditures. In other words, the estimations of fiscal multipliers may be distorted by virtue of the, at least partial, endogenous response of government spending to changing macroeconomic conditions.

Another important problem is given by the large predictability of fiscal policy. This predictability relies on the simple fact that in modern democracies the approval of fiscal packages is usually associated with a public political process preceding the implementation of fiscal policy. As pointed out by, among others, Canova and Pappa (2007) in the presence of predictability of fiscal policy, standard structural VARs analysis might be unreliable.

Hence, any attempt to identify the exogenous movements in fiscal policy must imply a strategy aiming to tackle these problems.

In particular, in this review of the literature on the identification of fiscal shocks, we focus on investigations which adopt a multivariate time series approach. Two main identification strategies of the fiscal disturbances have emerged in this area of research in recent years referable, respectively, to the structural VAR (Vector Autoregression) methodology and to the "narrative approach".

The approach based on structural VARs was initiated by Blanchard and Perotti (2002). This approach essentially extends the methodology concerning the identification of monetary policy shocks, largely followed in the literature of the nineties, to the identification of fiscal shocks. By using a structural VAR, the exogenous component of fiscal (or, alternatively, monetary) policy is extracted from an equation, which is part of a system, defining (more or less explicitly) the policy rule followed by the responsible authority. Thus, in this context, the identified shock is nothing other than the unexpected, non-systematic, component of the policy rule.

Let us consider the following equation:

$$\Phi_t = F(\Omega_t) + \eta_t \tag{3.1}$$

where Φ_t is the policy instrument at time t, Ω_t represents the information set of the policy makers and F is the function describing the policy rule.[5] Φ_t is measured by a short-term interest rate or by an indicator of money supply, in the case of monetary policy instruments. Alternatively, by components of government expenditures or revenues in the case of fiscal rule instruments.

Through Eq. (3.1) a separation of the systematic component of policy, expressed by $F(\Omega_t)$, from the unexpected component, expressed by the stochastic term η_t, is allowed.

The information set, Ω_t, usually contains a combination of target variables, e.g. output and inflation, and a further set of macroeconomic variables, e.g. oil prices or a commodity price index, that are considered useful for predicting the behaviour of a selected set of key variables.

However, in order to trace the dynamic effects on nominal and real variables of the policy shocks, a set of economically meaningful identifying restrictions needs to be imposed.

As far as the identification of monetary policy shocks is concerned, Christiano et al. (1999) impose a contemporaneous causal structure relying on informational assumptions concerning the delayed effects of monetary policy on macroeconomic variables. Bernanke and Mihov (1998), using the VAR methodology, evaluate alternative indicators of monetary policy for the U.S. based on the Federal Reserve System's operating procedures and then measure the effects of policy innovations on macroeconomic variables.[6]

It is worth noting that predictability is likely to be less relevant in the case of monetary policy. Yet, although the decisions on interest rates by central banks are not subject to a parliamentary process, as instead is the case for government decisions concerning fiscal policy, there has been a steady increase in public communication on monetary policy choices and strategies in the last decades.

In regard to the literature concerning fiscal policy, starting with the classic work of Blanchard and Perotti (2002), the SVAR approach to the identification of fiscal shocks has relied on the assumption that fiscal variables respond with a delay to changes in macroeconomic conditions. This assumption seems quite reasonable, in particular in the light of the political process associated with fiscal policy decisions and in the presence of data available at quarterly frequency. Nevertheless, as stressed by the authors, when utilizing annual data this identifying restriction would sound much more questionable, implying an unrealistic delay in the response of fiscal policy. This

[5]Some examples of linear rules related to the conduct of monetary policy are given in Christiano et al. (1999). The authors review the research on monetary policy shocks in the previous decades.

[6]Beside the structural VAR approach to measure monetary policy, another large body of research has been devoted to modeling the central bank's "reaction function", i.e. estimating structural equations describing the systematic component of monetary policy. Following the seminal work of Taylor (1993), structural equations models have developed to analyze the systematic response of the nominal interest rate to changes in a small set of macroeconomic variables. The set of variables usually includes at least a measure of aggregate economic activity, such as the output gap, and a measure of inflation. See e.g. Clarida et al. (1998).

also seems to suggest the importance of collecting fiscal data at quarterly frequencies for empirical investigations.

An alternative approach to identification of fiscal shocks is based on narrative techniques, through which series of government expenditures or revenues, seen as exogenous with respect to current macroeconomic conditions, are created.[7] This approach originated by the work of Barro (1981), who was the first to use military expenditures as an instrument for government spending. The main idea is that by using historical military build-ups it is possible to undertake a sort of "natural experiment" aimed at measuring the effects on the economy of true exogenous movements in fiscal policy. He found that the fiscal multiplier in time of war exhibits keynesian features, its size being around one. In his article Barro also stressed the importance of separating temporary changes in defense purchases, mainly characterizing wartime, from permanent shifts in defense expenditures, which are usually associated with much lower government spending multipliers. Thus, Barro's main findings contrast with the traditional Keynesian view on fiscal policy as a useful tool for macroeconomic stabilization.

Ramey and Shapiro (1998) extended this approach by using narrative evidence in order to build a series of anticipated military spending. In Ramey (2011) there was a further refinement, based on the conclusion that big increases in government spending are often anticipated by economic agents before they become effective. This ability by agents to anticipate changes in government spending may lead to imprecise estimations of fiscal multipliers. According to Ramey, this represents an important weakness of the structural VAR approach to the study of fiscal policy. Thus the author builds some new series of government military spending shocks by using newspaper sources and the Survey of Professional Forecasters. The estimated fiscal multipliers are comprised between 0.6 and 1, a result in line with the findings of Barro (1981).

In Barro and Redlick (2011) new estimations based on annual data indicate a value below unity for the government expenditures multiplier.

Auerbach and Gorodnichenko (2012) disaggregate government expenditures variables in order to measure possible differences in the size of spending multipliers. They conclude that, as far the postwar US economy is concerned, military spending exhibits the largest multiplier.

Although the strategy of recovering fiscal shocks from the military spending and from the news narrative can help to improve the estimation of fiscal multipliers, some problems arise in extending this methodology to other countries. The first problem is that the natural experiment of large military buildup is difficult to export outside the United States and, in any case, is much more problematic for smaller economies, since in this case the assumption made for the US that wars influence the economic system only through the exogenous effects exerted by government spending clearly does not hold.

[7] A comprehensive survey of the literature on macroeconomic shocks, also including fiscal shocks, and their propagation mechanisms has recently been provided by Ramey (2016).

Moreover, when the investigation is based on multi-country models, as for instance in the present book, the time-series of news announcements is not readily available for larger sets of countries.

In a recent investigation (Barnichon and Matthes 2015) have stressed that the narrative approach may be subject to biases in the distribution between expansionary and contractionary shocks that do not seem to characterize other alternative structural VAR approaches, like the recursive identification scheme.

Other important critiques have recently been advanced of the narrative approach. Leeper et al. (2013) note that it is difficult to fully insert this approach within a theoretical model, by virtue of their particular treatment of information flows. Fisher and Peters (2010) point out two other important shortcomings: (1) It is necessary to assume that spending increases are known with certainty; (2) there is an unavoidable subjectivity in the identification of the relevant dates.

Fisher and Peters (2010) propose an identification strategy of government spending shocks aiming to tackle these shortcomings. The authors use innovations to the stock returns of big military contractors as an indicator of government spending shocks. They find that the cumulative response of output to a 1 percent increase of government spending is 1.5 over a period of five years.

3.3 Structural VARs and Identification of Fiscal Shocks

The dynamic relations among m macroeconomic variables can be expressed through a Vector Autoregression.

In general, a Vector Autoregressive Model (VAR) of order p for a $m-$dimensional vector of covariance-stationary variables, X_t, can be written as[8]:

$$X_t = A_1 X_{t-1} + A_2 X_{t-2} + \cdots A_p X_{t-p} + e_t \tag{3.2}$$

where e_t is the $m \times 1$ vector of error terms, such that $E(e_t) = 0$ and $E(e_t e_t') = \Sigma_e$. Let us rewrite (3.2) in the following way:

$$(I_m - A_1 L - A_2 L^2 - \cdots A_p L^p) X_t = e_t \tag{3.3}$$

or in a more compact form:

$$A(L) X_t = e_t \tag{3.4}$$

where $A(0) = I$. L is the lag operator, such that:

$$L X_t = X_{t-1}$$

$$L^2 X_t = X_{t-2}$$

[8]In order to simplify the notation, we omit constants and other deterministic components.

$$L^p X_t = X_{t-p}$$

From the autoregressive representation (3.4) and given the assumption that the vector process, X_t, is covariance stationary, we can recover the reduced-form Wold representation:

$$X_t = C(L)e_t \tag{3.5}$$

where $C(L) = A(L)^{-1}$.

We aim to identify the structural shocks driving the endogenous variables. The structural moving average representation is:

$$X_t = B(L)\varepsilon_t = \sum_{s=0}^{\infty} B_s \varepsilon_{t-s} \tag{3.6}$$

where: $B(L) = C(L)B$ and $\varepsilon_t = B^{-1}e_t$

The $m \times 1$ vector, ε_t, of the structural shocks contains orthonormal innovations, i.e. is such that $E(\varepsilon_t \varepsilon_t') = I$. There is the following relation between the vector of error terms and the vector of structural shocks:

$$e_t = B\varepsilon_t \tag{3.7}$$

Note that the covariance matrix of the error terms, Σ_e, can be expressed as:

$$E(e_t e_t') = \Sigma_e = BE(\varepsilon_t \varepsilon_t')B' = BB' \tag{3.8}$$

Equation (3.8) represents a system of equations through which, by virtue of the symmetry of the covariance matrix, Σ_e, $\frac{n^2+n}{2}$ restrictions are imposed on the n^2 elements of B. Hence, further $\frac{n^2-n}{2}$ restrictions need to be imposed on matrix B to recover the structural disturbances. This is a necessary order condition.

In the VAR approach, the additional $\frac{n^2-n}{2}$ restrictions, ideally based on some economic model, represents the bridge between theory and data.

The exogenous shocks driving the dynamics of the economic system are not directly observable and are obtained as a linear combination of the estimated error terms, by pre-multiplying the vector of error terms, e_t, for a non-singular matrix B^{-1}. This makes clear that the identification of a structural VAR model relies on the selection of a unique matrix B in such a way as to satisfy the formal conditions required for identification and at the same time to offer an economic interpretation of the $\frac{n^2-n}{2}$ imposed restrictions.

If we select B as the Cholesky factor of Σ_e, then B is the unique lower triangular matrix such that $BB' = \Sigma_e$. In this case, the researcher recovers a recursive (causal) contemporaneous VAR model. This identification strategy was followed by Sims (1980) in his well-known article pioneering the use of VAR models in applied macroeconomics.

Although the Cholesky orthogonalization is still widely used in the VAR literature, it often suffers from the difficulties of justifying the causal structure imposed on the data by appealing to theoretical models. Thus, this identification strategy is often labelled, with a misnomer, as "a-theoretical approach" to VAR identification.

However, let us notice that if we select B as the Cholesky factor of Σ_e, then any other orthogonalization can be obtained by postmultiplying B for a non-singular matrix V such that $VV' = I$.

In other words, any other structural VAR representation can be obtained as an orthonormal transformation of the Cholesky representation:

$$X_t = F(L)u_t = B(L)VV'\varepsilon_t \tag{3.9}$$

where F is such that $FF' = \Sigma_e$ and the zero restrictions imposed on the elements of F do not lead to a recursive structure.

Indeed, the label "structural VARs" has been historically attributed to models like those expressed by (3.9), characterized by non-recursive identification of structural disturbances.[9]

Let us note that by imposing at least $\frac{n^2-n}{2}$ restrictions, in adjoint to the $\frac{n^2+n}{2}$ underlying system (3.8), we have an exactly identified system.

The order condition is only a necessary condition for identification. For, as in traditional systems of simultaneous equations, a necessary and sufficient condition for identification (rank condition) is given by: $rank(\Sigma_e) = rank(BB')$.[10]

From the structural moving average representation (3.6) it is possible to obtain the impulse response functions, interpreted as the derivative with respect to the shocks:

$$\frac{\partial X_{t+k}}{\partial \varepsilon_t} = B_k \tag{3.10}$$

The element B_{ij} of B_k represents the response of variable i at the horizon $t+k$ to the shock ε_j which occurs in the period t. The response of variable i to a shock j, at various horizons, is usually presented in graphical form and represents the classical tool of structural VAR analysis.

In the present book, in Chaps. 4 and 5, we focus our investigation concerning the macroeconomic outcome of fiscal shocks on a selected group of small open Euro-area economies affected by high public and/or private debt. To accomplish this task, we will jointly model Euro-area and national variables. To this end, the VAR specification proposed by Cushman and Zha (1997) to identify monetary policy shocks in a small open economy (Canada) interacting with a large economy (United States) is of particular interest, since it allows the separation between an exogenous

[9] See, among others, Sims (1986) and Bernanke (1986).

[10] VAR models and identification of structural shocks are extensively treated in Canova (2007, Chap. 5). An important point stressed by Canova is that rank and order condition cannot rule out the possibility that more theoretical models are consistent with the estimated set of error terms. In other words, if rank and order condition are satisfied then we have local identification.

block, including area-wide variables, and an endogenous one, comprising the small open economy variables.

Starting with the autoregressive representation, $A(L)X_t = e_t$, a VAR model with block exogeneity restrictions has the following representation:

$$\begin{pmatrix} A_{11}(L) & 0 \\ A_{21}(L) & A_{22}(L) \end{pmatrix} \begin{pmatrix} X_{1t} \\ X_{2t} \end{pmatrix} = \begin{pmatrix} e_{1t} \\ e_{2t} \end{pmatrix} \tag{3.11}$$

where X_{1t} and X_{2t} have dimension, respectively, $m_1 \times 1$ and $m_2 \times 1$, $A_{11}(L)$ has dimension $m_1 \times m_1$, $A_{21}(L)$ $m_2 \times m_1$, $A_{22}(L)$ $m_2 \times m_2$. Moreover, $m_1 + m_2 = m$.

Thus, a near-VAR model has an exogenous block in which equations do not include local variables, i.e. the variables of the second block, whereas the equations related to local variables work as full VAR equations. In the presence of economic interaction between small and large open economies, this seems to be a proper specification of the VAR model that presents a further, important feature: although many different VAR models are estimated, one for each country considered in any empirical investigation, the set of area-wide shocks is not only common to all countries but also invariant.

We point out that, in the context of investigations conducted in Chaps. 4 and 5, we study the domestic effects of fiscal shocks and do not deal with the question of spillovers to other countries. Indeed, when studying spillovers, as in Chap. 6, more robust results may be obtained by using panel VAR models.

Peersman (2004) used the near-VAR model to investigate the transmission of monetary policy shocks to European countries. More recently, in Cavallo and Ribba (2015) this approach has been applied to study the propagation of Euro-area common shocks to a selected group of Euro-area economies. Other recent and interesting applications of the near-VAR methodology are provided by Boeckx et al. (2017), Cavallo and Ribba (2017), Conti et al. (2017).

Turning to identification of fiscal shocks, let us consider a vector X_t, 4×1, with $X_t = (G_t, T_t, P_t, Y_t)'$. Where G_t is a measure government spending, T_t is a government revenues variable, P_t is a price index and Y_t is a measure of aggregate output. VAR models utilized in the literature to study fiscal policy, generally include one or both the measures of fiscal policy, government expenditures and/or government revenues, and at least one indicator of the real activity, output and/or unemployment. Richer specifications may also include an instrument of monetary policy, private consumption and investment and/or open economy variables, such as exchange rate and net exports.

Starting with the seminal work of Blanchard and Perotti (2002), a crucial identifying restriction imposed by researchers is that fiscal variables do not respond within the quarter to GDP shocks. The political and economic motivation for this identifying restriction is that it requires time for policymakers to learn about a macroeconomic shock and to plan fiscal policy measures in response to shocks. Moreover, before implementing the measures parliamentary approval of the fiscal package is required. This seems a fairly convincing characterization of the fiscal policy process and, in fact, this identification strategy has been largely followed by the subsequent structural VAR literature. Nevertheless, it is worth stressing that imposing the zero restrictions on the contemporaneous response of fiscal variables makes much economic sense in the presence of quarterly data, whereas by utilizing annual data these restrictions are much less appealing, since they would imply an excessive inertia of policymakers to changes in economic conditions.

It is easily verified that, given the vector X_t, 4×1, the imposed delayed responses of G_t and T_t to macroeconomic changes do not give restrictions sufficient to just identify the VAR model. For, the relation $\Sigma_e = BB'$ gives 10 restrictions and two further zero restrictions come from the delayed responses of fiscal variables. We have a total of 12 restrictions whereas 16 are required for exact identification of the structural model. Indeed, to obtain the 4 additional restrictions required, it has become common practise in the fiscal VAR literature to adopt the Cholesky decomposition of matrix B, i.e. to impose a causal ordering to the variables, with the fiscal series ordered first.

A different identification strategy to recover the fiscal shocks is adopted in Canova and Pappa (2007) and in Mountford and Uhlig (2009). In these papers fiscal shocks are identified by imposing sign restrictions on the responses of some variables. Canova and Pappa (2007) recover a government expenditures shock by imposing that an increase in government expenditures causes an output increase on impact. Nevertheless, this identification strategy would be questionable for the Euro-area small open economies that we want to investigate in the present book, given the uncertainty detected in the literature not only on the size of fiscal multipliers but also on the sign of the response of aggregate output to fiscal expansions.

Mountford and Uhlig (2009) identify both government revenues and government expenditures shocks by using sign restrictions. This methodology is then applied to US quarterly data covering the period from 1955 to 2000. The sign restrictions imposed for tax and spending shocks are mild, since the response of the other, non-fiscal variables is not restricted. However, another novelty of this research is that the authors also identify monetary policy and business cycle shocks. The joint identification of monetary and fiscal shocks is a notable step ahead, in the light of the importance that theoretical models attribute to the stance of monetary policy in shaping the effects of fiscal shocks on the economy.

In particular, in Mountford and Uhlig (2009) the monetary policy shock is identified by imposing a positive sign in the response of interest rate and a negative sign in the response of prices to a decrease in money supply. Thus, while consistent with the conventional wisdom on the effects of contractionary monetary policy shocks on prices, this approach prevents in a (questionable) a-priori way the possible emergence of a price puzzle.[11]

In order to briefly discuss the methodology of identification based on sign restrictions, let us consider the covariance matrix of residuals, Σ_e, estimated from a reduced-form VAR representation like the one expressed by system (3.2) and recall that there

[11]The price puzzle is an age-old plague affecting VAR models aiming to study the dynamic effects of monetary policy shocks on nominal and real variables. The puzzle consists in the wrong sign in the response of prices to a monetary policy shock. In particular, it affects VARs in which shocks are identified by imposing contemporaneous, causal zero restrictions. See e.g. Christiano et al. (1999).

exists the following relation between the vector of estimated error terms, e_t, and the vector of exogenous shocks, ε_t: $e_t = P\varepsilon_t$. Given a factorization of the covariance matrix, $PP' = \Sigma_e$, by imposing sign restrictions on the responses of some variables to selected shocks, the researcher aims to identify an impulse vector p, such that $p = P\alpha$, where $||\alpha|| = 1$. The sign restrictions imposed would, ideally, be consistent with some macroeconomic model. This approach produces "weak identification": it does not impose an excessive strait jacket on data and allows a selection of a set of dynamic responses of variables to the identified structural shocks (see Uhlig 2005).

3.4 Alternative Definitions of Fiscal Multipliers

One of the main aims usually pursued by investigations on the effects of fiscal shocks concerns calculation of the so-called fiscal multipliers. There are alternative definitions adopted in the literature (see e.g. Spilimbergo et al. 2009). In this section we briefly present the most widely used definitions, on which are based calculations of fiscal multipliers.

The classic definition of output fiscal multiplier is:

$$Fiscal\ Multiplier = \frac{\Delta Y_{t+j}}{\Delta F_t} \tag{3.12}$$

Thus, the output fiscal multiplier is given by the ratio between the change j periods ahead of GDP, or other indicators of aggregate output, for a given change at time t of the fiscal variable, i.e. government spendings or, alternatively, government revenues.

If we take $j = 0$ we obtain the fiscal multiplier at impact:

$$Impact\ Fiscal\ Multiplier = \frac{\Delta Y_t}{\Delta F_t} \tag{3.13}$$

In some studies, the value of the fiscal multiplier is taken at peak, i.e. it represents the maximum value, at a detected horizon, of the change in output following a change in the fiscal variable at time t.

Instead, an alternative measure of fiscal multiplier, based on cumulative changes in Y and F, is given by:

$$Cumulative\ Fiscal\ Multiplier = \frac{\Sigma_{j=0}^{k} \Delta Y_{t+j}}{\Sigma_{j=0}^{k} \Delta F_{t+j}} \tag{3.14}$$

Hence, the cumulative multiplier at horizon j (see e.g. IMF 2009) is obtained as the ratio between the sum of changes in aggregate output over the period from t to $t + j$, and the sum of changes in fiscal variables over the same period.

Mountford and Uhlig (2009) also use a variant of the cumulative multiplier (3.14), expressed in terms of present value multiplier at given horizon, j:

$$Present\ Value\ Multiplier = \frac{\Sigma_{j=0}^{k}(1+i)^{-j}\Delta Y_{t+j}}{\Sigma_{j=0}^{k}(1+i)^{-j}\Delta F_{t+j}} \tag{3.15}$$

In order to calculate the present value multiplier, the authors use the average interest rate over the sample period.

Clearly, all these measures are potentially useful indicators of the effects of fiscal policy on output and are, as a consequence, widely used in the literature. It should be noted that the results obtained in empirical investigations are likely to be sensitive to the choice of one type of multiplier instead of another, and this may add a further dose of heterogeneity to the findings presented by researchers.

By looking at the definition of impulse response functions (see Eq. 3.10) and dealing with fiscal shocks, it is easy to recognize the close, conceptual and analytical, relation between the dynamic response of output to a fiscal shock and calculation of fiscal multipliers. Nevertheless, let us note that in most studies adopting the VAR approach both fiscal and other macroeconomic variables enter the model in natural logs. The implication is that the response of output to a fiscal shock, at selected horizons, returns an elasticity: the percent change in output in response to a one percentage change in government spendings (or revenues). In order to recover the measure of fiscal multiplier expressed in money-to-money terms, i.e. as the effect exerted on output by an increase in one unit of money in government expenditures (revenues), it is common practise in the literature to re-scale the result expressed as elasticity by the fiscal share, i.e. by F/Y. The usual choice for F/Y is the average fiscal share over the sample period. By considering that the fiscal share in the largest economies shows values comprised between 0.25 and 0.4, the conclusion is that fiscal multipliers are usually much larger with respect to measures based on elasticities.

Moreover, it is also worth observing that although this is a correct procedure from a mathematical point of view, when dealing with data spanning a long period of time, using the average value of F/Y may pose some problems if the series of fiscal share exhibits high variability. In other words, the results concerning the fiscal multiplier might be, at least partially, misleading.

Indeed, this critique may also apply to the studies included in the present book, since in order to calculate fiscal multipliers we will follow the procedure of rescaling for the fiscal share. However, we believe that the problem is less relevant in the context of our investigations: given our focus on the EMU period, we typically consider sample period covering, on average, around 17 years.

Turning to the alternative measures of fiscal multipliers presented in this section, in the various chapters of the present book we will mainly use the so-called cumulative multiplier. An important advantage of this measure is that it provides a synthetic indicator of the strength of the effects of fiscal policy on output and, at the same time, it conveys useful information on the persistence profile of fiscal shocks. Both the information are clearly of great interest for policymakers.

Finally, we have repeatedly stressed in this chapter (and also in others) that in recent decades not only has the size of fiscal multipliers been subject to debate among researchers and policymakers but even the time-honored view of a positive sign for the spending multiplier and a negative one for the tax multiplier has been challenged by non-Keynesian views, both on empirical and theoretical grounds. Nevertheless, it seems that the Great Recession has helped to revitalize the old view.

3.5 The Dynamics Effects of Fiscal Shocks in the US Economy

In Sect. 3.2 we have reviewed part of the literature using the narrative approach to identification of fiscal shocks. In this section and in the subsequent ones we mainly focus on research adopting the structural VAR approach to identification.

In Blanchard and Perotti (2002), X_t is a 3×1 vector, where $X_t = (T_t, G_t, Y_t)'$. T_t is a government revenues variable, defined as total taxes minus transfers; G_t is government spending, defined as government consumption plus government investment; and Y_t is a measure of aggregate output represented by GDP. The authors express all the variables in real, per capita, terms and use quarterly data from 1947 to 1997, though most estimations conducted in the paper cover the period 1960–1997.

As already discussed in the previous section, the crucial identifying restriction imposed by Blanchard and Perotti is that fiscal variables do not respond within the quarter to GDP shocks. The political and economic motivations underlying this restriction are summarizable in three points: (1) It requires time for policymakers to learn about a macroeconomic shock; (2) further time is required to plan fiscal policy measures in response to shocks; (3) before implementing the measures, a parliamentary approval of the fiscal package is needed in all modern democratic systems.

In order to exactly identify the three dimensional VAR model, a further restriction is required in addition to the 6 restrictions obtained by the relation $BB' = \Sigma_e$, linking the covariance matrix of error terms, Σ_e, to B, the 3×3 matrix containing the contemporaneous effects of the shocks, and two further restrictions deriving from the assumption that fiscal variables are not affected in the contemporaneous period by GDP shocks. The $9th$ zero restriction is obtained by imposing that government spending shocks do not have contemporaneous effects on taxes. Alternatively, the authors estimate VAR models in which there is the reverse restriction, i.e. that tax shocks have zero effects within the quarter on government spending. This set of restrictions leads to a lower triangular B matrix, and hence Blanchard and Perotti estimate structural VARs in which the orthogonalization of the shocks is obtained by adopting the Cholesky decomposition.

The main findings of the research are that in the US postwar economy fiscal shocks exert Keynesian effects on output: an unexpected increase of government spending causes an increase both of output and private consumption; an unexpected increase of taxes causes a contraction both in aggregate output and private consumption. However, the results concerning private investment are more difficult to reconcile with the Keynesian tradition, since an expansion in government expenditures provokes a decrease in private investment.

Blanchard and Perotti in their investigation find that the size of the government spending multiplier is around one at peak (or around -1 for the tax multiplier). However, there is some variability in the size of estimated multipliers which is related to the choice of the trend components, deterministic or, alternatively, stochastic.

Including both tax and expenditure variables in VAR estimations seems a proper choice, since omitting taxes (or expenditures) may bias the results. Nevertheless, some SVAR studies focus attention only on the effects of government spending shocks. Sometimes this is due to data limitations, in particular when studying a wider group of countries. For example, this is the case of Ilzetzki et al. (2013) who measure fiscal policy by estimating a Panel SVAR including 44 countries and focus on the effects of government expenditures.

Fatas and Mihov (2001) and Galí et al. (2007), by using structural VAR techniques and investigating the postwar US economy, confirmed the main results obtained by Blanchard and Perotti (2002). These two studies mainly focused on the response of consumption to government spending shocks and their conclusion is that there is an increase in aggregate consumption following an increase in government expenditures. In Galí et al. (2007) the estimated effects of fiscal shocks on aggregate output, i.e. the government spending multiplier, is 0.78 at impact and 1.74 at peak (reached after 8 quarters following the shock).

Mountford and Uhlig (2009), despite using a different methodological approach to identification of fiscal shocks, based on sign restrictions, obtain quite similar results with respect to Blanchard and Perotti (2002). The authors jointly identify monetary policy, fiscal policy and business cycle shocks. They obtain an estimation for the fiscal multiplier of 0.65, in the case where government spending is financed through deficit. Thus, although the implied spending multiplier is smaller, the conclusions of Blanchard and Perotti of keynesian effects of fiscal shocks exerted in the US postwar economy are substantially confirmed.

Canova and Pappa (2011) identify government consumption expenditure shocks by imposing sign restrictions and find for the US economy a positive fiscal multiplier at impact, conditional on an accommodative monetary policy stance, on where the latter is identified by a negative real interest rate associated with the increase in government spending.

This conclusion on the crucial role played by an accommodative monetary policy in order to generate large effects on output following government consumption increases is confirmed by Hall (2009) and Woodford (2011). Both studies use New Keynesian models to shed light on the dynamics effects of government spending shocks. However, as stressed by Canova and Pappa (2011), this conclusion on the role of monetary policy typically characterizes Keynesian models but is instead contrasted by neoclassical models, where the real rate of interest is independent of monetary policy and depends on saving and consumption decisions of the private sector. Hence, in neoclassical models, fiscal multipliers cannot be influenced by monetary policy choices of the central bank and the interest rate increases in response to expansionary fiscal policies.

Keynesian effects of fiscal policy for the postwar period are also detected by Monacelli et al. (2010). The authors estimate unemployment fiscal multipliers, using a structural VAR model identified by imposing a causal ordering, with government expenditures ordered first. The estimated unemployment multiplier equals 0.6 at the peak. Thus, according to Monacelli et al. (2010), an increase of 1 percent of government spending-to-GDP-ratio causes a maximum decrease of 0.6 percent in unemployment rate.

A quite different result is instead found in Brückner and Pappa (2012), since they conclude that fiscal expansions can increase unemployment, both in the US economy and in other OECD countries. In part, these contrasting results may be ascribed to different sample specifications. However, the authors maintain that the main explanation rests on the heterogeneity characterizing workers, separated in outsider and insiders. The increase in the overall unemployment is explained by an increase in outsider unemployment greater than the decrease in insider unemployment.

3.6 The Estimated Effects of Fiscal Shocks in the European Economy

Despite the extensive attention devoted in the last decade to studies on the macroeconomics outcome of fiscal policy shocks, are still limited in number investigations concerning the Euro Area as a whole and also specific member countries. Some researchers have indeed investigated the effects of government spending shocks at the aggregate Euro-area level (e.g. Canova and Pappa 2011; Burriel et al. 2010). However, an important problem posed by such aggregated studies is that a fiscal policy conducted at the Euro-area level has not been effective in the last decades and is still not. Thus, it is difficult to provide a sound economic interpretation of the identified fiscal shocks. Maybe even more important, in these studies data are aggregated for different national fiscal variables over a period of around 30 years, and hence with samples covering both the pre- and post-EMU period. Once again given the momentous upheaval, both economic and political, that has characterized the Euro Area from the start of currency union, it is not easy to provide a consistent interpretation of the estimated fiscal shocks.

Let us recall that in the previous chapter we have provided an estimation of government spending multipliers at the Euro-area level, and thus on this front we are potentially subject to the same critique. Nevertheless, our sample period covers the last 15 years, i.e. the EMU period. In our opinion, considering a more homogeneous period, in which all countries share a set of common fiscal policy rules and are subject to the same common monetary policy regime, helps to provide a more sound economic interpretation of the aggregate fiscal shocks recovered.

Burriel et al. (2010), for the period 1981–2007, estimate a (cumulative) spending multiplier around 1 at peak. This result contrasts with the conclusion of Canova and Pappa (2011), who find, instead, evidence of a large spending multiplier, considering the period 1993–2008, but only in the presence of an accommodative monetary policy. At least in part, these different results might be explained by the alternative identification strategies followed: sign restrictions in the work by Canova and Pappa, and the Cholesky decomposition, in the spirit of Blanchard and Perotti (2002), in the case of Burriel et al. (2010).

Canova and Pappa find that under an accommodative monetary policy, with a negative real interest rate, an increase in government consumption expenditures has expansionary effects on the Euro-area economy. The fiscal multiplier, at impact, is around 2. However, the estimation is subject to uncertainty, and given the wide confidence bands obtained, the size of the multiplier may also be well below one.

Our findings are in line with the conclusion of Canova and Pappa, since we find that a relatively large spending multiplier (above 2 at peak) emerges in the Euro Area when the central bank simultaneously reduces the interest rates. However, unlike Canova and Pappa, we calculated a sizeable fiscal multiplier around 2 under an identification scheme in which the government expenditures shock is not associated with accommodative monetary policies.

Other studies, like Ilzetzki et al. (2013) use panel VAR techniques and thus include a group of Euro-area countries in their investigation. Nevertheless, even in this case, the authors do not obtain an estimate of fiscal multipliers at country level. Instead, they aggregate the European and non-European countries under alternative macroeconomic classifications. One of the most interesting findings of this research is that when the countries are classified on the basis of the public debt-to-GDP ratio, with high public debt countries above the threshold of 60 percent, the estimated government spending multipliers are negative for high debt countries. Clearly, a very important result, also in the light of the notable numbers of Euro-area countries, and in particular Southern countries, affected by high public debts.

However, in our opinion, the risk of obtaining spurious results is also present in this research, since the average responses to a government expenditures shock may hide substantial differences among the national economies. In Dallari and Ribba (2015) we have undertaken an investigation that considers only the EMU period and includes Mediterranean countries plus Ireland. By using structural VARs identified by imposing a recursive structure, we find that unemployment decreases in response to a positive government spending shock in Italy and Greece and instead decreases in Ireland and Spain. The important implication is that fiscal policy is effective in two high public debt countries, i.e. Italy and Greece, and ineffective in two high private debt countries, i.e. Ireland and Spain. This is a quite different conclusion with respect to Iltezky et al. (2013) who aggregate this group of countries without separating for high public and private debt.

Brückner and Pappa (2012), instead, found that in European countries like France, Italy and UK, the unemployment rate increases in response to government spending shocks. For France and Italy the sample period covered, with quarterly data, is 1980:1–2009:1, for UK is 1964:1–2009:1. Thus, the investigation covers both the pre- and post-EMU period, implicitly assuming that the currency union (in the case of France and Italy) does not imply an important historical break. In the light of the work by Ilzetzki et al. (2013), another shortcoming of this investigation concerns the different exchange rate regimes characterizing these countries over the sample period considered.

Giordano et al. (2007) have used the VAR methodology developed by Blanchard and Perotti (2002) to study the dynamic effects of government expenditure shocks on private GDP in Italy. The size of the estimated fiscal multiplier is 0.6 at peak (after 3 quarters). However, looking at the cumulative multiplier, the authors find a quite significant Keynesian effect exerted by government spending shocks on total output.

In a recent paper Gambetti and Gallio (2016) investigate fiscal policy coordination and spillovers from fiscal shocks in Germany, France, Italy and Spain. As for fiscal policy coordination, despite the high synchronization of business cycles characterizing these countries, the authors detect very low levels of fiscal coordination across countries.

3.7 Fiscal Shocks and International Spillover Effects

Another important theme, recently explored by the literature on fiscal policy, concerns the spillover effects associated with domestic fiscal shocks. For the Euro Area, the estimation of international spillovers is of particular interest, given the high degree of trade openness characterizing, on average, Euro-area economies and, not less important, considering the relevant macroeconomic imbalances affecting the currency area. In fact, a possible macroeconomic strategy suggested by some researchers and also by international institutions in recent years regards the proposal of a sizeable fiscal stimulus in Germany seen both as a tool for reducing the excessive domestic surplus in the current account and to boost growth in peripheral Euro-area countries, by stimulating an increase in their net exports.

Beetsma and Giuliodori (2004) and Beetsma et al. (2006) find that there are large trade spillovers deriving from fiscal shocks in a group of European countries, including Germany, Italy and France. The main propagation factor is given, according to the authors, by the trade channel. Trade flows, as key factors for significant spillovers, are also present in Global-VAR (GVAR) models (see, among others, Hebous and Zimmermann 2013; Belke and Osowski 2016; Ricci-Risquete and Hernández 2015).

Clancy et al. (2015) find that for a receiving country sizeable spillovers are generated when the country exhibits a high share of import content from abroad. Indeed, this seems quite a plausible macroeconomic condition.

Gambetti and Gallio (2016), explore spillovers in the Euro Area over the period 1995–2014. They use a time-varying coefficients VAR model and identify government expenditures shocks by imposing a Cholesky orthogonalization of the structural shocks. Their main finding is that local fiscal shocks in the four largest Euro-area economies, i.e. Germany, France, Italy and Spain, exert sizeable spillovers on the other countries. Interestingly, spillovers reach their peak at medium run horizons. Moreover, the authors detect stronger effects in periods of financial crisis.

However, according to the results presented in Blanchard et al. (2015), a fiscal expansion in the largest European economies generates significant spillovers in the peripheral countries in the presence of a zero-lower-bound of the interest rates.

Georgiadis and Hollmayr (2016), by using a Global-VAR (G-VAR) model, find that spillovers from fiscal policy shocks originating in France, Germany and Italy are significant in the Euro Area. Even in this study the trade channel plays an important role in transmitting the effects of domestic fiscal shocks.

Eller et al. (2017), estimate a Bayesian GVAR and recover a deficit-financed government expenditures shock by imposing sign restrictions. Their main finding is that the fiscal shock causes persistent and positive cross-border output spillovers.

Nevertheless, it is worth noting that in modern economies other relevant channels are likely to operate in the transmission of fiscal shocks. For example, it is well known that in recent decades the role of financial markets has strongly increased all over the world and, with regard to the Euro Area, there are large financial flows among the national economies.

It is also worth mentioning the research by Auerbach and Gorodnichenko (2013) who find evidence of asymmetric effects of spillovers from fiscal shocks. Their results are consistent with the conclusion that size of fiscal multipliers and spillovers effects are magnified in recessions.

In Chap. 6 we will provide an estimation of both the size of German fiscal multipliers and the spillovers in the Euro-area countries. As we will see, there are notable domestic macroeconomic effects exerted by government expenditures shocks in Germany and, not less important, sizeable spillovers from German fiscal shocks which propagate their effects in the other Euro-area economies. Moreover, we find that in some cases financial markets, as per Ireland, play a pre-eminent role in the propagation mechanism.

3.8 Macroeconomic Factors Shaping the Effects of Fiscal Policy

In recent years, research on fiscal policy has explored, both at the theoretical and empirical level, the role of some selected macroeconomic factors capable of significantly influencing the responses of output and unemployment to fiscal shocks. In this section we will briefly present the main conclusions on the role played by these factors, focusing on degree of openness, exchange rate regime, monetary policy stance and country financial conditions.

For, the heterogeneous results on fiscal multipliers shown in the empirical literature are less surprising in the light of the long tradition of theoretical studies on fiscal policy. For example, the famous Mundell-Fleming model predicts that for open economies the exchange rate regime is a crucial factor influencing the size of fiscal multipliers. In particular, the prediction is that fiscal multipliers are larger in economies characterized by a fixed exchange rate regime. According to the Mundell-Fleming model, the channel through which fiscal multipliers increase under fixed exchange rate is mainly the current account; for net exports decrease under flexible exchange rate regime following an increase in government spending. In turn, this contraction of net exports is a consequence of the predicted appreciation of national currency under a flexible exchange rate regime. Thus the fiscal multiplier is around zero in this context, since the contraction of net exports may counterbalance the increase in government expenditures.

Another age-old discussion on the outcomes of fiscal policy concerns the so-called crowding out effect, i.e. the decrease in private spending following an increase in government spending due to the possible rise of interest rates. The implication is that, holding constant other factors, the lower the increase in interest rates in response to positive fiscal shocks, the larger the value of fiscal multipliers. Clearly, this conclusion calls for analysis of the monetary policy stance: the size of fiscal multipliers grows in the presence of accommodating monetary policies.

A further, important factor shaping the macroeconomics outcome of fiscal shocks, stressed in recent years by the literature, concerns the country financial conditions - where, in turn, these conditions are closely related to the level of indebtedness, both of public and private sector. The main conclusions are that in the presence of high public debt the sign of the fiscal multiplier might be negative, i.e. an increase in government spending has recessionary effects on the economy (cf. Ilzetzki et al. 2013), while a high private debt affecting the economy might be associated with a larger size of the fiscal multiplier, i.e. an increase in government spending has more pronounced expansionary effects on output.

However, in the next chapters we will present some new results for a group of small Euro-area economies affected by high public and/or private debt which challenge these conclusions, since in the case of Greece and Italy, countries affected by high public debt, we find expansionary effects associated with positive fiscal shocks while for Ireland and Spain, countries affected by high private debt, we find contractionary effects associated with positive fiscal shocks. Thus, we find results in sharp contrast with the conclusions so far reached by the majority of researchers.

3.8.1 The Degree of Openness and the Exchange Rate Regime

The simple, textbook, Keynesian multiplier has a smaller size in open economies since part of the increase in aggregate income is used to buy foreign goods and services. Of course, the degree of openness to trade may vary across countries also as a consequence of trade barriers.

In a more general model, with endogenous exchange rates and interest rates, it becomes important to separate alternative exchange rate regimes. For, the

Mundell-Fleming model, i.e. the traditional IS-LM model extended to open economies, predicts that when the economy is operating under a fixed exchange rate regime, an increase in government spending produces a bigger increase in aggregate output with respect to a flexible exchange rate regime.

Let us note that, implicitly, this is a prediction on the different reaction of monetary policy in the two distinct regimes: under a fixed exchange rate regime, an increase in government spending must necessarily be accompanied by an expansionary monetary policy otherwise the increase in interest rates would cause undesired movements of the exchange rate. In other words, under a fixed exchange rate, in the presence of expansionary fiscal policies the stance of monetary policy should be necessarily accommodating. Instead, under flexible exchange rates and assuming a goal of price stability pursued by the central bank, there will be an increase in the interest rates which is depressive for the aggregate demand.

Nevertheless, the prediction of small, or at most null, effects of fiscal policy for open economies operating under flexible exchange rates has to pass the US test, where the great majority of studies share the conclusion that the government fiscal multiplier is greater than zero and, on average, around one. In fact, although the US economy in the last 40 years has been characterized by flexible exchange rates, the significant expansionary effects associated with fiscal stimuli are mainly explained by the size of the economic system, a large aggregation of 50 States operating under a single currency. Thus, given the size of its internal markets, the U.S. resembles a (relatively) closed economy.

It is also important to stress that, at least in the last decade, the fiscal stimulus has been largely accommodated by the so-called quantitative easing pursued by the Federal Reserve System.

The theoretical predictions concerning the exchange rate regimes and the degree of openness to trade, are largely confirmed by the investigation conducted by Ilzetzki et al. (2013). The analysis covers 44 countries over the sample period 1970–2007. However, due to availability of data, there are some differences in the sample data across countries. Fiscal stimuli are associated with positive and large fiscal multipliers only in economies characterized by fixed exchange rate regimes. Instead, in countries operating under flexible exchange rate regimes the multipliers are negative at all horizons.

As far as the degree of openness is concerned, the authors find a negative multiplier for a group of countries identified as "open" and, instead, a positive multiplier, in the long run around one, for a group of countries classified as "closed".[12]

We wish to emphasize that in the Euro-area Germany is a country exhibiting the following features: (a) It is the biggest Euro-area economy, with a relatively large domestic market; (b) It operates within a currency union (an extreme form of fixed exchange rate regime); (3) the Euro-area monetary policy stance is very

[12] In the article, an economy is classified as "open" if the ratio of import plus export to GDP is greater than 60 percent. This criterion leads to the separation of 28 open from 16 closed countries. Of course, it should be noted that these classifications suffer, unavoidably, from some degree of arbitrariness.

accommodative, given the aggressive "Quantitative Easing" undertaken since 2014 by the European Central Bank. The conclusion is that Germany has an ideal macroeconomic context, also considering the fiscal space associated with the budget balance, to adopt a fiscal stimulus that in the light of the results presented in these sections would likely be beneficial both for Germany and for the other smaller Euro-area economies.

At longer political horizons, the evidence on fiscal policy characterizing the United States suggests that in the presence of a fiscal union in the Euro Area, i.e. under a centralized fiscal policy aiming to manage aggregate demand for stabilization, fiscal policy would be quite effective.

It is worth adding that beside the large evidence available for the United States, there is growing, encouraging evidence of the sizeable effects of fiscal policy in the Euro Area. A contribution to this evidence is offered in the first chapter of this book.

3.8.2 *The Monetary Policy Stance*

The interaction between monetary policy and fiscal policy is another old and important theme of macroeconomic research. In the first twenty years following the Second World War the goal of full employment dominated the political agenda and in pursuing this goal in many countries monetary policy played an ancillary role with respect to fiscal policy. For example, in the United Kingdom the responsibility for the setting of interest rates was formally attributed to the Chancellor of the Exchequer, i.e. to the Government. In Italy, the central bank supported the government's fiscal policy by ensuring that bonds not absorbed by private investors at auctions would be purchased by the Bank of Italy.

More generally, and abstracting from the formal institutional design of the interaction between central bank and government characterizing the various countries, there was little doubt on the supremacy of fiscal policy in majority of industrialized countries from 1950 to 1970s.

However, after the stagflation experienced in the 1970s, and in particular after the second oil shock in 1979 which pushed the inflation rate to unprecedented levels in oil importing countries since the postwar period, the Friedmanian view on the role of monetary policy (cf. Friedman 1968) and on the macroeconomic risks of keeping the interest rates at excessively low levels in order to ensure full employment, became dominant.[13]

Fact and theories stimulated a deep rethinking of the role of monetary policy and the independence of central banks was strengthened, both in terms of laws and monetary policy rules followed by central banks. In Italy, in 1982 there was the

[13]In this article Friedman proposed the notion of natural rate of unemployment, explicitly inspired by the Wicksellian notion of natural rate of interest. The main argument is that if the central bank keeps the interest rate below the long-run equilibrium rate, i.e. the natural rate, in an attempt to reduce an undesidered high level of unemployment, will lose control of inflation.

so-called "divorce" between Bank of Italy and the Treasury. As for the United States, a law approved by Congress in 1978 attributed the Federal Reserve System a dual mandate consisting in pursuing the stability of both nominal and real variables. Nevertheless, there is little doubt that, starting with the appointment of Paul Volcker, the Fed has gained substantial autonomy with respect to government in the last 30 years.

Finally even the British government gave the Bank of England "operating responsibility for setting interest rates" (cf. Brown 1997).[14]

However, in more recent years, there were fears of deflation, rather than of inflation, and the unemployment rate rose to very high levels in many countries. This macroeconomic context contributed to a revival of fiscal policy and, as a consequence, to pay also a renewed attention to the interaction between fiscal policy and monetary policy.

Canova and Pappa (2011) have used a structural VAR model to study the effects of government consumption expenditure shocks on output in the United States, the Euro area and the United Kingdom. Fiscal shocks are identified by imposing sign restrictions. The authors conclude that the type of interaction between fiscal policy and monetary policy is very important in determining the macroeconomic outcome of fiscal packages. In particular, fiscal policy has significant and large effects on the real economy when negative real interest rates prevail, as a consequence of aggressive and accommodative monetary policy. Let us note that this is exactly the situation faced by these economies in more recent years.

Christiano et al. (2011) investigate the size of the government-spending multiplier when the central bank follows a Taylor rule and, alternatively when the nominal interest rate is kept constant. The authors study the case of constant rates associated with the zero lower bound on nominal interest rate. They conclude that in the presence of Taylor rules driving the monetary policy choices, the size of the spending multiplier decreases significantly.

The role played by accommodative monetary policies to magnify the macroeconomic effects of fiscal stimuli also characterizes the New Keynesian frameworks used by Hall (2009) and Woodford (2009).

In a more recent paper, (Leeper et al. 2015) utilized Bayesian estimates of fiscal multipliers for the US economy. The authors use a monetary DSGE model in order to estimate the fiscal multipliers by considering alternative monetary-policy stances. The conclusion of greater expansionary effects in the presence of accommodative monetary policies is confirmed.

---

[14]The chancellor Gordon Brown (Brown 1997) proposed to amend the Bank of England Act 1946 and to attribute independence to the Bank. "The New Monetary Policy Framework" (1997) in establishing objectives for the central bank stated that: "Price stability is a precondition for high and stable levels of growth and employment".

3.8.3 The Role of Public and Private Debt

What are the dynamic effects of fiscal shocks on aggregate output in countries affected by high debt? An attempt to give an answer to this question on the empirical ground is provided by Ilzetzki et al. (2013). The authors classify a country as affected by high public debt when the debt-to-GPD-ratio is above the threshold of 60 percent. The main finding is that the government spending multipliers are negative in the presence of high public debt. In other words, in these countries, if a government tries to stimulate the economy with a fiscal package it gets the opposite outcome: a recession.

Although Ilzetzki et al. (2013) do not build a theoretical model capable of explaining their empirical results, they suggest that the key factor is represented by debt sustainability: when the country is affected by high debt levels, an increase in government purchases may cause a reduction of both private consumption and investment if the private sector of the economy believes that problems of sustainability will induce future fiscal tightening.

In our opinion, on the whole, the results presented by Ilzetzki et al. (2013) on the importance of a set of macroeconomic factors in shaping the response of output to fiscal shocks are notable and help to shed light on some heterogeneous results characterizing the literature. However, we also believe that some findings are not robust to further investigation and analysis.

We stress that fiscal multipliers are not estimated country by country but the various economies are aggregated on the basis of the somewhat arbitrary threshold of 60 percent. Thus, since the authors estimate an average value of the multiplier for the aggregated countries, in principle, it is not possible to rule out the presence of countries with public debt above 60 percent that exhibit positive government spending multipliers. Let us for example consider the case of Italy in the last ten years, a country in recession, suffering from high public debt, above 100 percent, operating under a currency union and in a context in which the central bank is undertaking an aggressive expansionary monetary policy. The survey of the literature conducted in this chapter shows that with the exception of the debt level, the other macroeconomic factors act in favour of expansionary effects associated with fiscal stimulus. In this book we show that this last conclusion fits well with Italian data.

Another possible shortcoming affecting the investigation conducted by Ilzetzki et al. (2013) concerns the inclusion in the panel VAR of countries characterized by high private debt-to-GDP-ratio. This is the case, for example, of Ireland and Spain which under the EMU experienced average values of private debt above 150 percent with respect to GDP. Hence, the macroeconomic outcome of fiscal shocks in these countries may be significantly influenced not only by public by also by private debt. In this book, the analysis conducted at the country level will allow the separation of these factors.

It is also worth noting that in recent years the European Commission has proposed a threshold of 160 percent for private debt-to-GDP ratio as one of the indicators of macroeconomic imbalances (see European Commission 2012).

A high level of private debt may exert a macroeconomic influence in a twofold way: firstly, high private debt-to-GDP ratios contribute to exacerbate the recessionary effects of financial crisis: secondly, they contribute to shape the macroeconomic outcome of fiscal stimuli.

In a recent research (Andrés et al. 2015) study the size of government fiscal multipliers by developing a general equilibrium model with search frictions. They show that in the presence of private debt and impatient households the size of the multipliers is above one; however this result holds only under normal financial conditions, since the size of the multipliers decreases as financial conditions become more severe. The authors also find that their model fits some observed characteristics of the US economy relatively well.

We point out that these conclusions are partially in line with the results of our investigation, included in this book, since we find that the government fiscal multipliers in high private debt Euro-area countries are negative in the EMU period. Moreover, we find that fiscal policy becomes ineffective in these countries, i.e. government spending multipliers turn out to be negative, after the spread of the financial crisis. We conjecture that the recessionary effects of fiscal expansions in these countries might depend on: (a) In the presence of particularly high private debt-to-GDP ratio, fiscal expansions may trigger confidence in the private sector; (b) if fiscal expansions cause a worsening of the financial conditions, high private indebtedness may lead to negative response of private expenditure.

It is also worth stressing that our results concerning high private debt countries only partially confirm the conclusions reached in studies such as Giavazzi and Pagano (1990) and Alesina and Ardagna (2010). For, those studies emphasize the importance of credibility of consolidation plans in order to get non-Keynesian effects of fiscal policy. Instead, we find that there is a clear separation between high public debt and high private debt countries. In other words, credible or not, fiscal plans in countries like Greece and Italy tend to exert Keynesian effects, since fiscal consolidations are recessionary and government spending multipliers show positive signs.

3.9 Identification of Fiscal Shocks and Fiscal Foresight

Fiscal foresight consists in the ability of rational economic agents to anticipate future tax or government spending obligations. This ability poses problems for the correct identification of fiscal shocks in the structural VAR approach, since in the presence of foresight the information set of agents is larger than the econometrician's information set.

Indeed, a crucial assumption underlying the structural VAR approach is that fiscal shocks can be identified as linear combinations of current and past exogenous disturbances. However, fiscal packages are usually announced in advance of their implementation and agents with rational expectations will anticipate the effects of these packages, implying that fiscal shocks should be properly recovered as a combination of current, past and also future exogenous disturbances (see e.g. Leeper et al. 2013). Thus, a notable component of fiscal policy is predictable and this poses problems when shocks are recovered following the traditional VAR approach to identification.

Rational expectations equilibria are associated with non-fundamental moving average representation. In Leeper et al. (2013) an example of non-fundamentalness is related to the optimizing behaviour of agents who discount future taxes.[15]

Following Leeper et al. (2013), the problem of foresight in terms of VAR representations can be seen in the following way. Let us write the moving average representation:

$$X_t = \sum_{s=0}^{\infty} B_s \varepsilon_{t-s} \tag{3.16}$$

where (3.16) is a non-fundamental representation if the space spanned by $\{\varepsilon_{t-s}\}_{s=0}^{\infty}$ is larger than the space spanned by $\{X_{t-s}\}_{s=0}^{\infty}$. In this case the researcher, adopting the traditional VAR approach, will recover the shocks, ε_t^*, by imposing a set of identifying restrictions. However, the econometrician will not identify the structural shocks, ε_t, since the information set used for identification is smaller with respect to agents. Put in another way, the econometrician is conditioning on X_t while agents observe directly ε_t.

Clearly, the problem of possible information sets utilized by the econometrician which are smaller than those used by rational agents is relevant for the analysis of fiscal policy but is not restricted to this area of research.

With respect to the literature on fiscal shocks that we have analyzed in previous sections, if the problem of fiscal foresight is believed to be relevant, the conclusion is that the estimation of fiscal multipliers obtained by using the structural VAR methodology might be highly imprecise.[16]

Forni and Gambetti (2014) deal with this problem of "information deficiency" in VAR models. The authors derive necessary and sufficient conditions to fix the problem. These conditions essentially amount to testing that no state variables help to predict, i.e. Granger cause, the vector of variables used in the VAR estimation. The logic is straightforward: if all the relevant information is contained in the VAR, then no state variable is useful to predict the vector and hence the econometrician's

[15] The difficulties in interpreting structural VARs when agents have rational expectations, i.e. the problem of non-fundamentalness, were first discussed in Hansen and Sargent (1991). Another important example of non-fundamental representation was presented in Lippi and Reichlin (1993), in the context of structural VARs identified by imposing long-run restrictions (cf. Blanchard and Quah 1989). Lippi and Reichlin showed that a non-fundamental representation may be generated in the presence of particular diffusion processes of technological innovations.

[16] However, it is worth observing that the unreliability of fiscal multiplier estimations based on the structural VAR methodology rests mainly on the assumption of rational and intertemporally optimizing agents who can discount future fiscal obligations. More likely, only a small part of the families are able to discount such future fiscal obligations. In other words, the majority of agents follows a simpler rule of thumb rather than complicated intertemporally optimizing plans. As a consequence, it is possible that critiques of VAR identification of fiscal shocks are overestimated.

information set allows the structural shocks to be recovered using the traditional VAR approach.

Canova and Sahneh (2016) have recently suggested an alternative testing procedure for detecting fundamentalness, since Granger causality tests may produce spurious results. They find that adding the growth rate of consumers' confidence to a bivariate VAR including labor productivity and employment helps to recover a fundamental technological shock.

These results can be interpreted as a suggestion to include in the estimated VAR leading indicators of economic activity, which are likely to Granger cause the vector of variables of interest. For example, in Dallari and Ribba (2015) a stock price index was included to obtain better estimates of fiscal multipliers in the Mediterranean, EMU countries. In Cavallo and Ribba (2017) the identification of fiscal shocks for a selected group of Central and Eastern European countries was obtained by also including as exogenous variables a national index of stock prices and indexes of consumers confidence.

It is worth recalling that the strategy of recovering government spending shocks by relying on index of stock prices was first adopted by Fisher and Peters (2010). However it is important to stress that, in principle, leading indicators should be useful predictors of fiscal variables in order to correctly recover the fiscal shocks, and in fact Fisher and Peters utilize the excess return of stock index concerning a set of large military contractors.

In the next chapters we will estimate and identify structural VARs to measure fiscal policy in a group of small Euro-area economies affected by high public and/or private debt. In order to tackle the problem of fiscal foresight we will include in the estimated VARs a set of variables which are considered useful to predict changes in fiscal policy.

3.10 Conclusions

The main conclusion emerging from this survey is that despite the boost to research witnessed in the last decade, the literature measuring fiscal policy is still far from a shared conclusion on the macroeconomic outcomes associated with fiscal shocks. There is heterogeneity in the results concerning the responses of macrovariables to fiscal shocks and, closely related, a wide dispersion in the size of estimated fiscal multipliers. We have argued that the bulk of the explanation for the heterogenous results obtained in empirical studies rests on the sensitivity of the responses of macrovariables to some selected macroeconomic factors affecting the propagation of fiscal shocks in the economic system. These macroeconomic factors that include, among others, the monetary policy stance, the exchange rate regime under which the economy is operating and the country financial conditions, should not be neglected, of course for different reasons, by both researchers and policy makers.

In this survey we have also stressed one possible shortcoming affecting (part of) the literature investigating the Euro-area economy and that concerns the use of sample periods which often include quite different monetary and institutional regimes. To take one example, Italy and some other Euro-area member countries underwent a dramatic change of regime in 1999 and thus analyzing fiscal policy over a period of 30 or 40 years without regarding this change is likely to produce, at least partially, unreliable results. In fact, it is worth pointing out that in the first years of EMU researchers had to face important data constraints which made it very difficult to undertake investigations based on only a few years of data available. However, around 19 years have by now elapsed since the outset of the Euro and hence we begin to dispose of sufficient observations. Consistently with this view, in the present book and as far as possible, we will mainly use sample data covering the EMU period.

As far as the overall Euro Area is concerned, we have briefly reported that there is a growing number of studies supporting the evolution of Euro Area towards a complete Monetary and Fiscal Union and that one of these studies has been recently published by the European Commission (2017).

In the first chapter we have explored the potential effects of fiscal shocks derived at the area-wide level and then studied the response of output and prices. We concluded that a centralized fiscal policy might be a powerful tool for the macroeconomic stabilization of the Currency Area. Nevertheless, a possible objection to this investigation strategy might be that a Euro-area fiscal budget does not yet exist and hence one would need to aggregate over national fiscal variables in order to obtain an aggregate Euro-area expenditures or revenues variable. We believe that studying the dynamic effects of area-wide fiscal shocks allows a first evaluation of the ability of the (future) Fiscal Union to manage aggregate demand in response to adverse, common Euro-area shocks. Let us recall that our main findings are that a positive government expenditures shock would produce significant expansionary effects on aggregate output and that even more sizeable effects would be obtained in the presence of an accommodative monetary policy. The finding on the role played by the stance of monetary policy is in line with the conclusions reached in their investigation by Canova and Pappa (2011) and seems to contrast the implications deriving from neoclassical models concerning the inability of monetary policy to influence the real output outcomes of fiscal shocks.

Another important area of research on fiscal policy regards the investigation of spillover effects associated with national fiscal shocks. We have briefly reviewed part of this literature in Sect. 3.7. Not surprisingly, this strand of literature, too, shows heterogeneity in the results obtained. Besides the macroeconomic factors recalled at the start of this section, the state of the economy, recessionary or expansionary contexts, have been identified as another crucial factor in determining the size of spillovers.

In order to investigate size of spillovers and channels of propagation of fiscal shocks, in Chap. 6 we will (implicitly) take German spending shocks as a proxy for Euro-area government expenditures shocks and estimate both the size of the fiscal multiplier in Germany and the spillover effects on the Euro-area economies. This seems a good first approximation of a centralized Euro-area budget, given the role and size of Germany in the currency union. To anticipate the main results, the German fiscal multiplier is large (above one) and, moreover, it seems that a vigorous fiscal expansion in Germany might boost growth in the Southern Eurozone economies.

We have stressed that most of the literature regards trade as the main channel for the transmission of fiscal policy shocks. However, since Euro-area countries also exhibit highly integrated financial markets, this may represent another important channel of domestic fiscal shock propagation.

References

Alesina A, Ardagna S (2010) Large changes in fiscal policy: taxes versus spending. In: Tax policy and the economy, vol 24. NBER, Cambridge, pp 35–68

Andrés J, Boscá EJ, Ferri J (2015) Household debt and fiscal multipliers. Economica 82:1048–1081

Auerbach AJ, Gorodnichenko Y (2013) Output spillovers from fiscal policy. Am Econ Rev 103:141–146

Auerbach AJ, Gorodnichenko Y (2012) Measuring the output responses to fiscal policy. Am Econ J Econ Policy 4:1–27

Barnichon R, Matthes C (2015) Stimulus versus austerity: the asymmetric government spending multiplier. CEPR discussion paper 10584

Barro RJ (2009) Government spending is no free lunch. Wall Street J

Barro RJ (1981) Output effects of government purchases. J Polit Econ 89(6):1086–1121

Barro RJ, Redlick CJ (2011) Macroeconomic effects from government purchases and taxes. Q J Econ 126(1):51–102

Belke A, Osowski T (2016) Measuring fiscal spillovers in EMU and beyond: a global VAR approach. CEPS working paper no. 428

Bernanke BS (1986) Alternative explanations of the money-income correlation. In: Carnegie-Rochester conference on public policy, vol 25, pp 49–99

Bernanke BS, Mihov I (1998) Measuring the monetary policy. Q J Econ 113:869–902

Beetsma R, Giuliodori M (2004) What are the spill-overs from fiscal shocks in Europe? An empirical analysis. ECB working paper no. 325

Beetsma R, Giuliodori M, Klaassen F (2006) Trade spillovers of fiscal policy in the European Union: a panel analysis. Econ Policy 21(48):641–687

Blanchard OJ, Erceg CJ, Lindé J (2015) Jump starting the Euro Area recovery: would a rise in core fiscal spending help the periphery? NBER working papers, no. 21426

Blanchard O, Perotti R (2002) An empirical characterization of the dynamic effects of changes in government spending and taxes on output. Q J Econ 117:1329–1368

Blanchard OJ, Quah D (1989) The dynamic effects of aggregate demand and supply disturbances. Am Econ Rev 79:655–673

Blinder AS, Zandi M (2010) Stimulus worked. Financ Develop

Boeckx J, Dossche M, Peersman G (2017) Effectiveness and transmission of the ECBs balance sheet policies. Int J Cent Bank 13:297–333

Brown G (1997) The new monetary policy framework. Letter from the Chancellor, Gordon Brown, to the Bank of England Governor, May 1997

Brückner M, Pappa E (2012) Fiscal expansions, unemployment and labor force participation: theory and evidence. Int Econ Rev 53:1205–1228

Burriel P, De Castro F, Garrote D, Gordo E, Paredes D, Perez JJ (2010) Fiscal policy shocks in the Euro Area and the US: an empirical assessment. Fisc Stud 31(2):251–285

Canova F (2007) Methods for applied macroeconomic research. Princeton University Press, Princeton

Canova F, Pappa E (2007) Price differentials in monetary unions: the role of fiscal shocks. Econ J 117:713–737
Canova F, Pappa E (2011) Fiscal policy, pricing frictions and monetary accommodation. Econ Policy 26:555–598
Canova F, Sahneh MH (2016) Are small-scale SVARs useful for business cycle analysis? Revisiting non-fundamentalness. Working papers 2/2016, BI Norvegian Business School
Canzoneri M, Collard F, Dellas H, Diba B (2016) Fiscal multipliers in recessions. Econ J 126:75–108
Cavallo A, Ribba A (2017) Measuring the effects of oil price and Euro-area shocks on CEECs business cycles. Department of Economics 0111, University of Modena and Reggio Emilia
Cavallo A, Ribba A (2015) Common macroeconomic shocks and business cycle fluctuations in Euro Area countries. Int Rev Econ Financ 38:377–392
Clancy D, Jacquinot P, Lozej M (2015) Government expenditure composition and fiscal policy spillovers in a small open economy within a monetary union. ESM working paper series no. 4
Cogan JF, Cwik T, Taylor JB, Wieland V (2010) New Keynesians versus old Keynesians government spending multipliers. J Econ Dyn Control 34(3):281–295
Christiano L, Eichenbaum M, Evans CL (1999) Monetary policy shocks: what have we learned and to what end? In: Taylor JB, Woodford M (eds) Handbook of macroeconomics, vol 1. North Holland, Amsterdam, pp 65–148
Christiano L, Eichenbaum M, Rebelo S (2011) When is the government spending multiplier large? J Polit Econ 119:78–121
Clarida RJ, Galí J, Gertler M (1998) Monetary policy rules in practise: some international evidence. Eur Econ Rev 42(6):1033–1067
Conti AM, Neri S, Nobili A (2017) Low inflation and monetary policy in the Euro Area. Working paper series, European Central Bank
Cushman D, Zha T (1997) Identifying monetary policy in a small open economy under flexible exchange rates. J Monetary Econ 39:433448
Dallari P, Ribba A (2015) Economic shocks and their effects on unemployment in the Euro Area periphery under the EMU. Department of Economics No 114, University of Modena and Reggio Emilia
De Grauwe P, Ji Y (2016) How to reboot the Eurozone and ensure its long-term survival. In: Baldwin R, Giavazzi F (eds) How to fix Europe's monetary union: views of leading economists, VoxEU.org eBook. CEPR Press
Eller M, Feldkirchner M, Huber F (2017) How would a fiscal shock in Germany affect other European countries? Evidence from a Bayesian GVAR model with sign restrictions. Austrian Central Bank. Focus on European Economic Integration, vol 1, pp 54–57
European Commission (2017) Reflection paper on the deepening of the Economic and Monetary Union
European Commission (2012) First alert mechanism report on macroeconomic imbalances in member states. MEMO/12/104
Fatas A, Summers LH (2016) The permanent effects of fiscal consolidations. NBER working paper no. 22374
Fatas A, Mihov I (2001) The effects of fiscal policy on consumption and employment: theory and evidence. CEPR discussion papers 2760
Fisher JDM, Peters R (2010) Using stocks returns to identify government spending shocks. Econ J 120:414–436
Forni M, Gambetti L (2014) Sufficient information in structural VARs. J Monet Econ 66:124–136
Friedman M (1968) The role of monetary policy. Am Econ Rev 58:1–17
Galí J, Lopez-Salido JD, Valls J (2007) Understanding the effects of government spending on consumption. J Eur Econ Assoc 5:227–270
Gambetti L, Gallio F (2016) Measuring fiscal policy spillovers in the Euro Area. ADEMU WP 2016/044
Georgiadis G, Hollmayr J (2016) Fiscal spillovers in the Euro Area: sign, size and determinants. mimeo

Giavazzi F, Pagano M (1990) Can severe fiscal contractions be expansionary? Tales of two small European Countries. NBER chapters. In: NBER Macroeconomics Annual 1990, pp 75–122
Giordano R, Momigliano S, Neri S, Perotti R (2007) The effects of fiscal policy in Italy: evidence from a VAR model. Eur J Polit Econ 23:707–733
Gros D, Belke A (2015) Banking union as a shock absorber: lessons for the Eurozone from the US. CEPS, Bruxelles
Hall RE (2009) By how much does GDP rise if the government buys more output? Brookings Pap Eco Ac 2:183–231
Hansen LP, Sargent TJ (1991) Two difficulties in interpreting vector autoregressions. Ration Expect Econ 1:77–119
Hebous S, Zimmermann T (2013) Estimating the effects of coordinated fiscal actions in the Euro Area. Eur Econ Rev 58:110–121
Ilzetzki E, Mendoza EG, Végh CA (2013) How big (small?) are fiscal multipliers? J Monet Econ 60:239–254
IMF (2009) Fiscal multipliers. IMF staff position note, No. 09/11
Leeper EM, Traum N, Walker TB (2015). Clearing up the fiscal multipliers morass: prior and posterior analysis. NBER working paper 21433
Leeper EM, Walker TB, Yang S-CS (2013) Fiscal foresight and information flows. Econometrica 81:1115–1145
Lippi M, Reichlin L (1993) The dynamic effects of aggregate demand and supply disturbances: comment. Am Econ Rev 83:644–652
Monacelli T, Perotti R, Trigari A (2010) Unemployment fiscal multipliers. J Monet Econ 57:531–553
Mountford A, Uhlig H (2009) What are the effects of fiscal policy shocks? J Appl Econom 24:960–992
OECD (2009) The effectiveness and scope of fiscal stimulus. Economic outlook interim report
Peersman G (2004) The transmission of monetary policy in the Euro Area: are the effects different across countries? Oxford B Econ Stat 66:285–308
Pissarides C (2016) Rebooting Europe: closer fiscal cooperation needed. In Baldwin R, Giavazzi F (eds) How to fix Europe's Monetary Union: views of leading economists. VoxEU.org eBook. CEPR Press
Ramey VA (2016) Macroeconomic shocks and their propagation. In: Taylor JB, Uhlig H (eds) Handbook of macroeconomics, vol 2. North Holland, Amsterdam, pp 71–162
Ramey VA (2011) Identifying government spending shocks: it's all in the timing. Q J Econ 126:1–50
Ramey VA, Shapiro M (1998) Costly capital reallocation and the effects of government spending. In: Carnegie-Rochester conference on public policy, vol 48, pp 145–194
Ricci-Risquete A, Ramajo-Hernández J (2015) Macroeconomic effects of fiscal policy in the European Union: a GVAR model. Empirical Econ 48(4):1587–1617
Romer C, Bernstein J (2009) The job impact of the American recovery and reinvestment plan
Sapir A, Wolff G (2015) Euro Area governance: what to reform and how to do it. Bruegel policy briefs
Sims CA (1986) Are forecasting model usable for policy analysis? Q Rev Win:2–16
Sims CA (1980) Macroeconomics and reality. Econometrica 48:1–48
Smets F, Wouters R (2007) Shocks and frictions in U.S. business cycles: a bayesian DSGE approach. Am Econ Rev 97:586–606
Spilimbergo A, Symansky S, Schindler M (2009) Fiscal multipliers. IMF staff position note no 09/11
Tabellini G (2016) Building common fiscal policy in the Eurozone. In: Baldwin R, Giavazzi F (eds) How to fix Europe's Monetary Union: views of leading economists. VoxEU.org eBook. CEPR Press
Taylor JB (1993) Discretion versus policy rules in practise. In: Carnegie-Rochester conference on public policy, vol 39, pp 195–214

Uhlig H (2005) What are the effects of monetary policy on output? Results from an agnostic identification procedure. J Monetary Econ 52(2):381–419
Woodford M (2011) Simple analytics of the government expenditure multiplier. Am Econ J Macroecon 3:1–35
Woodford M (2009) Convergence in macroeconomics: elements of the new synthesis. Am Econ J Macroecon 1(1):267–279
Wyplosz C (2005) Fiscal policy: institutions versus rules. Natl Inst Econ Rev 191(1):64–78

Chapter 4
The Macroeconomic Effects of Fiscal Shocks in High Debt Euro Area Countries

Abstract The aim of this chapter is to characterize the response of prices and GDP to monetary policy and fiscal shocks in a group of Euro-area countries affected by high public and/or private debt-to-GDP ratio. We utilize the structural near-VAR methodology, by jointly modeling Euro area-wide and national variables. We find that during the EMU period, in Italy, Greece and Portugal a fiscal tightening caused a contraction of aggregate output. Instead, for Ireland, Netherland and Spain we find an opposite result: fiscal austerity exerted expansionary effects on the economy. However, in almost all the countries included in this investigation, fiscal shocks explain only a small part of the variability of both output and prices, while a greater role seems to have been played by monetary policy shocks and, more generally, by Euro-area common shocks. The exception is represented by Greece, where fiscal shocks played a notable role as drivers of aggregate output fluctuations.

4.1 Introduction

In this chapter we investigate the causal relations among domestic fiscal policy shocks, Euro-area monetary policy shocks and macroeconomic outcomes in a group of European economies which includes Greece, Ireland, Italy, Netherlands, Portugal and Spain. We consider the period 1999–2016, i.e. the EMU period, and focus on the response of national GDP and prices to the set of identified structural shocks.

In the last decade these countries have been affected by a number of strong, adverse economic shocks, starting with the financial crisis which hit the world economy in 2007. Moreover, since these countries were characterized by high debt-to-GDP ratio, in particular high public debt for Italy and Greece and high private debt for Ireland, Netherlands and Spain, they were also subject to a series of confidence shocks concerning the sustainability of public finances. These confidence shocks had their main sources in the need to recapitalize domestic financial institutions, in the high private debt countries, and in the cost of financing welfare policies, in the southern economies.

In this adverse economic context, European policymakers faced unemployment at the highest levels since the mid-Nineties, when the common monetary system was

© Springer International Publishing AG 2018
A. Cavallo et al., *Fiscal Policies in High Debt Euro-Area Countries*,
https://doi.org/10.1007/978-3-319-70269-8_4

not yet operational. It is worth recalling that even as a consequence of the economic and social difficulties experienced by these countries, the viability of the Economic and Monetary Union has been repeatedly put into question in recent years.

This sequence of events has stimulated both a public debate and a strand of research focused on the relationship between the centralized conduct of monetary policy and the role of domestic fiscal policies. For, still at this stage of evolution of the Eurozone institutional design, the Euro Area does not have a centralized fiscal capacity, while fiscal policies are decided at the national level within a set of common, supranational rules.

In this chapter we adopt a structural near-VAR approach and study the dynamic effects of both Euro-area and national macroeconomic shocks in this group of countries during the first eighteen years of the EMU. In particular, we focus on Euro-area common monetary policy shocks and local fiscal policy shocks. Indeed, beside measuring fiscal policy, another aim pursued in this investigation is to derive some useful insights for policy actions.

Blanchard and Perotti (2002) were among the first to apply the structural VAR methodology to investigate the effects of fiscal shocks on aggregate output. They found that in the postwar US economy the fiscal policy has played a role in stabilizing business cycle fluctuations, i.e. Keynesian results have characterized expansionary fiscal policies in the USA.

Mountford and Uhlig (2009) use a structural VAR model identified by imposing sign restrictions on the responses of the variables. Their results on the macroeconomic effects of fiscal shocks substantially confirmed the conclusions presented in Blanchard and Perotti.[1]

Another interesting strand of research has investigated the relations between fiscal shocks and the conduct of monetary policy. Canova and Pappa (2011) investigated the response of real activity to government expenditure shocks in the United States, the Euro area and the United Kingdom and found that there is a close relation between large effects exerted by fiscal shocks and accommodative monetary policies.

In related research, Christiano et al. (2011) have found that the size of the government-spending multiplier increases in the presence of a constant nominal interest rate. In particular, the authors study a case of constant nominal rates related to a binding zero lower bound on the nominal interest rate.

In a more recent paper, Leeper et al. (2015) have explored the role played by alternative monetary-policy stances in influencing the size of the fiscal multipliers. The important conclusion, consistent indeed with the results of Christiano et al. (2011), is that the size of fiscal multipliers increases with accommodative monetary policies.

Canzoneri et al. (2016) have recently argued that fiscal multipliers can be state-dependent. They develop a theoretical model of the business cycle which includes costly financial intermediation and conclude that fiscal multipliers are much larger in recessions. On the empirical side, Auerbach and Gorodnichenko (2012) find evidence

[1]We have extensively discussed the main results shown in the literature on the macroeconomic outcomes of fiscal shocks in Chap. 3.

of different size of spending multipliers in expansion and in recession for the postwar US economy. Their results confirm the conclusion that fiscal policy exerts stronger effects on output when the economy experiences negative phases of business cycle.

Evidence of heterogeneity of the results concerning fiscal multipliers is provided by Ilzetzki et al. (2013) in an empirical investigation on the macroeconomic effects of fiscal stimuli in 44 countries. They find that the sign of fiscal multipliers is strongly related to some selected key country macroeconomic factors. In particular, fiscal multipliers are negative, i.e. fiscal expansions have recessionary effects, in countries affected by high public debt.

The conclusion that output fiscal multipliers may exhibit a non-Keynesian sign is not new in the literature, since it dates back to the research by Giavazzi and Pagano (1990), concerning the expansionary effects of fiscal consolidations in two small European economies, i.e. Denmark and Ireland, in the 80s. Similar conclusions have more recently been presented by Alesina and Ardagna (2010).

Nevertheless, Dallari and Ribba (2015) provide only a partial confirmation for the conclusions reached by Ilzetzki et al. (2013); for, they characterize the response of unemployment to fiscal shocks in peripheral EMU countries under the EMU and find that following a government spending shock unemployment decreases in Italy and Greece but instead increases in Ireland and Spain. Thus, at least according to these results, it seems that not only is sovereign debt a potential, important factor in explaining "perverse" effects of government spending shocks but also private debt is likely to play a significant role.

Moreover, the results obtained by Dallari and Ribba also contrast with the conclusion reached by Canzoneri et al. (2016), and based on a theoretical model, that fiscal multipliers are larger when the economy faces a recession. According to the empirical results of Dallari and Ribba (2015), it is important to take into account some relevant macroeconomic factors since public and private debt levels, jointly with country financial conditions, also matter in determining size and signs of fiscal multipliers: at a pinch, in the presence of high levels of debt the sign of fiscal multipliers could be reversed.

Of course, we would need sound, and possibly operational, definitions of high public or, alternatively, private debt. However, it is interesting to point out that in the context of the "Procedure to prevent and correct the macroeconomic imbalances", the European Commission has established a threshold for the private debt of 160% of GDP besides the well known threshold of 60% of GDP for general government sector debt (see European Commission 2012).

In this chapter we use block exogeneity restrictions and thus we treat the national systems as small open economies which are part of the European Monetary Union (EMU). In other words, although the national economies interact with the area-wide economy, there is unidirectional causality running from the Euro-area variables to national variables.

Cushman and Zha (1997) used the near-VAR to model the interaction between a small open economy, i.e. Canada, and a large one, i.e. the United States. They aimed to obtain a sounder identification of the monetary policy shocks affecting the small open economy, given a flexible exchange-rates regime. A recent application of this methodology is found in Cavallo and Ribba (2015). The authors, in the context of EMU, identify a structural near-VAR model to study the dynamic effects of monetary policy shocks on industrial production in a group of Euro-area countries in the first decade of the Euro.[2]

To anticipate the main results of this chapter. We find that in Italy, Greece and Portugal, in response to expansionary fiscal shocks, there is an increase in aggregate output. More ambiguous are the results concerning the response of prices. Instead, as far as Ireland, Netherlands and Spain are concerned, expansionary fiscal shocks are recessionary, since there is a decrease both in output and prices. Nevertheless, in almost all the countries included in this investigation, both spending and revenue shocks play a limited role in driving output fluctuations at the business cycle frequencies. Instead, a more important role is played by Euro-area, common shocks and in particular by monetary policy shocks. However, this result does not hold for Greece, where we find that fiscal shocks turned out to be important drivers of business cycle fluctuations under the EMU. Of course, this finding is far from surprising in the light of the repeated austerity plans carried out by the Greek government in recent years. Indeed, our results seem to support the conclusion that austerity was one of the main factors underlying the deep and persistent economic crisis which has hit Greece for a decade.

Another important finding of this investigation concerns the size of fiscal multipliers: even in those countries showing expansionary effects on the economy following a positive government spending shock, the fiscal multiplier, though not small, is below one. Given this moderate size of fiscal multipliers, it follows that in order to obtain a notable effect on GDP, a quite strong expansion of the government deficit would be required. Clearly, in the present European environment, and in light of high public debt affecting these countries, this is a non-viable strategy for the national economies.

Also related to the quite limited fiscal space available in southern Euro-area economies and to persistent macroeconomic imbalances characterizing the Euro Area, in Chap. 6 we will explore the possibility that a fiscal expansion in Germany may exert positive spillover effects in the Euro-area countries. It is indeed worth recalling that Germany exhibits a persistent current account surplus to GDP, above the threshold of 6% recently indicated by the European Commission as one indicator of potential macroeconomic imbalances. Nevertheless, despite the frequent international calls to the German government to undertake expansionary fiscal policies, there is still lack of evidence on the importance of these measures for the other Euro-area economies.

The rest of the chapter is organized as follows. In Sect. 4.2 we report some descriptive statistics for the national economies. The econometric approach is described in Sect. 4.3. In particular, in this section we present the estimated near-VAR model and describe the identification strategy adopted in order to recover the structural disturbances. Section 4.4 presents the econometric evidence. Section 4.5 is devoted to the

---

[2] In Peersman (2004) a near-VAR model is adopted to study the transmission of monetary policy shocks in European countries. Recent applications of this methodology to investigate Euro-area and European economies include Boeckx et al. (2017), Cavallo and Ribba (2017), Conti et al. (2017).

presentation of the sources of fluctuations in prices and GDP through the lens of variance decomposition analysis. In this context we also discuss the degree of integration of national business cycles in the European one, implied by our estimations. Section 4.6 concludes.

4.2 Some Descriptive Statistics for the National Economies

In this section we present, and briefly discuss, some descriptive statistics covering the period 1999–2016 and concerning the six national economies included in this investigation.

As shown in Table 4.1, the average rate of inflation, over the sample period, is similar for the six countries, and around two percent.[3] Nevertheless, the average value hides the very different variability of the inflation rate which characterized these economies in the first eighteen years of EMU. For example, in the case of Ireland, given an average value of 1.8% over the period, the minimum in the inflation rate was observed in the last quarter of 2009, at a negative value of −2.9%, while the maxim value was reached in the third quarter of 2000, with the inflation rate near 6%. As for Italy, the minimum value of −0.3% was recorded in the second quarter of 2016, with a maximum in the third quarter of 2008 at 4%. Instead, Greece and Spain show a minimum in inflation, respectively, of −2.2% in the last quarter of 2013 and −1.1% in the first quarter of 2015. As for the maximum value of inflation, these two countries exhibit values, respectively, of 5.5 and 4.8%.

A similar variability of the inflation rate characterized the Netherlands (maximum value of 5.2 in the second quarter of 2001 and a minimum value of −0.5 recorded in the first quarter of 2015) and Portugal (maximum and minimum values given by, respectively, 4.7 in the first quarter of 2001 and −1.5% in the first quarter of 2009). However, although negative values for the inflation rate have been common to Euro-area countries following the Great Recession, also according to more recent information on the evolution of prices in the various countries, the risk of persistent deflations might be behind us.

Greater differences among countries are instead observed in the average growth rate of real GDP, with the poor performance of Greece, Italy and Portugal compared to the more sustained average growth experienced by Ireland, Netherlands and Spain. Let us note that, as shown in Table 4.1, these last three countries have had a notable private debt-to-GDP ratio over the period 1999–2016. Thus, and maybe not by mere

[3] An important area of research concerns the convergence (and the divergence) of inflation rates in the Eurozone. Some results are presented in Cavallo and Ribba (2014). The authors use monthly data and investigate the convergence of inflation rates in the Euro Area over the period 1999:1–2011:12. The main findings are that only a small number of countries, including France, Italy and Belgium exhibits convergence of inflation dynamics. Thus, diverging results have characterized the inflation differentials in the Euro Area in the first 13 years of Monetary Union. Nevertheless, it should be pointed out that in recent years, mainly through painful deflations in the Mediterranean countries, further improvements in the reduction of inflation differentials have been achieved.

Table 4.1 Descriptive statistics for the national economies, 1999–2016

Variables	Greece	Ireland	Italy	Netherlands	Portugal	Spain
π_t	2.2 (1.9)	1.8 (2.0)	1.9 (1.1)	1.9 (1.3)	2.0 (1.5)	2.2 (1.6)
$\frac{\Delta y_t}{y_t}$	0.2 (4.8)	4.7 (6.4)	0.3 (2.2)	1.5 (2.1)	0.6 (2.3)	1.8 (2.7)
$\frac{g_t}{y_t}$	27 (2.9)	20 (2.7)	22 (0.98)	28 (2.1)	23 (1.9)	22 (1.6)
$\frac{t_t}{y_t}$	19 (5.5)	15 (4.5)	16 (0.70)	18 (1.6)	18 (2.4)	17 (3.6)
$\frac{publ.debt_t}{y_t}$	129 (33)	59 (35)	112 (12)	55 (8.2)	85 (31)	61(22.4)
$\frac{priv.debt_t}{y_t}$	95 (33)	214 (56)	102 (20)	215 (12)	175 (28)	154 (39.1)
$spread_t$	443 (581)	128 (192)	107 (114)	20 (15.6)	195 (274)	101 (126)

Note The table presents for each series the mean and the standard deviation (in parenthesis). π_t is built as the annual rate of inflation based on the CPI. $\frac{\Delta y_t}{y_t}$ is the GDP annual growth rate. $\frac{g_t}{y_t}$ and $\frac{t_t}{y_t}$ are the ratios, respectively, of government spending and government revenues to GDP. Government spending is obtained as the sum of government consumption and government investment. Revenues are obtained by subtracting from total revenues, transfers and interest expenses. Private sector debt, in consolidated terms, is the stock of liabilities held by the sectors Non-financial corporations and households. The spread is built as the difference between the yield on 10-year national government bond and the corresponding German bond

chance, the economies exhibiting higher growth rates are also the economies characterized, in the period under investigation, by high private debt. Moreover, it is also important to point out that despite the collapse of growth in the period 2008–2012, the three high private debt countries have again experienced strong GDP growth rates in more recent years, well above the average growth of the Euro Area.

On the other hand, the countries affected by high public debt experienced an average rate of growth near zero over the period 1999–2016. Since the small Euro-area countries have been hit by the same global negative shocks in the EMU period, we may conjecture that fiscal consolidations of recent years have played a sizeable role, jointly with national specific more structural factors, in determining these so poor performances.

Let us note that as far as private debt is concerned, Portugal shows values in line with those observed in the other high private-debt countries. Yet Portugal also exhibits an average value of pubic debt-to-GDP ratio well above the threshold of 60%. In fact, in terms of macroeconomic growth outcome, Portugal has behaved more similarly to Greece and Italy.

Important differences among the six countries are also observed in the level of debts with respect to GDP. More precisely, Greece and Italy were affected in the period considered (and, indeed, are still affected) by high public debt. "High" in the twofold sense of being well above the threshold of 60% established within the European rules and around twice with respect to the values characterizing the other investigated countries. Nevertheless, it should be noted that from 1999 to 2007 the public debt was below 60% and declining in all "low debt" countries, whereas it steadily increased following the Great Recession. In other words, at least for the period under investigation, there is a negative correlation between public and private debt in these countries. This negative correlation is particularly marked in Spain over the period 2008–2016. Of course, this is far from surprising, given the pressure on public resources exerted as a consequence of the financial difficulties in the private sector of the economic systems.

As for the ratio of private debt to GDP, data show a quite different situation, with a group of countries including Ireland, Netherlands, Portugal and Spain affected by much higher values with respect to Greece and Italy. In particular Ireland, Netherlands and Portugal are, on average, well above the threshold level of 160% (see European Commission 2012), while Spain is quite near, still on average, to this level implying that in the last decade the country has repeatedly experienced values above the threshold.

Indeed, it is well known that in the first decade of the Euro, the favorable borrowing costs and cross-border financial integration under the EMU produced large capital inflows in peripheral Euro-area countries. Moreover, these large capital inflows were associated with growing current account deficits. Of course, and symmetrically, growing current account surpluses have characterized northern Euro-area economies and Germany in primis.

These large capital inflows also represented an important factor underlying bubbles in real estate prices in the first part of 2000s. It is well known that such bubbles exposed these countries to serious financial fragilities. For, as a consequence of the financial crisis which hit the world economy in 2007, these countries found themselves exposed to a series of confidence shocks on the solidity of the financial system and on the sustainability of public finances.

4.3 The Econometric Approach

We estimate a near-VAR in order to model the dynamic interaction between Euro-area variables and national variables. We start with the estimation of the reduced-form, near-VAR model:

$$X_t = A(L)X_{t-1} + e_t \tag{4.1}$$

where X_t is a 8×1 vector of macroeconomic variables, including both Euro-area and national variables, and e_t is the 8×1 vector of error terms, such that $E(e_t) = 0$ and $E(e_t e_t^{'}) = \Sigma_e$.

The vector X_t includes the following variables:

$$X_t^{'} = \left(p_t \ y_t \ i_t - i_t^* \ \varepsilon_t \ g_{it} \ t_{it} \ p_{it} \ y_{it}\right)$$

$A(L)$, the 8×8 matrix polynomial in the lag operator L, has the following structure:

$$\begin{pmatrix} A_{11}(L) & A_{12}(L) & A_{13}(L) & A_{14}(L) & A_{15}(L) & 0 & 0 & 0 \\ A_{21}(L) & A_{22}(L) & A_{23}(L) & A_{24}(L) & A_{25}(L) & 0 & 0 & 0 \\ A_{31}(L) & A_{32}(L) & A_{33}(L) & A_{34}(L) & A_{35}(L) & 0 & 0 & 0 \\ A_{41}(L) & A_{42}(L) & A_{43}(L) & A_{44}(L) & A_{45}(L) & 0 & 0 & 0 \\ A_{51}(L) & A_{52}(L) & A_{53}(L) & A_{54}(L) & A_{55}(L) & A_{56}(L) & A_{57}(L) & A_{58}(L) \\ A_{61}(L) & A_{62}(L) & A_{63}(L) & A_{64}(L) & A_{65}(L) & A_{66}(L) & A_{67}(L) & A_{68}(L) \\ A_{71}(L) & A_{72}(L) & A_{73}(L) & A_{74}(L) & A_{75}(L) & A_{76}(L) & A_{77}(L) & A_{78}(L) \\ A_{81}(L) & A_{82}(L) & A_{83}(L) & A_{84}(L) & A_{86}(L) & A_{86}(L) & A_{87}(L) & A_{88}(L) \end{pmatrix}$$

The sample covers the period 1999–2016.[4]

This is a near-VAR model since there are two distinct blocks: in the first block, the equations of the Euro-area variables do not include lags of the national, macroeconomic variables; in the second block, the equations of the national variables instead include lags of all the variables of the dynamic system. Thus, this block exogeneity restriction implies that the national variables are unidirectionally caused by the Euro-area variables.

It is worth pointing out that although we estimate six different VAR models, one for each country, the set of the identified euro-wide shocks is invariant. The important implication is that this allows the domestic dynamics to be investigated, conditional on common disturbances.

In particular, the first block includes the following macroeconomic variables: Euro-area consumer price index, p_t; the real gross domestic product, y_t; the differential between the Eonia and the federal funds rate, $i_t - i_t^*$, the nominal exchange rate, ε_t, defined as US dollars per currency units.

By including the differential between the Euro area and US short-term interest rate we specify the reaction function of the ECB in terms of a monetary policy rule for an open economy.[5] As standard in the literature, we adopt the short-term interest rates to measure the stance of monetary policy (see e.g. Bernanke and Mihov 1998 and Taylor 1999).

The second block of the model comprises national series. These are government expenditures, g_{it}; government revenues, t_{it}; the domestic consumer price index, p_{it}; and the real gross domestic product, y_{it}.

Government expenditures are given by the sum of government consumption and government investment. Government revenues are given by total revenues minus transfers and interest expenses. Hence, we choose the same aggregates for the fiscal series adopted by Blanchard and Perotti (2002). The rationale behind this choice is that public spending on goods and services influences aggregate demand directly, while transfers and taxes have their first impact on the amount of disposable income, and therefore on the savings-investment decisions.

---

[4]More precisely, due to data availability the sample starts in 2002:Q1 for Ireland. For all the other countries the data start in 1999:Q1. The sample ends in 2016:Q3 for the six countries included in this investigation.

[5]There is evidence of a notable interaction between the ECB and the Fed over the EMU period. See e.g. Scotti (2011) and Ribba (2012).

The interest rate differential enters the model in basis points. Instead all the other variables are taken in natural logs. More precisely, in order to obtain the response of variables in percentage points, given a generic variable z_t, we take $log(z_t) * 100$.

The lag length is set to one.

System (4.1) is estimated by using Seemingly Unrelated Regression (SUR) methods (Zellner 1962). Moreover, the impulse response functions together with the confidence bands are obtained by utilizing Monte Carlo integration techniques and the Gibbs sampling (Doan 2010).

We recover the structural shocks in the following way. We first obtain the reduced-form moving average representation of system (4.1):

$$X_t = C(L)e_t \tag{4.2}$$

where $C(0) = I$.

Then, the structural disturbances are obtained by imposing a contemporaneous recursive structure to the estimated VAR model:

$$X_t = B(L)\eta_t \tag{4.3}$$

where $B(L) = C(L)B$ and $\eta_t = B^{-1}e_t$. B is the Cholesky factor of Σ_e, i.e. is the unique lower triangular matrix such that $BB' = \Sigma_e$.

Thus, for the Euro area-wide block, we impose that a monetary policy shock does not impact either the price level or GDP within the period; a demand shock does not influence prices in the contemporaneous period; the exchange rate exerts a delayed effect on the interest rate and on the other Euro-area variables.

It is worth stressing that this identification strategy is widely adopted in this area of research (see, for example, Christiano et al. 1999; Eichenbaum and Evans 1995). A more recent example of recursive identification strategy, in the context of studies on the effects of fiscal shocks, is provided by the structural VAR investigation on the US economy conducted by Monacelli et al. (2012)

As far as the domestic block is concerned, fiscal shocks are ordered first. This assumption implies that the government does not react within the quarter to changes in national macroeconomic conditions.[6] This seems a reasonable choice also considering, in particular, the difficulties for fiscal variables to react in the contemporaneous period to a changing state of the economy. More precisely, there are components of total government expenditures and revenues, the so-called automatic stabilizers, that endogenously react to business cycle fluctuations. Instead, changes in other components such as public investments and purchases of goods that requires the interaction between government and parliament do not happen within quarter.

However, this identification may imply a non-fundamental representation if economic agents foresee the fiscal shocks. Indeed, it is well known that fiscal choices are often announced in advance and moreover there are delays in the process of

[6]Similar identifying restrictions are adopted by, among others, Blanchard and Perotti (2002) and Monacelli et al. (2012).

parliamentary approval. In these contexts, agents may respond to them anticipating the effective occurrence of the fiscal shock.

An interesting example of fiscal foresight is given in Leeper et al. (2013). The authors use tax policies as an example of foresight and show that output multipliers for taxes will be distorted if the researchers neglect modelling foresight.

In order to overcome the non-fundamentalness, an alternative identification strategy may consist in a narrative approach, as in Ramey (2011). Whatever the merits of this approach, it is important to stress that the time-series of news announcements is not always easily available for the countries included in our investigation. Moreover, as emphasized by Barnichon and Matthes (2015) the narrative approach might suffer from its own problems. For example the authors note that the narrative approach may be biased in the distribution between expansionary and contractionary shocks. These potential problems do not seem to affect our recursive identification scheme.

Leeper et al. (2013) note that, given the peculiar treatment of information flows, problems arise in building models capable of incorporating the information flows underlying the narrative approach.

Forni and Gambetti (2014) suggest that leading indicators, like stock prices and business confidence indexes, may add useful information for recovering the structural shocks. To this end, we add the composite index of the domestic stock market and the Economic Sentiment Indicator (ESI) as exogenous variables to each country VAR model.[7]

Adopting structural VARs, it is important to check the robustness of results obtained under a given identification scheme. In the next chapter we will undertake some sensitivity analysis and will recover the government spending shocks by imposing sign restrictions on the response of some variables.

4.4 Estimation Results: The Responses of Variables to Monetary and Fiscal Shocks

The responses of Euro-area and national variables to monetary policy and fiscal shocks are collected in four figures. Figure 4.1 reports the responses of Euro-area variables to a contractionary monetary policy shock, while Fig. 4.2 shows the dynamic effects exerted by the common monetary policy shock on national variables, i.e. on domestic prices and output. Finally, Figs. 4.3 and 4.4 report the responses of domestic prices and aggregate output to, respectively, national government expenditures shocks and government revenues shocks. The evidence concerning the dynamic effects of the identified shocks on domestic variables is presented in three distinct subsections.

It is useful to briefly present (and discuss) also the results concerning the effects exerted by unexpected movements in interest rates at the Euro-area aggregate level,

---

[7]The ESI is computed by the Commission's Directorate General for Economic and Financial Affairs as a composite confidence indicator.

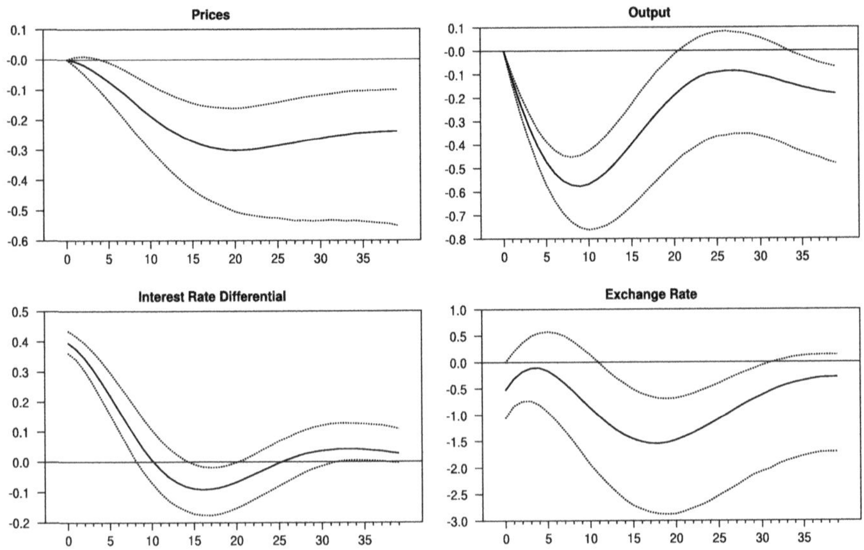

Fig. 4.1 Responses of Euro-area variables to a contractionary monetary policy shock. *Note* Impulse responses to a contractionary monetary policy shock. Solid line: median estimate; dashed lines: 68th percentile confidence interval

since on the one hand this helps the evaluation of the identification strategy and, on the other, allows a comparison with the results obtained in the responses to monetary policy shocks at the country level.

Median responses are reported together with the error bands. Following the suggestion of Sims and Zha (1999) we consider the 16th and the 84th percentiles.

Let us recall that given our specification of the monetary policy rule for large open economies, a monetary tightening is associated with an increase in the differential between the European and the US policy rates.

As shown in Fig. 4.1, a contractionary monetary policy shocks causes recessionary effects in the Euro Area, since in response to the increase in interest rates there is a contraction of both aggregate output and price index. Moreover, the effects exerted on the macrovariables turn out to be quite persistent. In particular, as far as the response of output is concerned, the contractionary effects exerted by the monetary tightening vanish after around four years since after then they become statistically non-significant.

As for the size of the effects, Fig. 4.1 reports the response of variables to a one standard deviation shock and shows that a 40 basis points increase in the differential between the European Overnight Rate and the Federal Funds Rate leads to a maximumnegative effect on Euro-area output of −0.55% after 9 quarters. In other words, a 1% increase in EONIA, holding constant the Federal funds rate, causes a decrease of 1.3% of output at an horizon of two years. Indeed, a quite remarkable real effect.

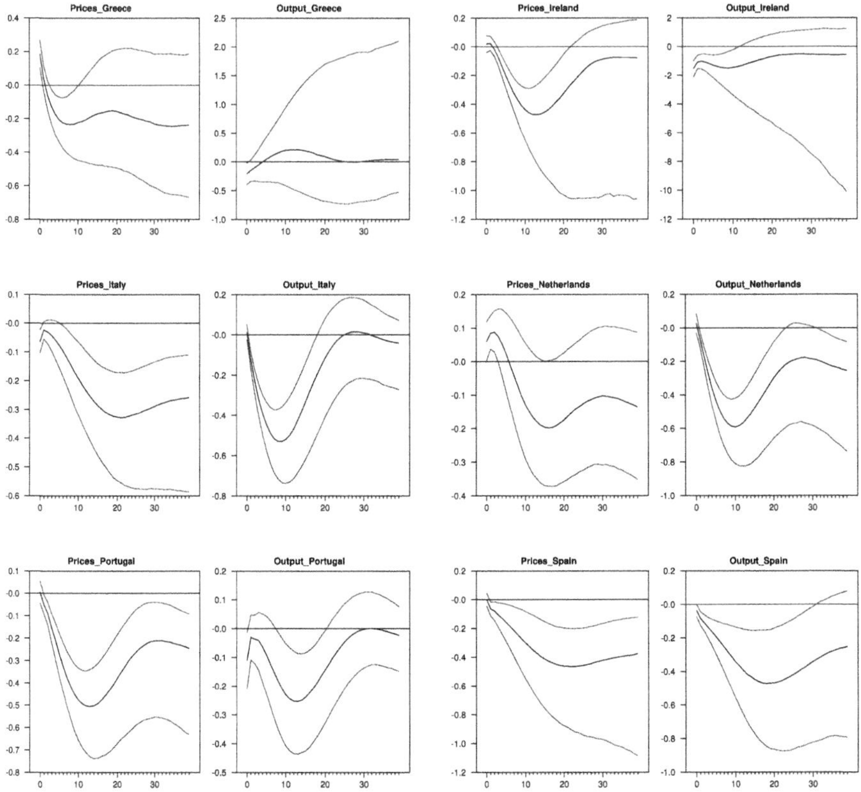

Fig. 4.2 Responses of national variables to a contractionary common monetary policy shock. *Note* Impulse responses to a common contractionary monetary policy shock. Solid line: median estimate; dashed lines: 68th percentile confidence interval

Thus, a first important conclusion is that monetary policy matters at the Euro-area aggregate level, in the sense that it exerts significant effects on both nominal and real variables. The dynamic effects are also persistent, since they last for years.

It is important to point out that our identification approach is not plagued by the so-called price puzzle: the response of prices to monetary policy shocks exhibits the expected sign, i.e. there is a decrease in the price level following a monetary tightening. We believe that this result supports the identification strategy followed in this investigation to recover the structural disturbances.[8]

As for the reaction in the exchange rate, the Uncovered Interest Parity predicts that in response to a contractionary monetary policy shock the national currency should appreciate for some quarters while, over time, the response of the exchange rate

[8]Or, at a minimum, the identification strategy adopted allows an appreciable characterization of the dynamic effects of monetary policy shocks on nominal and real variables. The emergence of the price puzzle is not uncommon in VAR models in which structural disturbances are identified by imposing a contemporaneous causal structure. See, among others, Christiano et al. (1999).

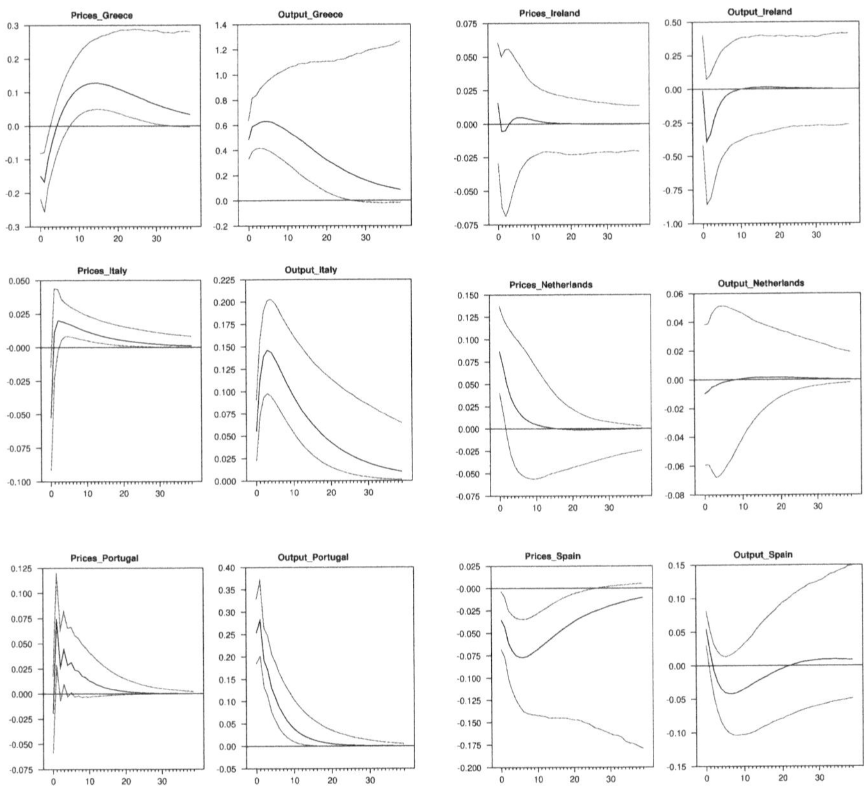

Fig. 4.3 Responses of national variables to a domestic government spending shock. *Note* Impulse responses to a positive government spending shock. Solid line: median estimate; dashed lines: 68th percent confidence interval. Government expenditures defined as government consumption plus investment

should change its sign. Our finding is only partially aligned to this prediction, since in the short run, given the estimated error bands, the response of the national currency is not significant. Instead, we detect a significant depreciation of the domestic currency starting three years after the shock which is consistent with the theoretical prediction.

4.4.1 The Response of National Variables to a Contractionary Common Monetary Policy Shock

As shown in Fig. 4.2, a monetary tightening provokes a persistent economic recession in all the Euro-area countries considered with the exception of Greece, since there is a significant contraction of both the aggregate output and the Consumer Price Index which lasts for many quarters.

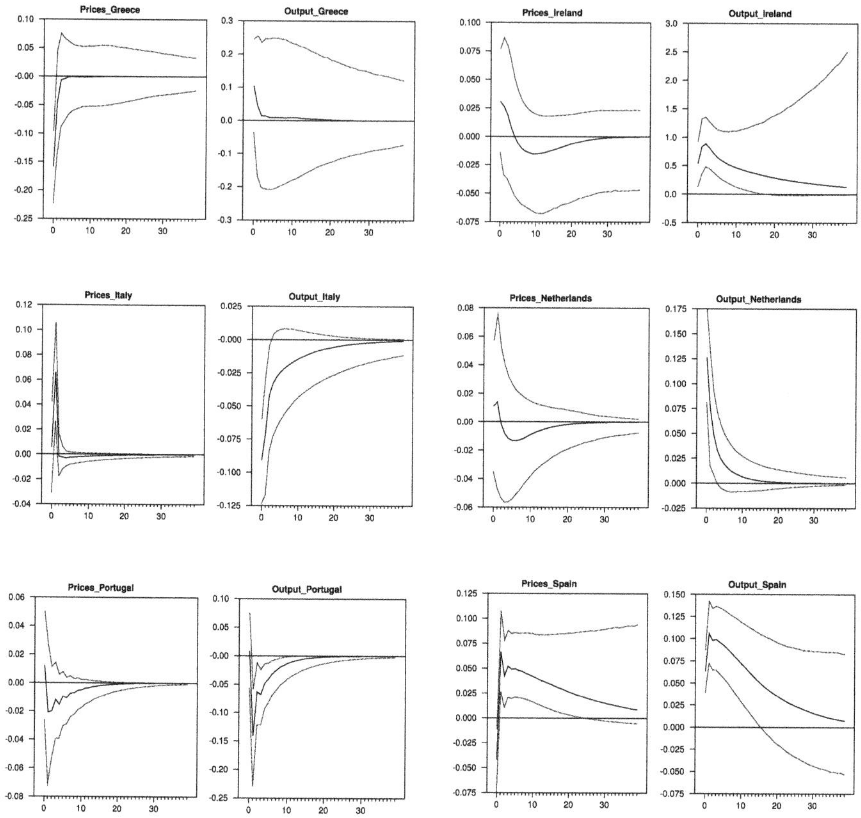

Fig. 4.4 Responses of national variables to a domestic government revenues shock. *Note* Solid line: median estimate; dashed lines: 68th percent confidence interval. Government revenues are defined as total revenues minus transfers and interest expenses

Regarding the responses of Greek variables, starting from the second quarter following the monetary tightening there is a contraction of prices and after around three years the effects become statistically non-significant. Instead, as for aggregate output, although there is a small negative contemporaneous impact the effects exerted by the common Euro-area monetary policy shock are non-significant at all the other horizons. Indeed, the channels through which changes in short-term interest rate may propagate their effects on the economy are mainly related to the demand of the private sector. However, as stressed by Keynes in the 30s of the 20th century, it is unlikely that a reduction of interest rates may stimulate aggregate demand in the context of a depressed economy.

As far as the other five countries are concerned, the recessionary effects of the monetary tightening are common and, moreover, the size of the maximum effect on the aggregate output is quite similar among countries. Nevertheless, the effects turn out to be particularly persistent in Spain and Netherlands, since in these countries it requires around 6 years for the effects of monetary policy shocks to vanish.

Thus a second, important conclusion is that monetary policy matters not only at the aggregate Euro-area level but, largely, even at the country levels. For, we find that in five out of six countries included in the present investigation there are significant real effects exerted by monetary policy shocks. Another result which is worth stressing is that the size of the effects exerted by unexpected changes in the policy rate on output are, on average, quite large. Let us consider, for example, the case of Italy: in order to obtain around 1.2% increase (decrease) of output, a decrease (increase) of 100 hundred basis points in the differential between Eonia and the federal funds rate is required. Quite similar results hold for Netherlands and Spain, while Ireland exhibits the strongest negative reaction of output and Portugal, on the opposite side, the smallest one.

A third conclusion is that not only is the profile of dynamic responses for Italy, Netherlands and Portugal similar to the one characterizing the Euro Area as a whole, but even the size of the responses is quite close.

On the whole these results, obtained with structural methodologies, seem indeed to contrast with the anecdotal evidence developed in recent years on the difficulties faced by the ECB in promoting a sound reprise of both inflation towards 2% and of output growth in the Euro area.[9] These findings are also a notable complement to the conclusions reached in Cavallo and Ribba (2015), where significant real effects exerted by monetary policy shocks were detected in the national business cycle component of industrial production.

4.4.2 The Response of National Variables to a Domestic Government Spending Shock

Figure 4.3 shows the responses of national prices and GDP to a government spending shock.

A positive government spending shock causes an increase of output in Greece, Italy and Portugal, i.e. there are expansionary macroeconomic effects associated with the increase in government expenditures. Instead, in Ireland, Netherlands and Spain, the increase in government spending does not produce significant effects on aggregate output. More precisely, the response of output in Spain exhibits a positive sign on impact but this positive effect quickly vanishes just after one quarter. The median response in Ireland is negative for around two years, however the error bands are so wide as to lead to the conclusion that the fiscal shock exerts non-statistically

[9] Of course, we are implicitly maintaining that our estimated linear model allows a proper representation of the economic and monetary dynamics in the Euro Area and that, as a consequence, asymmetric effects of monetary policy (in terms of different effects exerted in expansionary with respect to recessionary phases of the economy) are negligible.

significant effects on output at all horizons. The same result also holds for the response of prices.

A similar analysis characterizes the impulse response functions in the Netherlands, though in this case there is a contemporaneous positive response of prices.

These results seems to confirm, at least partially, the conclusion of Dallari and Ribba (2015), who conduct an empirical investigation to characterize the responses of unemployment to fiscal shocks in the peripheral European countries under the EMU and find that Italy and Greece exhibit Keynesian results associated with government spending shocks. Conversely, the results obtained by Ilzetzki et al. (2013), concerning the negative sign of the fiscal multiplier for high public debt countries, are not confirmed by ours, since for the Mediterranean countries considered in the present investigation - notoriously high public debt countries - we detect a positive response of output to the fiscal expansion.

The dynamic responses of prices to the spending shock are less clear in terms of macroeconomic interpretation: in all the three "Keynesian countries" there is a contemporaneous negative sign in response to the positive expenditure shock. However, after a few quarters the response of prices becomes positive and thus they increase, consistently with the expansionary effects exerted by the fiscal shock on output.

In the next section we will provide an analysis of the sources of fluctuations in aggregate output in the national economies and, as we will see, the results obtained are consistent with the conclusion of a limited role played by national fiscal shocks.

Summing up the results concerning the dynamic effects of government spending shocks in this selected group of countries: there is a clear separation into two distinct groups, with the first one which includes Greece, Italy and Portugal and the second one which includes Ireland, Netherlands and Spain. Over the same sample period, i.e. a large part of the EMU period, and thus under the same monetary regime with a supranational central bank conducting the monetary policy, the two groups exhibit quite different macroeconomic outcomes associated with expansionary fiscal policies: a Keynesian, expansionary macroeconomic outcome in Greece Italy and Portugal and instead a more muted response of macrovariables in the remaining three countries.

How to explain these different results? The Mediterranean countries characterized by Keynesian outcomes of their fiscal policies are affected by high public debt-to-GDP ratio, ranging from an average value over the sample period of 130% of Greece to 85% in Portugal, and hence well above the traditional threshold of 60% established in the Euro Area. The other three countries, which exhibits non-Keynesian effects associated with fiscal policies are instead affected by high private-to-GDP ratio, with Ireland and Netherlands showing an average value under the EMU above 200% and Spain, over the same period, with an average value near to 160%, i.e. the threshold indicated by the European Commission.

Since all these countries share a common monetary policy and a common currency, an explanation for the quite different responses to fiscal shocks lies on the reaction of financial markets and private sector to changes in domestic fiscal policy. In the next chapter we further explore these different responses of the macrovariables to fiscal shocks by paying closer attention to the reaction of consumption and other domestic variables in the presence of high indebtedness at the government level or, alternatively, at the private sector level.

4.4.3 The Response of National Variables to a Domestic Government Revenues Shock

Figure 4.4 reports the responses of national variables to a positive government revenues shock. The fiscal austerity, i.e. the increase in government revenues, has recessionary effects for Italy and Portugal, since GDP decreases for some quarters following the fiscal shock. Regarding Greece, contrary to the results obtained in the case of government spending shocks, the response of aggregate output is statistically non-significant at all horizons. Instead, prices decrease in response to the tax shock. Thus, only for Italy and Portugal are the "Keynesian" conclusions of the previous subsection fully confirmed.

However, as far as Italy is concerned, it remains difficult to interpret the positive response of prices to the tax shock. We conjecture that this result may be explained by the composition of the fiscal tightening in Italy, which was repeatedly based on increases of value added tax, VATs, in the 2000s.[10]

For the group of high private debt countries, Ireland, Netherlands and Spain, the results unambiguously show the "non-Keynesian" effects of fiscal austerity: in response to the increase in government revenues there is a significant, expansionary effect exerted on GDP. These expansionary effects turn out to be particularly persistent in Ireland and Spain, where the increase in aggregate output is statistically-significant for around five years.

The median response of prices is positive for some quarters in Ireland and Netherlands. Nevertheless the responses are non-significant at all horizons, given the estimated error bands. Instead, as for Spain, the response of the aggregate price level is fully consistent with the expansionary effects exerted by government revenues shocks on output: following the fiscal austerity, there is a persistent increase in prices and the effects vanish after around 5 years.

Thus, studying the dynamic effects of government revenues shocks, we find again the separation between a group of high public debt countries and a group of high private debt countries, with quite different macroeconomic outcomes associated with the fiscal shocks.

---

[10]We have also checked the robustness of the estimated results shown in this section to changes in the setting of confidence bands. We find that the results do not change significantly if we set the error bands to the 10th and the 90th percentiles.

Table 4.2 Fraction of the forecast error variance at various horizons of national GDP attributable to the common, Euro-area monetary policy shock

Horizon	Greece	Ireland	Italy	Netherlands	Portugal	Spain
1	2.6	10.7	0.3	0.6	2.5	2.6
4	2.4	11.2	15.3	11.6	2.5	12.8
8	3.7	15.3	40.9	41.9	5.3	22.7
12	5.5	18.4	50.6	55.6	11.9	30.7
24	12.0	22.3	48.0	48.0	24.6	39.8

Note The table presents the fraction of variability of GDP at various horizons and for each country which is due to the Euro-area monetary policy shock

4.5 Estimation Results: Sources of Business Cycle Fluctuations in the Six Countries

Given the structural representation (4.1), we can recover the error in forecasting X_t for each horizon k in the following way:

$$X_{t+s} - E_t X_{t+s} = B_0 \eta_{t+s} + B_1 \eta_{t+s-1} + B_2 \eta_{t+s-2} + \dots + B_{s-1} \eta_{t+1} \quad (4.4)$$

From (4.4), it is easily seen that the variance of the forecasting error is:

$$Var(X_{t+s} - E_t X_{t+s}) = B_0 B_0' + B_1 B_1' + B_2 B_2' + \dots + B_{s-1} B_{s-1}' \quad (4.5)$$

From Eq. 4.5 one may obtain a decomposition of the total variance of the forecast error for each variable and hence investigate the sources of national business cycle fluctuations. In particular, given the focus of the present research on fiscal shocks, it is worth measuring the relative importance of government spending and government revenues shock in driving fluctuations of GDP at short and medium horizons. Moreover, let us note that the identified near-VAR model also allows the importance of the set of Euro-area common shocks to be estimated. This last estimation may be interpreted as an evaluation of the degree of integration of national business cycle in the European one.

Table 4.2 shows that the common Euro-area monetary policy shocks are an important driver of output fluctuations in the majority of the countries considered. This result confirms the conclusion of Sect. 4.3 that monetary policy matters in the Euro area.

Monetary policy shocks explain an important part of the variability of aggregate output at different horizons in Italy, Netherlands, Spain and Ireland. In particular, in Italy and Netherlands around 40% of the forecast error variance of output is explained by the monetary shock at horizons of 8 quarters. Although in these two countries we detect the most notable results exerted by monetary policy shocks, even Ireland and Spain have from one fifth to one third of the variance of output explained between the 8th and the 12th period.

Table 4.3 Fraction of the forecast error variance of GDP attributable to fiscal shocks and to other national shocks: Greece

Horizon	Expenditures	Revenues	Supply	Demand
1	12.9	0.8	0.5	58.6
4	18.8	1.3	1.2	52.7
8	18.4	1.2	2.2	42.7
12	16.1	1.0	2.7	34.0
24	10.8	0.7	2.6	20.6

Note For each country, the total variance of the forecast error for GDP is computed and then decomposed in the part attributable to each structural shock (cf. formula 4.5). The table presents the fraction of variability at various horizons which is due to the four national macroeconomic shocks

A less important role seems to have been played by changes in monetary policy at the aggregate Euro-area level in Greece and Portugal in the first 16 years of EMU: for the first 8 periods we find that monetary policy shocks explain a maximum of variability of output which reaches, respectively, around 4% in Greece and 5% in Portugal. The ability of monetary shocks to drive aggregate output fluctuations in these two countries grows over longer horizons but, on average, there are smaller values with respect to the other countries.

From Tables 4.3, 4.4, 4.5, 4.6, 4.7 and 4.8 we collect, for each country, the forecast error variance at various horizons, ascribable to fiscal shocks and to the other national shocks. In all the countries investigated fiscal shocks do not seem to be among the main drivers of aggregate output fluctuations. Nevertheless there are significant differences among countries.

In the case of Italy and the Netherlands both the spending and revenues shocks give a rather limited explanation for output fluctuations. In particular, their joint contribution to business cycle fluctuations is comprised between 1 and 6% at all horizons.

A more important role in the first sixteen years of EMU has been exerted by government revenues shocks both in Ireland and Spain, where the variance explained is around 10% in specific quarters. A more limited role is instead attributable to government spending shocks in these countries.

Regarding Greece and Portugal, the forecast error variance analysis tells a different story. First, government spending shocks play a pre-eminent role (with respect to government revenues shocks); Second, spending shocks are important drivers of business cycle fluctuations. As for Greece, around one fifth of output variability is explained by changes in government expenditures at horizons comprised between 4 and 8 quarters, whereas for Portugal the values are only slightly lower. Instead, a quite negligible role has been played in the last decades by changes in government revenues.

Another important finding concerns the role of national demand shocks that, with the exception of Italy, exhibit a primary role as drivers of output fluctuations at very short horizons. For, the variance explained by national demand shocks in the contemporaneous period ranges from 58.6 of Greece and to 34.7% of Netherlands.

Table 4.4 Fraction of the forecast error variance of GDP attributable to fiscal shocks and to other national shocks: Ireland

Horizon	Expenditures	Revenues	Supply	Demand
1	0.6	4.4	0.9	48.8
4	2.0	13.6	1.0	27.2
8	1.7	11.4	1.1	17.2
12	1.3	9.1	0.9	13.1
24	0.8	6.4	0.6	9.1

Note See Table 4.3

Table 4.5 Fraction of the forecast error variance of GDP attributable to fiscal shocks and to other national shocks: Italy

Horizon	Expenditures	Revenues	Supply	Demand
1	1.1	2.9	0.2	19.0
4	5.3	1.5	1.3	12.7
8	5.0	0.8	0.9	7.8
12	4.0	0.5	0.7	5.4
24	2.8	0.3	0.4	3.7

Table 4.6 Fraction of the forecast error variance of GDP attributable to fiscal shocks and to other national shocks: Netherlands

Horizon	Expenditures	Revenues	Supply	Demand
1	0.4	5.5	2.9	34.7
4	0.7	2.7	3.9	18.9
8	0.5	1.3	2.8	9.1
12	0.4	0.7	1.9	5.2
24	0.2	0.3	1.0	2.5

Table 4.7 Fraction of the forecast error variance of GDP attributable to fiscal shocks and to other national shocks: Portugal

Horizon	Expenditures	Revenues	Supply	Demand
1	12.1	0.4	7.9	37.2
4	14.6	2.4	5.3	27.0
8	12.9	1.9	4.2	21.1
12	9.7	1.5	3.5	17.0
24	6.7	1.0	2.5	11.8

Note See Table 4.3

Table 4.8 Fraction of the forecast error variance of GDP attributable to fiscal shocks and to other national shocks: Spain

Horizon	Expenditures	Revenues	Supply	Demand
1	5.1	6.5	0.5	49.2
4	2.1	10.1	1.7	38.3
8	1.7	6.4	2.8	24.7
12	1.3	3.8	3.3	15.4
24	0.8	1.3	3.1	5.4

Note See Table 4.3

Nevertheless, and maybe even more important, after two years the set of national shocks explain only a minor part of the variability of output in all the countries except Greece.

On the whole, the results presented in this section tell us two main things: (1) fiscal shocks have exerted statistically-significant but economically-limited effects in Italy, Spain and in the majority of small Euro-area economies from the onset of the euro; (2) the important (and maybe expected) exception is represented by Greece, where the effects of government spending shocks are significant and explain a notable part of movements in aggregate output. A similar conclusion also holds for Portugal.

4.5.1 *The Degree of Integration of Domestic Business Cycle in the European One*

In this investigation we have identified two separate sets of structural shocks for each country: a first set of exogenous sources of fluctuations in macrovariables which includes disturbances at the Euro-area level; a second one instead including the domestic sources of fluctuations. Moreover, the set of area-wide shocks is invariant, given the adopted methodology based on near-VARs.

The results presented in Tables 4.2, 4.3, 4.4, 4.5, 4.6, 4.7 and 4.8 also allow the following question to be investigated: is the pre-eminent source of domestic output fluctuations ascribable to area-wide macroeconomic shocks or do the local shocks play the dominant role?

Clearly, in the presence of dominant domestic factors which explain the dominant bulk of business cycle fluctuations at different frequencies, the conclusion should be that the national economy is not well integrated in the European business cycle. This finding would thus signal that relevant asymmetries (still) characterize business cycles in the Euro Area.

In order to exhibit a good degree of integration in the European business cycle it is not strictly required that local shocks exert negligible effects at all horizons but, rather, that their relative importance in driving output and price fluctuations decrease quite rapidly.

These conditions of business cycle convergence, i.e. of dominant role of exogenous area-wide shocks and/or quick decrease of relative importance of domestic shocks, are clearly satisfied only in the case of Italy, Netherlands, Portugal and Spain, since in these four countries after 4 quarters only around 20–25% of aggregate output variance is explained by national shocks. Ireland is in an intermediate position since, on impact, around 53% of variability is explained by national shocks but even after four quarters 43% of variability is still explained by the set of domestic macroeconomic shocks. However starting from the fourth quarter there is a rapid increase in the relative importance of Euro-area shocks.

As far as Greece is concerned, the degree of integration in the Euro-area business cycle is clearly unsatisfactory: at the horizon of four quarters over 70% of output variability is explained in Greece by local factors and domestic shocks keep a pre-eminent role even at horizons of 12 quarters.

Thus, while at horizons of around one year there is a notable role exerted by local shocks in almost all countries (Italy represents an exception), after two years around 70% of output fluctuations are driven by Euro-area common shocks in Ireland and Spain. In Portugal, Euro-area shocks explain around 60% of domestic output fluctuations at the same horizons. Instead in Italy, at horizons of 8 periods onwards, over 90% of variability of national output is explained by area-wide shocks.

As for the Netherlands, local shocks are minor drivers of business cycle fluctuations: they explain a sizeable part of national output variability only at very short horizons; after one year, 75% of variability is due to external Euro-area shocks.

On the basis of these results, we are led to conclude that these small open economies exhibit business cycle fluctuations well integrated in the European business cycle, in the sense that, apart from very short-run fluctuations, national fluctuations have mainly a common rather than a local source. Thus, the important conclusion is that there is no evidence of a big role played by asymmetric shocks in shaping business fluctuations at the national level.

However, we would stress once more that this conclusion does not hold for Greece, where local shocks explain the pre-eminent part of variability in aggregate output.

4.6 Conclusions

The results presented in this chapter, based on structural near-VARs estimated for the EMU period, show that contractionary fiscal policy shocks, i.e.decreases in government expenditures or increases in government revenues, have exerted heterogeneous effects on prices and output in a selected group of Euro-area countries in the period 1999–2016. More precisely, these shocks produced mainly expansionary effects in Ireland, Netherlands and Spain, with an increase in output which lasts for some quarters, and mainly contractionary effects in Greece, Italy and Portugal, with a persistent decrease in the aggregate output level.

In our opinion, these results concerning the dynamic effects of fiscal shocks in a group of Euro-area countries affected by high (public and-or private) debt, suggest that is worth further exploring the role played by debt in shaping the reaction of macroeconomic activity to fiscal policy decisions made by national governments.

In their interesting paper, Ilzetzki et al. (2013) showed, by using panel VAR techniques, that in countries characterized by high public debt, fiscal shocks exert non-Keynesian effects, i.e. contractionary fiscal policies produce expansionary macroeconomic effects. Our empirical results, while confirming the importance of some key national factors, public debt included, in explaining the macroeconomic outcome of fiscal shocks should induce, on the other hand, some caution on the conclusion that these non-Keynesian results hold always and everywhere. For, although our investigation covers a different sample period with respect to Iltezsky et al. and hence there is some problem in comparing the results directly, we found that a high public debt-to-GDP ratio does not necessarily prevent positive effects on output of expansionary fiscal policies. Let us recall that Italy and Greece have systematically experienced debt-to-GDP ratio well above 100% in the EMU period.

It seems also to be worth exploring, within the national economies, the nexus between "perverse" effects of fiscal policies and heavy indebtedness of households and corporate sectors.

It should be noted that at least in the case of Portugal, too the public debt is particularly high and above 100% of GDP.

Nevertheless, as also shown by the simple descriptive analysis of Sect. 4.2, there is a significant (cor)relation between public and private debt, at least in recent years: countries with high private debt in the first part of the 2000s, i.e. Ireland and Spain, have experienced a steady increase of public debt during the Great Recession. This is far from surprising in the light of the recapitalization of domestic financial institutions and in the rising costs of welfare policies required in the face of the crisis.

Another result of this research which is worth pointing out is that despite the Keynesian effects of fiscal policies observed for southern countries (with the exception of Spain), fiscal shocks do not explain a pre-eminent part of the observed variability of output and prices. Instead, we find that the monetary policy shocks and the other common Euro-area shocks are important, exogenous drivers of business cycle fluctuations in all the countries included in this investigation, in particular at short and medium-run horizons.

However, the conclusions concerning the limited role of fiscal shocks and of Euro-area shocks do not hold for Greece: the severe austerity imposed in the last decade had a significant role in the deep recession experienced by this country and, related, local disturbances are more important in relative terms with respect to area-wide shocks. In other words, asymmetric shocks have played a dominant role in the Greek economy in the EMU period.

On the whole, these results seem to suggest that in the case of the small, and highly indebted, Euro-area countries, excessive confidence should not be placed in the ability of fiscal policies to stabilize the economic system or, on an even more ambitious ground, to rely on expansionary fiscal policies to promote a sound recovery of the economies.

Instead, a more promising European strategy might rely on a more expansive stance of fiscal policy in the large Euro-area economies, *in primis* Germany. Indeed, in the light of the surveillance of macroeconomic imbalances by the European Commission, Germany has a prominent and persistent surplus in the current account, above the identified threshold of 6%. Thus, also considering that the public debt and the government budget balance are kept well below the thresholds established by European fiscal rules, there is a positive fiscal space for an increase in government spending and in tax reduction.

Of course, it should not be taken for granted that expansionary fiscal policies in Germany would exert significant spillover effects in the Euro area. To this end, in Chap. 6 we aim to measure these spillover effects by identifying fiscal shocks in Germany and by characterizing the responses of prices and output both at the wide area level and at the level of small countries.

In reality, the perspective target of a fiscal capacity at the aggregate Euro-area level could be the key for proper management of aggregate demand, at least in the presence of adverse shocks of particular virulence. Let us recall that in Chap. 2 we have shown that a centralized conduct of fiscal policy, in particular in coordination with monetary policy, might be a strong political and economic stabilizer for the Eurozone.

Further, an interesting by-product of the empirical investigation conducted in this chapter concerns the conclusion that Ireland, Italy, Netherlands, Spain, and to a lesser extent Portugal, exhibit business fluctuations with a high degree of integration with the Euro-area business cycle. This conclusion is related to the finding that the set of local shocks explains only a small part of the variability of national aggregate output at horizons longer than two years. Once again this conclusion does not hold for Greece.

Data Appendix

- Euro-Area Variables
  - **Prices**: Euro Area (19 Countries) Harmonised Index of Consumer Prices is collected from European Central Bank at a quarterly frequency. Data are seasonally adjusted by using the moving average technique. The reference year is 2015.
  - **Output**: The real gross domestic product for the Euro Area (19 Countries), Chain linked volumes (2010), is collected from Eurostat by using the GDP and main components database at a quarterly frequency. Data are already available adjusted for seasonality.
  - **Interest rate differential**: The variable is the difference between the European overnight interest rate (Eonia) and the US Federal Funds rate, both series have a quarterly frequency. The former is the short term interest rate collected from Eurostat by using the Money market interest rates database. The latter is retrieved from FRED, Federal Reserve Bank of St. Louis.
  - **Exchange rate**: The Euro/ECU exchange rate is collected from Eurostat. Data are quarterly and expressed as US dollars per currency unit.

- Countries Variables:
  The countries included in this investigation are Greece, Ireland, Italy, Netherlands, Portugal and Spain. For each country the following variables are used:
  - **Government expenditures**: The government expenditures variable is obtained, for each country, as the sum of government consumption and government investment. Data are collected from Eurostat, using the Quarterly non-financial account for general government. After collecting data at a quarterly frequency, firstly, they were seasonally adjusted and transformed in real terms using country GDP deflator; secondly, the sum of government consumption and government investment was made in order to obtain the government spending variable.
  - **Government revenues**: The government revenues variable is obtained, for each country, by subtracting from total revenues, transfers and interest expenses. Data are collected from Eurostat, using the Quarterly non-financial account for general government. After downloading data at a quarterly frequency, firstly, they were seasonally adjusted and transformed in real terms using country GDP deflator; secondly, the government revenues variable, for each country, was built by subtracting transfers and interest expenses from the total revenue stream.
  - **Prices**: The Harmonised Index of Consumer Prices of each country is collected from European Central Bank at a quarterly frequency. Data are seasonally adjusted by using the moving average technique. The reference year is 2015.
  - **Output**: The real gross domestic product, chain linked volumes (2010), is collected, for each country, from Eurostat by using the GDP and main components database at a quarterly frequency. Data are already available adjusted for seasonality.
  - **Economic sentiment indicator**: The Economic Sentiment Indicator series, for each country, come from the European Commission - Directorate general for economic and financial affairs (DG ECFIN). In order to obtain quarterly frequency, data have been aggregated through a simple average of monthly values. Data were already available adjusted for seasonality.
  - **Domestic stock market index**: Domestic stock market indexes are collected from Datastream at a quarterly frequency. In particular, for Greece we use the GR Athens Stock Exchange General Share Price Index; for Ireland we use the IR Price Index; for Italy we use the FTSE MIB INDEX, for Netherlands the AEX Index; for Portugal we use the PSI 20 Index and for Spain we use the IBEX 35 Index. Data were adjusted for seasonality by using the moving average technique.
  - **Private sector debt**: The Private sector debt, in consolidated terms, is the stock of liabilities held by the sectors Non-financial corporations and households. Data are collected from Eurostat by using the Financial Sheet database at a yearly frequency. Data were converted from a yearly to a quarterly frequency by using the Chow-Lin method.
  - **Public sector debt**: The Public sector debt, in consolidated terms, is the government gross debt. Data are provided, for each country, by Eurostat using the Quarterly government debt database.

- **Spread**: The spread is built as the difference between the yield on 10-years national government bond and the corresponding German bond. Data come from Eurostat by using EMU convergence criterion database at a quarterly frequency.

References

Alesina A, Ardagna S (2010) Large changes in fiscal policy: taxes versus spending. Tax policy and the economy, NBER 24:35–68

Auerbach AJ, Gorodnichenko Y (2012) Measuring the output responses to fiscal policy. Am Econ J Econ Policy 4:1–27

Barnichon R, Matthes C (2015) Stimulus versus austerity: the asymmetric government spending multiplier. CEPR discussion paper 10584

Bernanke BS, Mihov I (1998) Measuring the monetary policy. Q J Econ 113:869–902

Blanchard OJ, Perotti R (2002) An empirical characterization of the dynamic effects of changes in government spending and taxes on output. Q J Econ 117:1329–1368

Boeckx J, Dossche M, Peersman G (2017) Effectiveness and transmission of the ECBs balance sheet policies. Int J Cent Bank 13:297–333

Canova F, Pappa E (2011) Fiscal policy, pricing frictions and monetary accommodation. Econ Policy 555–598

Canzoneri M, Collard F, Dellas H, Diba B (2016) Fiscal multipliers in recessions. Econ J 126:75–108

Cavallo A, Ribba A (2014) Euro area inflation as a predictor of national inflation rates. J Policy Model 36:1048–1065

Cavallo A, Ribba A (2015) Common macroeconomic shocks and business cycle fluctuations in Euro area countries. Int Rev Econ Financ 38:377–392

Cavallo A, Ribba A (2017) Measuring the effects of oil price and Euro-area shocks on CEECs business cycles. Department of Economics 0111, University of Modena and Reggio Emilia

Christiano L, Eichenbaum M, Evans CL (1999) Monetary policy shocks: what have we learned and to what end? In: Taylor JB, Woodford M (eds) Handbook of macroeconomics. North Holland, Amsterdam, pp 65–148

Christiano L, Eichenbaum M, Rebelo S (2011) When is the government spending multiplier large? J Polit Econ 78–121

Conti AM, Neri S, Nobili A (2017) Low inflation and monetary policy in the Euro Area. Working paper series, European Central Bank

Cushman D, Zha T (1997) Identifying monetary policy in a small open economy under flexible exchange rates. J Monet Econ 39:433448

Dallari P, Ribba A (2015) Economic shocks and their effects on unemployment in the Euro Area periphery under the EMU. Department of Economics No 114, University of Modena and Reggio Emilia

Doan TA (2010) RATS users manual, Version 8, Estima, 1560 Sherman Avenue, Suite 510. IL, Evanston, p 60201

Eichenbaum M, Evans CL (1995) Some empirical evidence of shocks to monetary policy on exchange rates. Q J Econ 110:975–1010

European Commission (2012) First alert mechanism report on macroeconomic imbalances in member states. MEMO/12/104

Forni M, Gambetti L (2014) Sufficient information in structural VARs. J Monet Econ 66:124–136

Giavazzi F, Pagano M (1990) Can severe fiscal contactions be expansionary? tales of two small European countries. NBER chapters, NBER Macroeconomics Annual 1990:75–122

Ilzetzki E, Mendoza EG, Végh CA (2013) How big (small?) are fiscal multipliers? J Monet Econ 60:239–254

Leeper EM, Walker TB, Yang S-CS (2013) Fiscal foresight and information flows. Econometrica 81:1115–1145
Leeper EM, Traum N, Walker TB (2015) Clearing up the fiscal multipliers morass: prior and posterior analysis. NBER working paper 21433
Monacelli T, Perotti R, Trigari A (2010) Unemployment fiscal multipliers. J Monet Econ 57:531–553
Mountford A, Uhlig H (2009) What are the effects of fiscal policy shocks? J Appl Econom 24:960–992
Peersman G (2004) The transmission of monetary policy in the Euro Area: are the effects different across countries? Oxford B Econ Stat 66:285–308
Ramey VA (2011) Identifying government spending shocks: it's all in the timing. Q J Econ 126:1–50
Ribba A (2012) The federal funds rate and the conduction of the international orchestra. Econ Bull 32:2983–2990
Scotti C (2011) A bivariate model of Federal Reserve and ECB main policy rates. Int J Cent Bank 7:37–78
Sims CA, Zha T (1999) Error bands for impulse responses. Econometrica 67:1113–1156
Taylor JH (1999) A historical analysis of monetary policy rules. In: Taylor John H (ed) Rules monetary policy. National Bureau of Economic Research, Chicago
Zellner A (1962) An efficient method of estimating seemingly unrelated regressions and tests for aggregation bias. J Am Stat Assoc 57(298):348–368

Chapter 5
A Further Look To Macroeconomic Outcomes of Fiscal Austerity in High Debt Countries

Abstract According to the results presented in Chap. 4, fiscal policy exhibits the traditional Keynesian sign in a group of southern Euro-area economies, i.e. Greece, Italy and Portugal, affected by high public debt. Instead, a non-Keynesian sign was detected in another group of countries, i.e. Ireland, Nerherlands and Spain, characterized by high private debt over the EMU period. In this chapter we aim to give a closer look to the dynamics of domestic output in response to contractionary fiscal shocks. To this end, we estimate VAR models at the national level and adopt an alternative identification strategy, based on sign restrictions. We also see this investigation as a robustness analysis for the main results of the previous chapter. We focus on the response of private consumption, typically the largest component of aggregate demand, to domestic government spending shocks. We find the largest output multipliers, but of opposite sign, respectively in Greece and Ireland. Thus, the conclusion is that the main findings of the previous chapter are largely confirmed.

5.1 Introduction

In Chap. 4 we found that fiscal policy generates quite different macroeconomic outcomes in a group of small and medium-size European economies. In some cases fiscal stimuli cause expansionary effects on aggregate output, while in others they generate recessionary outcomes. The somehow surprising result (compared to some recent findings of the literature) is that expansionary effects are found for a group of Euro-area countries that suffer from persistent high public debt. The group includes Greece, Italy and Portugal. These results support the conclusions reached by Dallari and Ribba (2015), who measure the effects of fiscal shocks on domestic unemployment, but contrast with the conclusion achieved by Ilzetzki et al. (2013), whose main finding is that government spending shocks exhibit non-Keynesian effects on aggregate output in economies affected by high public debt. In Ilzetzki et al. (2013) a debt-to-GDP ratio exceeding 60 percent is the threshold used to select the set of high debt countries.

© Springer International Publishing AG 2018
A. Cavallo et al., *Fiscal Policies in High Debt Euro-Area Countries*,
https://doi.org/10.1007/978-3-319-70269-8_5

Instead, again in Chap. 4, we have detected recessionary effects associated with fiscal stimuli in a group of Euro-area countries affected by high private debt. This last group includes Ireland, the Netherlands and Spain.[1]

In this chapter we focus on the dynamic responses to government spending shocks of a wider set of real and nominal macrovariables at the national level. In particular, we study the reaction of domestic aggregate consumption to government spending cuts. For, private consumption is usually the largest component of aggregate demand and hence the response of consumption plays a crucial role in shaping the overall response of output to fiscal shocks. Further, a positive response of output to fiscal austerity, that we have detected in high private debt countries, must necessarily rest on a positive response of the private sector of the economy to the fiscal contraction. In order to study the dynamic responses of a wide set of domestic macrovariables to government spending shocks, we estimate VAR models at country level. With respect to the near-VAR approach adopted in Chap. 4, in this investigation full interaction among endogenous variables is allowed. Moreover, fiscal shocks are identified by imposing sign restrictions on the response of some variables.

An updated survey of the literature on the dynamic effects of macroeconomic shocks, which also includes analysis of fiscal shocks, is provided by Ramey (2016).

Giavazzi and Pagano (1990) were the first to suggest that fiscal consolidations might produce expansionary effects on the economy. The authors found evidence of negative fiscal multipliers in the 80s in two small European economies, Denmark and Ireland. Their empirical results suggested that in the presence of credible fiscal consolidations - in particular consolidations based on cuts to government expenditures - expectations of the private sector may improve, thus determining a positive indirect effect on aggregate demand. At a pinch, the increase in private demand may dominate the decrease in the public one, determining expansionary effects associated with the fiscal contraction.

Similar conclusions on the possible existence of expansionary fiscal contractions - based on an investigation concerning a larger set of OECD countries over the period 1970–2007 - are reached by Alesina and Ardagna (2010). In particular, they found that fiscal consolidations based on permanent cuts in government expenditures or permanent increases in taxes may produce expansions rather than recessions.

Andres et al. (2015) have developed a general equilibrium model with search frictions and have shown that when financial conditions worsen the fiscal multipliers decrease. Our evidence for the EMU period points not only to a decrease of spending multipliers but, for high private debt countries, to a sign reversal.

---

[1]There is, of course, an unavoidable ambiguity in the identification of high private and/or public debt countries. In this research, we have taken as the reference threshold for private debt the indicator proposed by the European Commission (2012), which identifies a possible macroeconomic imbalance in the presence of a private debt-to-GDP ratio of 160%. Ireland and the Netherlands had average values above 200% over the EMU period (see Table 4.1 of the previous chapter). As for Spain, the average value of private debt-to-GDP ratio is just slightly below this reference value but over a number of years the value recorded has been above 200%. As far as high public debt countries are concerned, Greece and Italy had an average value of public debt-to-GDP ratio well above 100% during the EMU period (see Table 4.1).

As against that, more recently Fatas and Summers (2016) have argued that fiscal austerity in Europe may have caused a permanent contraction of aggregate output. Although the authors raise an important point, our investigation covers the period 1999–2016 and hence we deal with quite small samples. In this case there is little sense in trying to separate permanent from persistent effects exerted by macroeconomic shocks. Nonetheless, in the present chapter we find that spending cuts have significant effects, both in an economic and statistical sense, on output and consumption for around 3–4 years in Greece and Italy. The most persistent effects of government spending shocks are found in Spain, where it requires around 6 years for these effects to vanish. It should be added that, at least according to our results, fiscal austerity generated a quite persistent increase both in output and private consumption in Spain, i.e. in this country the output fiscal multiplier is negative.

To sum up: as far as measuring fiscal policy is concerned, the picture offered by our research is characterized by mixed results, since the macroeconomic outcomes of fiscal shocks in European economies are heterogeneous under the EMU and thus not reducible to one single macroeconomic interpretation.

This chapter is organized as follows. Section 5.2 presents the VAR model estimated for each country and the identification strategy adopted to recover the fiscal shocks. Section 5.3 shows the main results obtained in terms of responses of output, consumption and other national macrovariables to domestic government spending shocks. Section 5.4 presents and discusses the heterogeneous results obtained for the domestic output fiscal multipliers. Section 5.5 concludes.

5.2 The Estimated VAR Models

We estimate for each country a separate VAR model and identify the domestic government spending shock by imposing sign restrictions. The point of departure is the estimation of the reduced-form, VAR model:

$$X_t = A_1 X_{t-1} + e_t \tag{5.1}$$

where e_t is the 8×1 vector of error terms, such that $E(e_t) = 0$ and $E(e_t e_t') = \Sigma_e$. X_t is the 8×1 vector of endogenous variables. The variables included are: government expenditures, obtained as the sum of government consumption and government investment; government revenues, obtained by subtracting from total revenues, transfers and interest expenses; the domestic consumer price index; real gross domestic product; real private consumption; the spread, built as the difference between the yield on 10-years national government bond and the corresponding German bond; the economic sentiment indicator; domestic stock market index.[2]

[2]In the appendix to Chap. 4 we have provided a detailed description of the included series and of their sources.

Of course, also in this chapter the definitions adopted for the fiscal series are in line with Blanchard and Perotti (2002), since the robustness analysis conducted in this chapter is essentially based on a different specification of the VAR model and of the identification strategy of the government spending shock rather than on alternative definitions of fiscal series.

The spread enters the model in basis points while all the other variables enter the model in natural logs. More precisely, we take $log(z_t) * 100$ for any variable z_t.

As already emphasized in previous chapters, in order to tackle the potential problem of fiscal foresight it is important to enlarge the VAR specification with series that are useful to predict the fiscal series and the other macrovariables included in the VAR.[3] Indeed, according to the permanent income hypothesis, consumption is a good long-run predictor of income while the stock market index and the economic confidence indicator are both leading indicators of the business cycle evolution.

In order to recover the government spending shock, we follow the sign restrictions approach proposed by Uhlig (2005).[4] In particular, given the covariance matrix of error terms, Σ_e, the matrix is randomly drawn from the posterior distribution of the matrix of the VAR coefficients.

System (5.1) is a reduced-form VAR model. Let us note that given a factorization of the covariance matrix, $PP' = \Sigma_e$, imposing sign restrictions on the responses of selected macroeconomic variables to a government spending shock implies identification of a vector p such that $p = P\alpha$, where $||\alpha|| = 1$. The sign restrictions imposed are usually selected in the literature by virtue of their consistency with theoretical models. In the context of investigations concerning identification of fiscal shocks, a quite standard set of contemporaneous sign restrictions is the following: (i) government expenditures decreases; (ii) deficit decreases; (iii) output decreases. For example, Canova and Pappa (2011) impose this set of restrictions on impact and, equally important, also show that this identification strategy is supported by a New Keynesian model.

However, in the study conducted in this chapter we will not follow this identification strategy and, in particular, we will not restrict the response of aggregate output. The main motivation for this choice derives from the controversial results obtained by a notable part of the empirical research on the sign characterizing the response of output to fiscal shocks. Indeed even our own results, presented in this book, show that domestic macroeconomic factors may influence both size and sign of output responses to government spending shocks. Hence, in light of the heterogenous results concerning the macroeconomic effects of fiscal shocks and given our goal to study how the presence of high private and/or public debt may shape the reaction of output, we leave free the response of output and other macrovariables to the

[3]On fiscal foresight see Leeper and Walker (2013). The importance of the selection of variables in the VAR specification useful to predict fiscal variables and aggregate output is shown by Forni and Gambetti (2014). See also Canova and Sahneh (2016).

[4]Mountford and Uhlig (2009) used the sign restrictions approach and identified more than one shock in the context of an investigation concerning the dynamic effects of fiscal shocks in the postwar US economy.

government spending shock. Thus, our sign restriction consists simply in imposing a negative sign, on impact, to government expenditures.

The confidence bands are calculated by following the Bayesian approach, as in Sims and Zha (1999) (see also Doan (2010)). We take 5000 draws from the posterior.[5]

Related to this identification strategy, an important question is the following: is it possible that by imposing a negative sign only on impact we might underestimate the (positive) response of consumption? In other words, in the view of those economists supporting the thesis of non-Keynesian effects of fiscal austerity, a crucial role is played by credibility, i.e. persistence of consolidation plans (see e.g. Giavazzi and Pagano (1990), Alesina and Ardagna (2010). This could indeed suggest to restrict the sign of government spending not only on impact but for several periods. To this end we have undertaken some robustness analysis, by restricting the negative sign of the fiscal variable over 4 or, alternatively, over 8 periods. Let us recall that we have already followed these alternative restriction strategies in Chap. 2, in order to test the robustness on some conclusions concerning the effects of fiscal shocks measured at the Euro-area wide level. However, as far as the investigation conducted in the present chapter is concerned, the results obtained in this chapter do not substantially change under different choices on the restriction horizons. To save space and figures we do not report the impulse response functions obtained.

As in the previous chapter, the sample covers the period 1999 – 2016.[6]

5.3 The Responses of Consumption to Government Spending Shocks

Private consumption is usually the most important component of aggregate demand. In the group of investigated Euro-area countries it ranges from an average of 45 percent in Ireland to 65 percent in Portugal, over the selected sample period. Thus, it seems a reasonable choice to focus on the reaction of consumption to unexpected decreases in government spending, since the response of this variable is one of the keys to understand the overall effects on output of fiscal shocks.

In fact, as for example maintained in Giavazzi and Pagano (1990) and Alesina and Ardagna (2010), permanent fiscal adjustments perceived as credible by consumers may improve expectations over lifetime income thus generating an increase in current consumption. In terms of dynamic response of private consumption to a contractionary government spending shock, this is translated into a positive reaction of consumption at some horizons. Therefore, these authors do not maintain that fiscal

---

[5] Inferential techniques based on this approach may be subject to problems of inaccuracy. A possible solution lies in increasing the number of draws, as shown among others by Liu et al. (2016). A choice of 5000 draws seems to be appropriate in the context of the present investigation. See also Uhlig (2005).

[6] It is worth recalling that due to data availability the sample starts in 2002:Q1 for Ireland. For all the other countries data start in 1999:Q1 and ends in 2016:Q3.

austerity is always and everywhere expansive, but that there may be circumstances in which improvement in expectations may dominate the contractionary effects of cuts in government expenditures. On the other hand, the conclusions of this strand of research put in discussion the traditional Keynesian view of fiscal policy, seen as an important tool to stabilize business cycle fluctuations. However, we agree with these authors on the argument that the presence in a given country of Keynesian effects, or not, of government spending cuts is mainly a matter of empirical investigation.

Another relevant macroeconomic factor that may explain "perverse" signs of fiscal multipliers is represented by the reaction of interest rates. Let us recall that we are considering economies affected by high public and/or private debt and hence particularly sensitive to the evolution of real interest rates. A credible fiscal consolidation, by increasing the confidence in the sustainability of debt, may cause a significant decrease in interest rates paid on domestic government bonds. In our VAR specification this would cause a decrease in the spread, i.e. the yield differential between domestic and German bonds. Once again, current private demand may increase in response to the interest rate contraction; for, although private demand is not directly influenced by interest rates paid on government bonds, interest rates are likely to move in the economic system following a communicating vessels principle and hence there might be a reduction in interest rates paid on the credit markets by consumers and firms.

Indeed, the rapid propagation of shocks among financial markets, both at the domestic and the international level, turned out to be one of the most important (and unpleasant) features experienced in the last financial crisis.

We have collected the evidence concerning the responses of domestic consumption, and other relevant macroeconomic variables, to government spending shocks in six distinct subsections, one for each country. As in the previous chapters, we report median responses together with the error bands, set at the 16th and the 84th percentiles.[7]

5.3.1 Greece

As shown in Fig. 5.1 a contractionary fiscal shock causes an economic recession in Greece, since both aggregate output and private consumption decrease for many quarters after the spending cut. These results are substantially in line with those obtained in Chap. 4. However, an important difference is represented by the persistence of the effects exerted by government spending shocks on output: in the previous chapter, by using a near-VAR model with interaction between Euro-area and domestic variables and recovering the fiscal shocks by imposing a causal ordering, we found that it requires around six years for the effects of government spending shocks to vanish, i.e.

[7]We have also checked the robustness of the estimated results shown in this section to changes in the setting of confidence bands. We find that the results do not change significantly if we set the error bands to the 10th and the 90th percentiles.

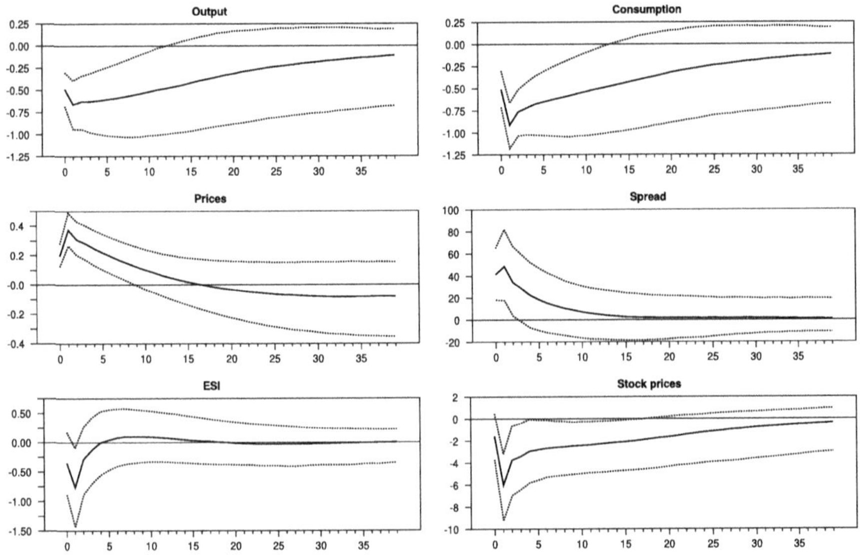

Fig. 5.1 Responses of domestic variables to a negative government spending shock: Greece *Note* Impulse responses to a negative government spending shock. Solid line: median estimate; dashed lines: 68th percent confidence interval. Government expenditures defined as government consumption plus investment

to become statistically non-significant. Instead, in the present chapter, by adopting an alternative identification strategy based on sign restrictions and considering only domestic variables, we find that the dynamic effects of government spending shocks, though keeping a notable degree of persistence, vanish after around four years.

Domestic interest rates paid on government bonds increase in response to cuts in government expenditures. This is an important result since, at least according to our estimations, it seems that fiscal consolidations in Greece rather than generating confidence in the sustainability of public finance, have generated the opposite result during the EMU period.

Regarding the response of stock prices, consistently with the recessionary effects caused by the fiscal austerity, there is a significant decrease which lasts for around four years.

The confidence index, ESI, does not show significant reactions to fiscal shocks at almost any horizon. A statistically-significant effect is detected only in the second quarter after the shock. However, this result is not robust to alternative selections of confidence intervals.

As far as the response of the domestic price index (Consumer price Index) is concerned, there is an increase in response to the government spending contraction which lasts for around two years. Given the overall picture obtained for Greece, the response of prices is difficult to reconcile with a recessionary context.

Summing up on Greece: fiscal consolidations conducted over the EMU period turned out to be costly, in terms of output losses, for this country. Clearly, and assuming the soundness of the results obtained in our investigation, something went wrong with the strategy of fiscal consolidation imposed by European and international institutions. The dynamic responses presented in Fig. 5.1, imply that a 1% decrease in government expenditures generated a cumulated negative effect on output of around −0.4% at horizons of two years. Although this result, taken in isolation, may not explain the Greek economic depression experienced in the last decade, it should be considered that the country, as a EMU member State, was also lacking exchange rate flexibility and monetary policy independence. Therefore, with the fiscal policy also oriented to a contractionary stance, the country had to face a deadly combination of adverse economic shocks.

Another important point which is worth stressing is that although there is little doubt on the necessity for Greece to reduce public deficit and debt after the economic and financial crisis started in 2008, we believe that on a macroeconomic ground the pursuit of an aggressive expansionary fiscal policy conducted at the Euro-area level might have helped to mitigate the costs of recession in Greece as well as in other national economies. After all, in the last decade we have experienced the worst economic and social crisis since the Great Depression of 1929. In this sense, the existence of a fiscal union might have played an important stabilizing role during the recent Great Recession. While hoping that the Great Recession is behind us, it is equally worth hoping that the Euro Area will be able to tackle the next recession with more appropriate, and above all centralized, fiscal policy tools.

5.3.2 *Italy*

Figure 5.2 shows the responses of selected Italian macrovariables to a negative government spending shock. The overall picture is rather similar to that of Greece: following a contractionary government spending shock, there is a persistent decrease of aggregate output and the effects of the fiscal contraction become non-significant after around four years. The dynamic behaviour of domestic consumption mirrors, both in terms of response profile and quantitative effects, the reaction of domestic output, i.e. private consumption significantly decreases for around four years.

The spread, i.e. the difference between the yield on 10-year Italian government bond and the corresponding German bond, increases. It is worth pointing out that with respect to Greece, the contractionary government spending shock exerts a more persistent effect on the spread. This result confirms that in the case of high public debt Euro-area countries fiscal austerity has produced the quite paradoxical effect of increasing interest rates, thus worsening the economic recession. Also in the light of the high exposure of the Italian banking system to government debt, an increase in the interest rates paid on government bonds is likely to generate negative effects even in interest rates paid on loans by households and private firms. This is, therefore,

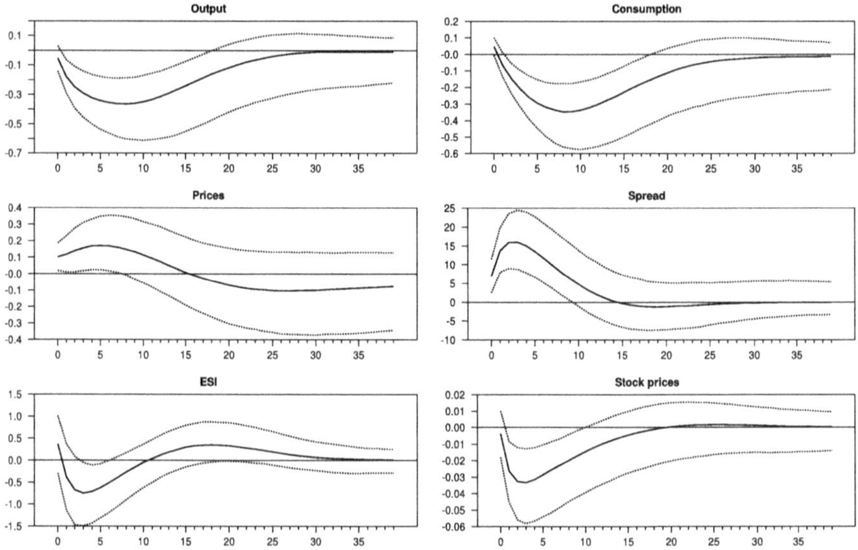

Fig. 5.2 Responses of domestic variables to a negative government spending shock: Italy
Note Impulse responses to a negative government spending shock. Solid line: median estimate; dashed lines: 68th percent confidence interval. Government expenditures defined as government consumption plus investment

another important channel through which fiscal consolidations may have exerted tough recessionary effects in these countries.

The confidence index shows a mute reaction at almost all horizons. There is a negative, statistically-significant response only at the horizon of one year. However, as in the case of Greece, this significant response is not robust to alternative selection of the confidence bands.

The stock price index moves in the same direction as government expenditures, i.e. there is a decrease, on average, of domestic stock prices. In this case, too, the decrease is quite persistent since the effects of the fiscal shock vanish after around three years.

Even in the case of Italy the dynamic response of the price index is relatively inconsistent with the recessionary effects generated by the government spending shock. The median response shows an increase in the Consumer Price Index for some quarters after the contractionary shock. However, looking at the confidence bands, the proper conclusion is that the response of prices is nearly non-significant. More precisely, by considering alternative confidence intervals, the response of prices become statistically non-significant.

In an investigation on the effects of fiscal shocks on a set of Italian macrovariables over the period 1982–2004, Giordano et al. (2007) found that an exogenous 1% increase in government spending causes an increase of private GDP of 0.6% at horizons of three quarters. Thus, although the sample period considered in the present study is quite different, covering 1999–2016, i.e. the EMU period, and there are some differences in the variables included in the estimated VAR model, we reach a similar conclusion. Indeed, the most important difference from the research by Giordano et al. (2007) is that we detect more persistent effects exerted on GDP and private consumption by government spending shocks. We also detect a smaller reaction of GDP to the fiscal shock, since in our study the percentage response of GDP to a 1% exogenous increase in government expenditures is around 0.4% compared to 0.6% in Giordano et al. (2007).

Thus, and summing up, fiscal consolidations turned out to be painful also for Italy, since significant (both economically and statistically) recessionary effects were generated during the EMU period. As in the case of Greece, starting with the financial crisis of 2008, the country has been hit by a sequence of large adverse shocks and in this challenging environment fiscal policy has acted in a pro-cyclical way, making economic conditions worse.

Let us note that this conclusion is the same as the previous chapter, where we adopted a recursive identification strategy to recover the government spending shock, in line with the approach of Blanchard and Perotti (2002). The important conclusion is that the Keynesian effects of fiscal policy detected for Italy under the EMU seem to be robust to alternative identification strategies.

5.3.3 Portugal

Figure 5.3 reports the responses of national variables to a negative government spending shock for Portugal. For this country, too, the overall picture is consistent with a recessionary outcome. For, as a consequence of the government spending cut there is a contraction in output, private consumption and the stock price index. The responses of the other domestic macrovariables are substantially non-significant at all horizons, with the exception on an increase, on impact, shown by the ESI index.

Although the results obtained in Chap. 4 are confirmed also in the case of Portugal, it is important to point out that when we recover the government spending shock by imposing sign restrictions, as in the present chapter, we find that the fiscal shock has more limited effects on aggregate output. In the previous chapter we had detected significant effects of the government spending shock, lasting for around three years, while in the present investigation we find that after one year the effects become statistically non-significant.

The recessionary effects exerted by the negative fiscal shock in Portugal are smaller and also exhibit less persistence with respect to both Greece and Italy. As we will see in the next section, calculations of government spending multipliers reinforce this conclusion.

To sum up on Portugal: the results clearly point to Keynesian effects of fiscal policy; nonetheless, it is worth stressing that this country exhibits both an average high public debt over the period 1999–2016 (around 85%), and an average high private debt over the same period (around 175%).

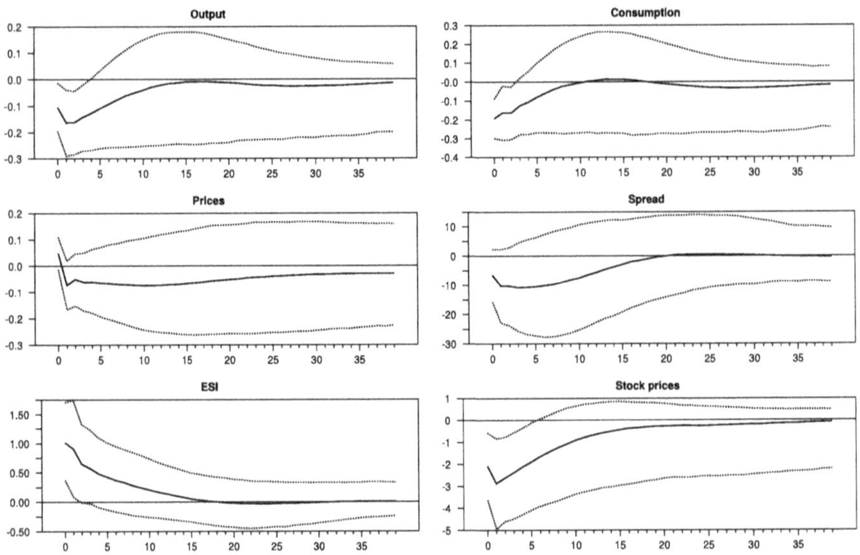

Fig. 5.3 Responses of domestic variables to a negative government spending shock: Portugal *Note* Impulse responses to a negative government spending shock. Solid line: median estimate; dashed lines: 68th percent confidence interval. Government expenditures defined as government consumption plus investment

5.3.4 Ireland

The responses of Irish variables to a negative government spending shock are shown in Fig. 5.4. On the whole, there is evidence of expansionary effects generated by the fiscal contraction. Both aggregate output and consumption exhibit statistically significant responses at horizons comprised between 8 and 20 quarters. Moreover, consumption shows an increase on impact, too.

In Ireland, the Consumer Price Index, consistently with the expansionary effects, increases for many quarters, i.e. the negative government spending shock has a positive persistent effect on prices.

The response profile of stock prices closely resembles that of the other, real and nominal, Irish macrovariables since there is an increase in the stock market index which lasts for around three years.

Instead, we detect a more muted response of interest rates to the contractionary fiscal shock. After four quarters the median response of the spread becomes negative and remains so for more than three years. Nonetheless, given the estimated confidence bands, the response is non-significant. Given the overall picture obtained for Ireland, this result may sound a little surprising, since the implication is that the only propagation mechanism of fiscal shocks is represented by an improvement in expectations which, in turn, causes an increase in private consumption. However, when we restrict the sign of government expenditures for more quarters, which amounts

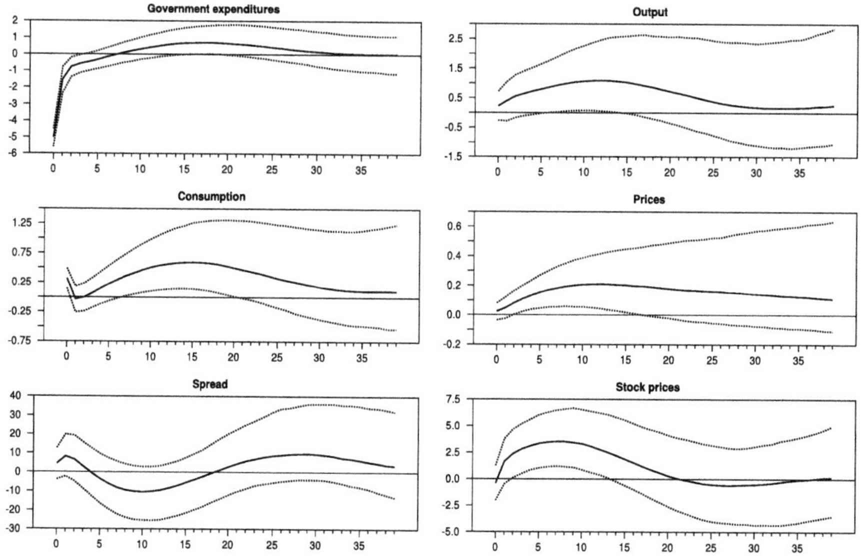

Fig. 5.4 Responses of domestic variables to a negative government spending shock: Ireland
Note Impulse responses to a negative government spending shock. Solid line: median estimate; dashed lines: 68th percent confidence interval. Government expenditures defined as government consumption plus investment

to assuming a more persistent and thus credible fiscal consolidation, we find a significant contraction of interest rates paid on government bonds which lasts for some quarters.[8] Therefore, a further propagation channel of fiscal shocks, related to the reaction of financial markets in terms of reduction of interest rates, is likely to have occurred in Ireland in the last decades, in a similar way, as we will see, to what detected for Spain.

It is worth recalling that Giavazzi and Pagano (1990) found non-Keynesian effects of fiscal policy in Ireland in an investigation concerning fiscal consolidations in the 80s. Thus, it seems that their conclusion is confirmed for the more recent period, indeed also characterized by a quite different monetary policy and exchange rate regime. Nonetheless, we would like to reiterate that one of the main findings of our study is that a credible fiscal consolidation is not sufficient to obtain negative signs of the government spending multipliers and that, instead, a crucial role is played by the indebtedness of the private sector. This conclusion is related to the findings that fiscal contractions have exerted Keynesian effects in countries like Greece and Italy. These countries share EMU membership with Ireland, and hence also share the same monetary policy and exchange rate regime. Thus, we are logically led to conclude that the relevant macroeconomic factors capable of explaining the quite different outcomes of fiscal policy in these countries lie in the different nature of

[8]However, as said in the previous section, we do not report the results of this further analysis.

high indebtedness which characterizes them: private for Ireland and Spain, public for Greece and Italy.

5.3.5 Netherlands

As far as the Netherlands is concerned, the contractionary fiscal shock generates a persistent contraction of output: it requires around four years for this negative effect to disappear. More ambiguous are the results concerning the response of consumption, since there is a significant increase on impact while between the sixth and the tenth quarter consumption show a statistically-significant decrease. Nonetheless, the decrease of consumption, given the estimated confidence bands, does not appear to be a robust result. Hence, an important conclusion is that the results obtained in the previous chapter are not confirmed in the case of the Netherlands. For, in this chapter we have detected Keynesian effects exerted by fiscal policy shocks.

Both the economic sentiment indicator and the stock price index decrease for around two years, consistently with the recessionary macroeconomic outcome. Instead, as for prices and spread, the responses to the negative government spending shock are non-significant at all horizons.

It is worth recalling that the Netherlands is a country characterized by high private debt and that this macroeconomic feature is shared with Ireland and Spain. Summing up, we find contrasting evidence on the possible existence of non-Keynesian effects in the Netherlands: when we identify government spending and revenues shocks by imposing a Cholesky decomposition, the findings, though not particularly strong, are in favour of non-Keynesian signs; when, as in the present chapter, we estimate a VAR which includes only domestic variables and identify the government spending by sign restrictions, we find a reverse sign characterizing the response of output to the fiscal shock (Fig. 5.5).

5.3.6 Spain

Figure 5.6 reports the responses of macrovariables to a negative government spending shock concerning Spain. As in the case of Ireland, the fiscal consolidation causes an increase both in consumption and output, i.e. in response to the spending cut there is an expansion of the economy. However, some important differences characterize the response of variables in Spain.

The first striking difference concerns the more persistent effects that the government spending shock has in Spain: we find evidence of economically and statistically significant effects on output and private consumptions which last for 5 years. The second important difference regards the reaction of interest rates paid on government bonds: in Spain, contrary to Ireland, there is a decrease in interest rates or, more precisely, there is a reduction in the spread between interest rates paid on domestic

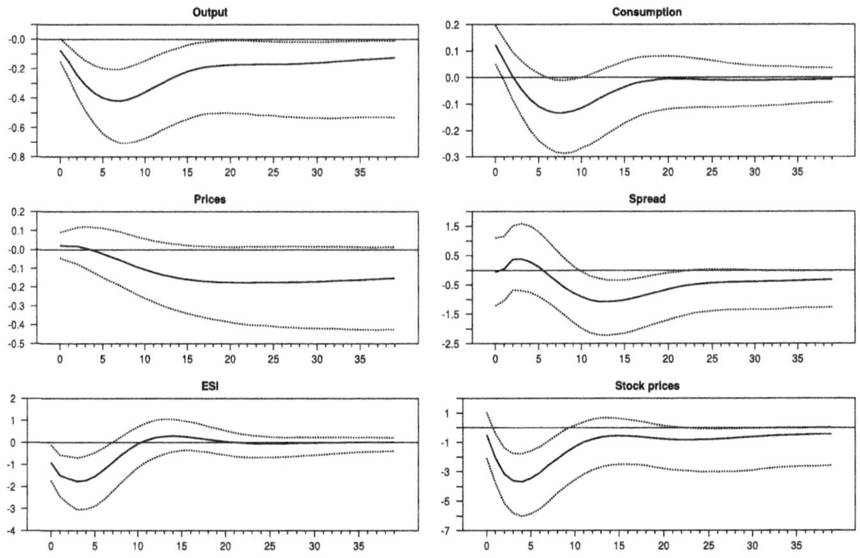

Fig. 5.5 Responses of domestic variables to a government spending shock: Netherlands *Note* Impulse responses to a negative government spending shock. Solid line: median estimate; dashed lines: 68th percent confidence interval. Government expenditures defined as government consumption plus investment

bonds and interest rates paid on correspondent German bonds, even in the case where the sign restrictions are imposed only on impact. Thus, in Spain we unambiguously detect two possible channels through which the effects of contractionary fiscal shocks propagate their effects in the economic system. The first is represented by the positive reaction of current consumption; the second one is represented by the interest rate channel which, indirectly, may boost private expenditure through its reduction. Let us recall that Spain and Ireland in the 2000s have been affected by price bubbles in the housing sector and that economic activity in this sector is particularly sensitive to the evolution of interest rates.

Consistently with this expansionary picture, the Economic Sentiment Index shows a positive reaction, which is statistically significant for two years. As for the stock index, there is a contraction on impact which is statistically significant at the selected confidence interval but is not robust to alternative confidence intervals. Nevertheless, after the first quarter we do not detect significant effects exerted by the negative government spending shock on the stock index. Finally, the response of the CPI to the government spending cut is non-significant at (almost) all horizons. In fact, given the estimated confidence bands, after 8 years there is a weak positive sign in the response of prices but this result is not robust to alternative choices of the confidence bands.

Hence, the conclusions reached in the previous chapter on the non-Keynesian effects of fiscal policy in Spain seem to be reinforced: by adopting a sign restrictions

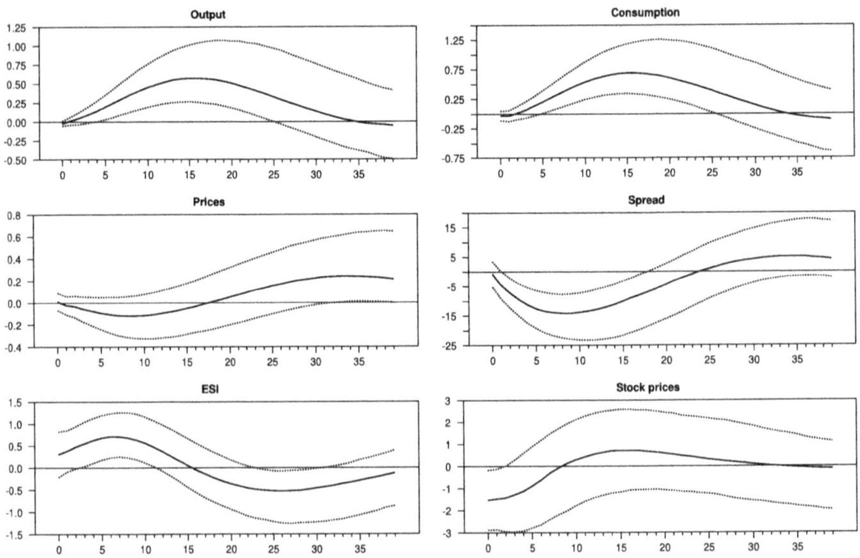

Fig. 5.6 Responses of domestic variables to a government spending shock: Spain
Note Impulse responses to a negative government spending shock. Solid line: median estimate; dashed lines: 68th percent confidence interval. Government expenditures defined as government consumption plus investment

approach, with a minimum set of restrictions imposed on government expenditures, we find sizeable expansionary effects generated by the fiscal austerity.

5.4 Estimation Results: Output Fiscal Multipliers

In this section we report the estimated domestic fiscal multipliers at different horizons. We calculate the cumulative multipliers at horizons of one and two years. Moreover, we also present fiscal multipliers on impact.

Let us recall that the impact multiplier is calculated as:

$$Impact\ \ Fiscal\ \ Multiplier = \frac{\Delta Y_t}{\Delta F_t} \tag{5.2}$$

where Y_t is aggregate output and F_t is the fiscal variable, in this case government expenditures. While the cumulative multiplier is calculated in terms of ratio of cumulative changes in Y and F (see e.g. IMF (2009)):

$$Cumulative\ \ Fiscal\ \ Multiplier = \frac{\Sigma_{j=0}^{k} \Delta Y_{t+j}}{\Sigma_{j=0}^{k} \Delta F_{t+j}} \tag{5.3}$$

Table 5.1 Government expenditures multipliers in Euro-area high debt countries under the EMU.

	Greece	Ireland	Italy	Netherland	Portugal	Spain
Impact	0.3*	−0.2	0.1	0.2	0.1*	0
1 year	1.1*	−1.3	0.8*	0.6*	0.4*	−0.1
2 years	1.5*	−3*	1.4*	1.2*	0.5	−0.7*

Note The table presents cumulative fiscal multipliers at various horizons for the national economies. * indicates a statistically-significant multiplier

We have presented and briefly discussed these alternative measures of fiscal multipliers in the third chapter. As shown in Table 5.1, the largest output fiscal multipliers are detected, respectively, for Greece and Ireland. Nonetheless, and paradoxically, in the two countries the multipliers exhibit opposite signs: positive in Greece and negative in Ireland. A negative government spending shock has contractionary effects on output at all selected horizons in Greece. For example, after two years following the implementation of the fiscal package, a one euro cut in government spending generates around €1.50 of aggregate output reduction. The fiscal multiplier is quite large, thus confirming the conclusion that fiscal austerity has exerted strong recessionary effects in Greece under the EMU.

A similar pattern, though with (relatively) smaller values, is shown by the fiscal multiplier in Italy. More precisely, the spending multiplier is around zero on impact but grows over quarters, being around 1 at the horizon of one year and significantly above one, 1.4, after two years.

Let us note that both sign and size of the estimated government spending multiplier in Greece and Italy are similar to those obtained in some studies concerning the Unites States (e.g. Romer and Bernstein (2009), Blinder and Zandi (2010)). Our results on the size of fiscal multipliers instead contrast with the conclusion of Barro (1981), according to whom exogenous increases in government expenditures have sizeable effects on output only in war periods, i.e. periods in which notable military build-ups are at the root of the expansionary effects on aggregate output (see also Barro and Redlick (2011)).

The government spending multiplier is above one in the Netherlands, too, at horizons of two years. Moreover, the multiplier has a positive sign, thus placing the Netherlands among the Keynesian countries. This result contrasts with the conclusion reached in Chap. 4.

In reviewing the relevant literature investigating the macroeconomic outcomes of fiscal policy, in Chap. 3 we have recalled some studies in which a relation is established between macroeconomic conditions experienced by the economy and the size of fiscal multipliers. Our results seems consistent with theoretical models predicting a larger size of fiscal multipliers in recessions (e.g. Canzoneri and Collard (2016)). On the empirical front Auerbach and Gorodnichenko (2012) have found that in the postwar US economy the government spending multiplier is more sizeable in recessions. We stress that although we have estimated linear models in this research, the specific historical period considered, from the start of EMU to 2016, has been characterized by large and persistent recessions in countries like Greece and Italy.

The government spending multiplier is quite large also in Ireland but with a negative, non-Keynesian sign. We detect a statistically non-significant multiplier at impact and at one year horizon. Nevertheless, after two years, the calculated size of fiscal multiplier implies that a decrease of one euro in government spending generates a statistically significant increase of aggregate output of around three euros. It is worth recalling that the estimated confidence bands are wide in the case of Ireland and hence there is a certain degree of uncertainty characterizing the size of the multiplier (but not the sign).

Finally, Spain is the other country that exhibits a negative spending multiplier. The calculated multiplier is small and non-significant at shorter horizons, on impact and at one year, but after two years from the fiscal shock it shows a significant value of −0.7. Thus, the analysis concerning the domestic government spending multipliers largely confirms the separation between countries exhibiting Keynesian effects of fiscal policy (Euro-area countries affected by high public debt) and countries characterized by non-Keynesian effects (some Euro-area countries affected by high private debt).

5.5 Conclusions

The investigation conducted in this chapter has largely confirmed the conclusions reached in Chap. 4 on the Keynesian effects associated with fiscal policies for Greece, Italy and Portugal. In the case of Greece, both impulse responses and fiscal multipliers indicate persistent and sizeable negative effects on output and private consumption caused by contractionary fiscal packages implemented over the EMU period. The same conclusion substantially holds for Italy. Nonetheless, in the case of Italy we have also detected a significant increase of the interest rates paid on government bonds. Thus the fiscal austerity, by exacerbating the recession, has also caused a worsening of the country's financial conditions which, in turn, has generated deeper recessionary effects.

As for fiscal multipliers, we have calculated a value of government spending multiplier well above 1 at horizons of two years both in Greece and Italy. Sizeable and statistically significant values of fiscal multipliers are also detected in Portugal. The first conclusion is that at least in the case of these southern Euro-area economies plagued by public debt notably above the threshold of 60 percent of GDP, fiscal austerity turned out to be very costly in terms of the output losses suffered by economies. Moreover, and indeed not surprising, we see from the reaction of private consumption, that cuts in government expenditures also caused significant contractions in consumption in all the three countries.

On the other hand, the presence of non-Keynesian effects of fiscal austerity has been detected in a selected group of Euro-area countries affected by high debt in the private sector of the economy during the EMU period. In particular, in the present chapter we have focused on the role played by private consumption towards contractionary fiscal shocks, and the main finding is that aggregate consumption increases in response to a contractionary government spending shock both in Ireland and Spain.

Among high private debt countries investigated in this book, only in the case of the Netherlands we were not fully able to confirm previous findings, since in this chapter, by adopting a different identification strategy of the fiscal shocks with respect to Chap. 4, based on sign restrictions, we find that cuts in government expenditures cause decreases both in aggregate output and consumption.

Recently, Fatas and Summers (2016) have argued that fiscal austerity in Europe may have caused a permanent contraction of aggregate output. However, in the light of the overall findings presented in this book, the picture in Euro-area economies seems to be more articulated. For, we often find evidence of persistent effects of fiscal shocks at country level, and our results show that in particular Greece and Italy have experienced deep and painful recessions following fiscal austerity. Nonetheless, for some small Euro-area economies, we also find evidence of persistent effects of opposite sign with respect to those conjectured by Fatas and Summers. For example, in the case of Spain we find that it requires some years for the effects of government spending shocks to vanish, but for five years following the shock there is an expansion of output and not a contraction. Although the effects of fiscal shocks on output exhibit less persistence with respect to Spain, the same non-Keynesian result is found for Ireland, too.

In this research we have often quoted the work by Ilzetzki et al. (2013). The importance of their research is also related to the conclusion that countries affected by high public debt show non-Keynesian effects of fiscal shocks. It is worth emphasizing that both in the current and in the previous chapter we have instead found robust evidence contrasting this result and hence the conclusion that public debt is a crucial factor in shaping non-Keynesian effects of fiscal policy needs to be reconsidered.

Instead the overall results presented in this book confirm the main findings of Dallari and Ribba (2015), who have studied the responses of unemployment to fiscal shocks in a group of small Euro-area economies, concluding that Ireland and Spain, contrary to Greece and Italy, show non-Keynesian effects of fiscal policy.

Our findings concerning the effects of fiscal shocks in Ireland under EMU seems to confirm the main conclusions reached by Giavazzi and Pagano (1990), who analyzed fiscal consolidation in the 1980s, i.e. a quite different historical period. However, following the so-called "German view", they interpreted their non-Keynesian results in terms of a positive reaction of the private sector to credible fiscal consolidations (see also Alesina and Ardagna 2010). Instead, according to our findings, persistence and credibility were not at all sufficient to avoid unpleasant Keynesian results in countries like Greece, Italy and Portugal. Moreover, given the presence of Spain in the group of countries exhibiting "perverse" signs of the fiscal multipliers, we are led to conclude that more than (or along with) credibility, it is the structure of a country's indebtedness that determines alternative outcomes of fiscal policy. In other words, the possible positive reaction of the private sector to fiscal contractions emerges in situations characterized by high indebtedness of households and firms. Against that, in the presence of high government debt, accompanied by relatively low levels of private debt, the macroeconomic outcomes of fiscal austerity are invariably of Keynesian sign.

References

Alesina A, Ardagna S (2010) Large changes in fiscal policy: Taxes versus spending. In Tax Policy and the Economy, NBER 24:35–68
Andres J, Bosca EJ, Ferri J (2015) Household debt and fiscal multipliers. Economica 82:1048–1081
Auerbach AJ, Gorodnichenko Y (2012) Measuring the output responses to fiscal policy. Am Econ J: Econ Policy 4:1–27
Barro RJ (1981) Output effects of government purchases. J Polit Econ 89:1086–1121
Barro RJ, Redlick CJ (2011) Macroeconomic effects from government purchases and taxes. Q J Econ 126:51–102
Blanchard OJ, Perotti R (2002) An empirical characterization of the dynamic effects of changes in government spending and taxes on output. Q J Econ 117:1329–1368
Blinder AS, Zandi M (2010) Stimulus worked. Finance and Development, Dec 2010
Canova F, Pappa E (2011) Fiscal policy, pricing frictions and monetary accommodation. Econ Policy 555–598
Canova F, Sahneh MH (2016) Are small-scale SVARs useful for business cycle analysis? Revisiting non-fundamentalness. Working Papers 2/2016, BI Norvegian Business School
Canzoneri M, Collard F, Dellas H, Diba B (2016) Fiscal multipliers in recessions. Econ J 126:75–108
Christiano L, Eichenbaum M, Rebelo S (2011) When is the government spending multiplier large? J Polit Econ 78–121
Dallari P, Ribba A (2015) Economic shocks and their effects on unemployment in the Euro Area periphery under the EMU. Department of Economics No 114, University of Modena and Reggio Emilia
Doan TA (2010) RATS user's manual, Version 8, Estima, 1560 Sherman Avenue, Suite 510. Evanston, IL, p 60201
European Commission (2012) First Alert Mechanism Report on macroeconomic imbalances in Member States. MEMO/12/104
Fatas A, Summers LH (2016) The permanent effects of fiscal consolidations. NBER Working Paper No. 22374
Forni M, Gambetti L (2014) Sufficient information in structural VARs. J Monet Econ 66:124–136
Giavazzi F, Pagano M (1990) Can severe fiscal contactions be expansionary? Tales of two small European countries. NBER Chapters, in NBER Macroeconomics Annual 75–122
Giordano R, Momigliano S, Neri S, Perotti R (2007) The effects of fiscal policy in Italy: Evidence from a VAR model. Eur J Polit Econ 23:707–733
Ilzetzki E, Mendoza EG, Vegh CA (2013) How big (small?) are fiscal multipliers? J Monet Econ 60:239–254
IMF (2009) Fiscal Multipliers. IMF Staff Position Note, No. 09/11
Leeper EM, Walker TB, Yang S-CS (2013) Fiscal foresight and information flows. Econometrica 81:1115–1145
Liu JD, Nordman DJ, Meeker WQ (2016) The number of MCMC draws needed to compute Bayesian credible bounds. Am Stat 70:275–284
Mountford A, Uhlig H (2009) What are the effects of fiscal policy shocks? J Appl Econom 24:960–992
Ramey VA (2016) Macroeconomic shocks and their propagation. In: Taylor JB, Uhlig H (eds) Handbook of Macroeconomics. vol 2. North Holland, Amsterdam, pp 71–162
Sims CA, Zha T (1999) Error bands for impulse responses. Econometrica 67:1113–1156
Romer C, Bernstein J (2009) The job impact of the American Recovery and Reinvestment Plan. Jan 8, 2009
Uhlig H (2005) What are the effects of monetary policy on output? Results from an agnostic identification procedure. J Monet Econ 52:381–419

Chapter 6
Can (And Should) Germany Do It? Spillovers of German Fiscal Policies in the Euro Area

Abstract In recent years, also in light of the economic and financial crisis that has affected Euro-area countries, the German government has received repeated calls for expansionary fiscal policies. Indeed, Germany exhibits both a conspicuous surplus in the current account and fiscal space. So far these calls have met with rather limited success. However, at this stage, we still lack firm evidence about the dynamic effects of German fiscal shocks on output of other Euro-area economies. In this chapter we therefore undertake an empirical investigation using a panel VAR which allows us to model cross-country interdependences and to study dynamic linkages. We show that a positive government spending shock in Germany has notable effects on national output and, moreover, exerts significant spillover effects on the other Euro-area countries. We also find that the government spending multiplier is greater than one and close to values found in the literature for investigations concerning the United States.

6.1 Introduction

In this chapter we empirically explore the following question: does a positive government spending shock in Germany exert significant spillover effects in the other Eurozone economies? Indeed, despite frequent international calls to German policymakers to undertake expansionary fiscal policies, also in light of the scope offered by the public budget balance and the conspicuous surplus account, there is still no thorough empirical evidence on the Euro-area effects of German fiscal shocks.[1]

In Chap. 2 we estimated the dynamic effects of government spending shocks in an aggregate VAR model of the Euro Area and found that a fiscal expansion at the Euro-area level might give a strong contribution to the stabilization of the economy. We also found that in the presence of an accommodative monetary policy the effects of fiscal policy are magnified. We interpreted those results as a good argument in support of the development of a fiscal union, seen as a substantive complement to the

[1] It is worth recalling that Germany exhibits a persistent value of the current account-to-GDP ratio above 6 percent and in fact the European Commission (2011) has established a threshold of 6 percent for the surplus in the current account as one indicator of potential macroeconomic imbalances.

© Springer International Publishing AG 2018

A. Cavallo et al., *Fiscal Policies in High Debt Euro-Area Countries*,
https://doi.org/10.1007/978-3-319-70269-8_6

monetary union. However, it is likely that for many years to come the Euro Area will not be equipped with a centralized fiscal capacity. Thus, in practise, the feasibility of fiscal stimulus in the Euro Area currently relies mainly on Germany, the largest EMU economy, and one characterized by sizeable fiscal space.

The argument in favor of expansionary fiscal policies adopted by Germany also rests on the relatively limited effectiveness that fiscal stimuli would likely have if implemented by other countries. In Chap. 4 we have studied the dynamic effects of fiscal shocks in high debt Euro-area countries and have concluded that fiscal multipliers are not always characterized by the expected sign and hence there is a good deal of uncertainty on the effects of fiscal policy in these small open economies. Indeed, the results concerning the possible emergence of non-Keynesian signs in fiscal multipliers has been confirmed in the investigation conducted in Chap. 5.

Another important problem is given by the large debt-to-GDP ratio affecting some of these countries. It is apparent that in the current European macroeconomic context, and under the existing fiscal rules, aggressive expansionary fiscal policies are a non-viable strategy for the great part of Euro-area member countries. Moreover, this is also not an advisable strategy for countries like Greece and Italy, given the high risk of unsustainable public debt dynamics.

Clearly, the proponents of expansionary fiscal policies in Germany support an open-economy Keynesian view. The prediction is that an increase of government spending in Germany, by expanding domestic output, would also have expansionary effects on output in other Euro-area countries characterized by significant flows in goods and services with Germany. Indeed, the existing literature finds that trade is typically the most relevant channel for the transmission of fiscal policy shocks. For example, Beetsma and Giuliodori (2004) and Beetsma et al. (2006) develop VAR models with a trade block. They find that trade spillovers resulting from fiscal impulses in Germany, as well as from Italy and France, can have statistically and economically significant spillovers. The trade channel is a key feature also in Global-VAR (GVAR) models, since the weighting scheme is usually based on trade interconnectedness across countries. Belke and Osowski (2016) find moderate spillover effects of fiscal policy shocks originating in Germany and France, but considerable variation in the magnitude of the spillovers among destination countries. They also find some evidence that spillovers generated by Germany or France are stronger for EMU than non-EMU countries in Europe.

Georgiadis and Hollmayr (2016) conclude that spillovers from country-specific fiscal policy shocks in the Euro Area are in general small, except for those from France, Germany, and Italy. Their analysis also indicates that the magnitude of fiscal spillovers depends on (i) the size of the domestic multiplier, (ii) the size of the domestic economy relative to the rest of the Euro Area, and (iii) the integration of the spillover-sender with the spillover-receiving economy through trade. Using a bayesian GVAR and sign restrictions to identify a deficit-financed government spending shock, Eller et al. (2017) conclude that the shock generates long-lasting positive cross-border output spillovers.

Finally, Gambetti and Gallio (2016) use a time varying coefficients VAR model covering 1995–2014 and find that country specific government spending shocks in

Germany, Italy, France and Spain generate significant effects. They also conclude that responses to spending across countries are heterogeneous and asymmetric, and that fiscal policy coordination in their sample appears to be small.

Recent studies using dynamic stochastic general equilibrium (DSGE) models typically agree with the Keynesian predictions of an increase in domestic output in response to an expansionary fiscal policy shock. Other things being equal, an increase in government spending leads to an increase in output from, depending on preference specifications, an increase in the labor supply or consumption. The responses of other variables, however are more uncertain. How these effects translate to the rest of the economy depends on a number of factors, including whether the fiscal impulse is permanent or transitory, which component of public spending is affected (Pappa 2009), the way it is financed, the monetary policy stance (Christiano et al. 2011), financial imperfections (Corsetti et al. 2012), the state of the economy (Auerbach and Gorodnichenko 2013), and whether consumers are optimizers or not (Galí et al. 2007).

DSGE models have also been used to study the spillover effects of fiscal policy shocks, beyond the domestic transmission channels. Using a two-country DSGE model, Corsetti et al. (2010) show that spending reversals - i.e. a decrease in future government spending and an increase in taxes to finance a fiscal stimulus today - can strengthen international spillovers. The main channels for the transmission of the shock are the expectation of lower future real interest rates stemming from the spending reversal, and the assumption that the country engineering the fiscal expansion is big enough to affect global rates. Cwik and Wieland (2010), using a structural model calibrated on the fiscal measures announced in Germany in 2009, report very small output spillovers in France and Italy. The reason is that the positive direct demand effect of German spending on other Euro-area economies is largely offset by the indirect negative effect of the euro appreciation. Spillovers to the Euro Area from fiscal shocks originating in Germany are small also in the three-regions structural model proposed by Gadatsch et al. (2015), irrespectively of whether public consumption, employment, or investment increase.

Blanchard et al. (2015) find that a fiscal expansion in core European countries can produce sizable positive spillovers in the periphery when the economy is at the zero-lower-bound. Veld (2013), (2016) employs the European Commissions QUEST model calibrated to capture crisis times, i.e. financially constrained consumers and effective lower bound on monetary policy rates. While the reported output spillovers are usually relatively small, he shows that spillovers are higher when fiscal impulses happen simultaneously in several member states. Clancy et al. (2015) show that a high share of import content from abroad is necessary to have large positive spillovers, even in case when government spending complements private consumption and increases the productivity of private investment. ECB (2014) presents an illustrative simulation to assess the size of fiscal spillovers across five largest Euro-area countries using the New Multi-Country Model (NMCM). In this simulation, countries are assumed to implement a permanent fiscal consolidation totaling one percent of GDP, with that consolidation being equally balanced between revenue and expenditure. The model controls for the downward impact of fiscal consolidation on domestic sovereign risk premia (the "sovereign risk channel") and fiscal spillovers operate mainly via the trade channel.

Overall, the empirical studies covered above find economically significant spillovers, although they are not uniformly expansionary, and heterogenity is sizeable. Instead, the endogenous increase in domestic interest rates that typically accompanies a fiscal expansion, prevails in standard model-based approaches, and determines smaller and sometimes negligible spillovers, from a combination of lower consumption and an appreciation of the exchange rate that lowers exports. Alternative assumptions, including with respect to the shocks process, the formation of expectations, the import content of government purchases, and the monetary policy response, can reverse that conclusion.

In order to investigate the spillover effects of German fiscal policy shocks, in this chapter we follow Dabla-Norris et al. (2017) and use a panel VAR, estimated over the sample 1999–2016, i.e. the EMU period. In the empirical analysis undertaken in the previous chapters, we have used structural VAR and near-VAR models. Nevertheless, while the near-VAR approach is suitable for investigations concerning the identification of macroeconomic shocks in small open economies acting in a monetary union, in the case of the transmission of fiscal shocks from large to small economies, the panel VAR methodology in Dabla-Norris et al. (2017) provides a better framework. In fact, it allows us to investigate the effects of fiscal shocks on both national and foreign variables while also allowing for cross-country independences and feedback loops, which can be important to capture spillback effects. Therefore, compared to other studies, we are in principle better able to capture the heterogeneity and complexity of the international transmission mechanism, and to provide more granular estimates of fiscal multipliers and spillovers, compared to an average result.

Our main findings can be summarized as follows: (a) The government spending multiplier is greater than one in Germany and it peaks at 1.45 after one year; (b) Fiscal spillovers are always positive, and they are sizeable especially in countries with strong trade ties with Germany, and in those with a smaller and less diversified economic base; (c) Spillovers to peripheral Euro-area countries are larger than those to France; (d) The trade channel is important but financial flows are also a relevant channel of spillover propagation; (e) These conclusions are robust to the selection of alternative sub-samples.

The chapter has the following structure. In Sect. 6.2 we present the estimated panel VAR model and the identification strategy of government spending shocks. Section 6.3 describes the data. Section 6.4 shows the results obtained both in terms of fiscal multipliers and responses of national and foreign economies to a positive government spending shock in Germany. Section 6.5 concludes.

6.2 The Estimated Model

We employ a large-scale panel VAR model of the form:

$$y_{it} = D_i(L)Y_{t-1} + F_i(L)W_t + e_{it} \tag{6.1}$$

where $i = 1, , N$ stands for countries, $t = 1, \dots, T$ for time, and L is the lag operator; y_{it} is a G $\times$ 1 vector of endogenous series for each i, and $Y_t = (y'_{1t}, , y'_{Nt})$; $D_{i,j}$ are $G \times NG$ matrices for each lag $j = 1, \dots, p$, $F_{i,j}$ are $G \times M$ matrices each lag $j = 1, \dots, q$; W_{it} is a $M \times 1$ vector of predetermined variables, $e_{it} \sim N(0, \Sigma_i)$ is a $G \times 1$ vector of disturbances. Since the variables we use are all demeaned and standardized, no deterministic variables are included.

Two features of the model are well suited for our investigation (see Canova and Ciccarelli 2013, for a discussion and a detailed derivation of the model's structure). First, the dynamic relationships and the variance of the error term are allowed to be unit specific. This is necessary since the units we are considering are likely to be heterogeneous in a number of dimensions. Second, whenever the $NG \times NG$ matrix $D(L) = [D_1(L), \dots, D_N(L)]'$, is not block diagonal for some L, cross-unit lagged interdependencies matter. Thus, dynamic feedbacks across countries are possible and this greatly expands the type of interactions the model can account for. Both features add realism to the model and avoid important specification errors. However, these features also increase complexity and the number of parameters to be estimated. To see this rewrite the model in regression format as:

$$Y_t = Z_t\delta + E_t \quad E_t \sim N(0, P \otimes \Omega) \tag{6.2}$$

where $Z_t = I_{NG} \otimes X'_t$; $X'_t = (Y'_{t-1}, Y'_{t-2}, \dots, Y'_{t-p}, W'_{t-1}, \dots, W'_{t-q})$, $\delta = (\delta'_1, \dots, \delta'_N)'$ and δ_i are $Gk \times 1$ vectors containing, stacked, the G rows of the matrix D_i and F_i, while Y_t and E_t are $NG \times 1$ vectors of endogenous variables and of random disturbances, $k = NGp + Mq$; finally, P is $N \times N$ and Ω is $G \times G$.

In a model with 10 countries, 5 variables, 2 lags and no predetermined variables, δ is 5000×1 vector and Ω has $(NG \times (NG - 1))/2 = 1125$ free parameters. Thus, the sheer dimensionality of the problem prevents any meaningful unconstrained estimation.

For this reason we assume that the vector δ is a function of a lower dimensional vector θ, and rather than estimating δ we estimate its vector of determinants. Let

$$\delta = \Xi\theta + u \qquad u \sim N(0, (P \otimes \Omega) \otimes V) \tag{6.3}$$

where Ξ is a matrix of zeros and ones, $dim(\theta) << dim(\delta)$, and u is a vector of disturbances capturing unmodelled features in the coefficient vector δ. Substituting (6.3) into (6.2) one obtains

$$Y_t = \sum_{j=1}^{r} \mathscr{Z}_{jt}\theta_j + v_t \tag{6.4}$$

where $\mathscr{X}_{jt} = Z_t \Xi_j$ and $v_t = E_t + Z_t u_t$. Thus, the factorization (6.3) transforms an overparametrized panel VAR into a parsimonious SUR model, where the regressors are averages of certain right-hand side VAR variables.

This approach is different from the strategy used in global VARs, where a factor capturing international spillovers is tagged on to country-specific VARs, since the latter implies proportionality restrictions on the spillovers across all countries, while (6.4) simply reparametrize the original panel VAR model so as to make it estimable.

It should be clear that our reparametrization strategy is also preferable to the one used with a collection of VARs or with bilateral VARs. On the one hand, the random pooling of cross sectional information in (6.3) helps to get more accurate estimates of the parameters and to reduce standard errors. On the other hand, if the momentum that the shocks induce across units is the result of a complicated structure of lagged interdependencies, it would instead emerge as "common shocks" in the two alternative frameworks.

In the specification, we use $\Xi\theta = \Xi_1\theta_1 + \Xi_2\theta_2 + \Xi_3\theta_3$ where Ξ_j are loading matrices of dimensions $NGk \times N$, $NGk \times G$, $NGk \times M$, $NGk \times p$ respectively; θ_j are mutually orthogonal factors capturing, respectively, movements in the coefficient vector which are country-specific; movements which are variable-specific; and movements which are specific to the lags.

Finally, we assume that the variance-covariance matrix has a Kronecker structure of the form $P \times \Omega$, where P is the country correlation matrix and Ω is the series correlation matrix. This structure implies that the shocks have the same instantaneous correlation structure across countries, and allows for parsimony in the number of estimated coefficients. In this application, the off-diagonal elements of P are left unrestricted, and are determined by the degree of correlation across countries. Zero restrictions are instead imposed on the diagonal element of P corresponding to the country where the shock is happening.

The model we consider has time invariant parameters and the VAR errors have fixed volatilities. Compared to those studies using estimated models where both the coefficients and the volatilities are time varying, our estimated model has an error term which is heteroskedastic, but time variations in the covariance matrix of the v_t are produced by the lags of the endogenous variables rather than by an independent, exogenous process. Moreover, we opt for a non parametric approach to address the possibility that there are structural breakes in the time series of the data. That is, rather than specifying a parametric law of motion for the evolution of the VAR coefficients, we estimate the model on several subsamples, starting from the Great Financial Crisis. A non-parametric approach to time variations is preferable because estimation of the model is, computationally, much less demanding.

Our approach to estimation is Bayesian, primarily because the sample size is small and we are interested in the exact small sample (rather than asymptotic) distribution of θ_j. To simplify the computations we assume $V = \sigma^2 I$, which makes sense given the fact the variables of the model have similar units. This implies that the error term of the model $v_t \sim N(0, \sigma_t \Omega)$, where $\sigma_t = (I + \sigma^2 X_t' X_t)$. Thus, the unknowns of the model are the vector of factors θ, their scale matrix σ^2, and the covariance matrix of the VAR shocks Ω.

We assume an independent prior for the three blocks and assume a semi-conjugate structure of the form

$$\theta \sim N(\theta_0, R_0) \tag{6.5}$$
$$\Omega^{-1} \sim W(NG, Q_0) \tag{6.6}$$
$$\sigma^{-2} \sim G(0.5, 0.5s^2), \tag{6.7}$$

where the hyperparameters $(\theta_0, R_0, Q_0, s^2)$ are treated as fixed quantities, W stands for Wishart distribution and G for Gamma distribution. We estimate θ_0, R_0 using averages of cross sectional data; Q_0 is estimated using the residuals of the country specific models, while s^2 is obtained using the average of variance of the residuals of $AR(p)$ regressions of the NG endogenous variables.

To obtain the posterior distribution for $\phi = (\theta, \Omega^{-1}, \sigma^{-2})$ we combine the prior with the likelihood of the data, which is proportional to

$$L \propto \left(\prod_t |\sigma_t \Omega|^{-1/2}\right) \exp\left[-\frac{1}{2}\sum_t (Y_t - \mathcal{Z}_t\theta)' (\sigma_t\Omega)^{-1} (Y_t - \mathcal{Z}_t\theta)\right]. \tag{6.8}$$

Let $Y^T = (Y_1, \ldots, Y_T)$ denote the available sample. Using Bayes' rule, we have $p\left(\phi \mid Y^T\right) = \frac{p(\phi)L\left(Y^T|\phi\right)}{p\left(Y^T\right)} \propto p\left(\phi\right) L\left(Y^T \mid \phi\right)$ and the posterior distribution for the elements of ϕ, can be obtained by integrating out the remaining elements from $p\left(\phi \mid Y^T\right)$.

For the model we use, the analytical computation of $p\left(\phi \mid Y^T\right)$ is impossible, because $p\left(Y^T\right)$ requires integration of the joint distribution of (ϕ, Y^T) with respect to ϕ. To draw sequences from the posterior without any need to compute them we use the Gibbs sampling. Each Gibbs sampling cycle requires $p\left(\theta|\Omega^{-1}, \sigma^{-2}, Y^T\right)$, $p\left(\Omega^{-1}|\theta, \sigma^{-2}, Y^T\right)$, $p\left(\sigma^{-2}|\Omega^{-1}, \theta, Y^T\right)$, the conditional posterior of each block of unknowns. Given the prior, it can be shown that

$$p\left(\theta|\Omega^{-1}, \sigma^{-2}, Y^T\right) \sim N\left(\theta_1, R_1\right) \tag{6.9}$$
$$p\left(\Omega^{-1}|\theta, \sigma^{-2}, Y^T\right) \sim W\left(\omega_1, Q_1\right) \tag{6.10}$$

where

$$R_1 = (R_0^{-1} + \sum_t \mathcal{Z}_t(\sigma_t\Omega)^{-1}\mathcal{Z}_t)$$

$$\theta_1 = R_1^{-1}(R_0^{-1}\theta_0 + \sum_t \mathcal{Z}_t(\sigma_t\Omega)^{-1}Y_t)$$

$$\omega_1 = NG + T$$
$$Q_1 = (\sum_t (Y_t - \sum_j \mathcal{Z}_{jt}\theta_{jt})(\sigma_t)^{-1}(Y_t - \sum_j \mathcal{Z}_{jt}\theta_{jt})') + Q_0$$

As is clear from (6.8), the conditional posterior for σ^{-2} does not have a standard format because of the Jacobian term $|\sigma_t \Omega|$. Thus, to compute this conditional posterior we use a Metropolis step where candidate draws are obtained from $\sigma^{2\dagger} = \sigma^{2i-1} + \nu$, where σ^{2i-1} is the previous draw and ν is distributed as a normal with mean zero and variance λ. The value of λ is selected to have an acceptance rate of the order of 25–35 percent.

Since our system satisfies the regularity conditions set up in Geweke (2000), cycling through the conditional distributions in (6.10) produces in the limit draws from the joint posterior of these unknowns. From these, the marginal distributions of θ can be computed averaging over draws in the nuisance dimensions. Convergence to the invariant distribution is checked with standard methods. The results we present are based on the last draw of 500 chains of length 1000 all starting in a small random interval of the last draw of a single (burn-in) chain of 10000 draws.

We summarize the posterior information contained in our sample using impulse responses and multipliers. Impulse responses are computed as the difference between two conditional forecasts, one where an orthogonal shock is set to one in period t and zero otherwise and another where the shock is zero at all t. Formally, let $\mathscr{F}_t^j$ be a conditioning set containing the initial conditions Y^T, draws from the posterior of ϕ, and a value of $\varepsilon_j = Hu$, $j = 1, 2, \ldots$ the structural shock of interest. Then, the impulse responses are

$$IR_y^j(t, \tau) = E(y_{t+\tau}|\mathscr{F}_t^1) - E(y_{t+\tau}|\mathscr{F}_t^2) \qquad \tau = 1, 2, \ldots \tag{6.11}$$

An expansionary government spending shock is identified using sign restrictions. In particular, similarly to the strategy adopted in Canova and Pappa (2007), we impose that (i) government spending increase, (ii) deficit increases, and (iii) domestic output increases on impact, while no additional restrictions are imposed in the following periods. Economic restrictions are imposed on the matrix Ω, which accounts for the general relationship among endogenous variables for, say, the average country. As commonly done in the literature, impulse responses are normalized by the ratio of government spending to GDP in order to convert the percentage changes to euro changes.

Compared to alternative identification strategies used in the literature, sign restrictions overcome some of the drawbacks of identification strategies based on a Cholesky factorization of the estimated residual covariance matrix. In particular, sign restrictions are not sensitive to the ordering of the variables in the VAR system, which instead can be problematic for identification schemes based on a recursive ordering, especially when the covariance between the residuals of the model is large. Also, sign restrictions identification is inspired by the predictions of micro-founded economic models, and is flexible enough to allow for the simulation of different alternative scenarios and shock processes. As such, they do not rely on a timing assumption of discretionary governmental policy interventions in response to developments in the business cycle. In fact, the sign restrictions approach entails generating many candidate structural relationships among the series of interest, rather than imposing a specific structural relationship a priori. Among the pool of generated candidate relationships, those satisfying certain quantitative or qualitative restrictions will be selected and used to estimate the effects of the shock.

6.3 Data

Germany, France, Netherlands, Belgium, Austria, Italy, Spain, Ireland, Finland, Portugal and Greece are the 11 Euro-area countries included in our sample.

We focus on post-1999 data to reduce the risk of measurement error due to the introduction of the euro, as well as other structural breaks.[2] The series that we decided to include in the model cover a wide range of macroeconomic aggregates: output, the current account and the real effective exchange rate, government spending, revenues and debt, and the yield on 10-years government bonds. Overall, these variables should give a good approximation of the true data generating process in the context of the international transmission of fiscal spillovers.

As we are mostly interested in the macroeconomic effects of changes to government spending, we jointly consider government consumption and investment. However, it is worth pointing out that different components of the public bill (consumption, investment, wages, interest expenses) can have heterogeneous effects on growth. As fairly standard in the literature, we consider government revenues net of transfers.

In order to control for the US monetary policy stance, the world and commodities cycle, we include the federal fund rate, world output, and oil price among the exogenous series in the panel-VAR.

All data enter the model in real per-capita terms and are logged, except for the interest rate series that enters the model in levels.

The government bond yield data were sourced from Datastream; the real effective exchange rate from the IMF International Financial Statistics data warehouse; and the crude oil average spot price from the HWWI Commodity Price Index. All other data series were retrieved from Oxford Economics.

6.4 Results

In this section we show the main results concerning the responses of variables to German government spending shocks and the related fiscal multipliers. There are alternative definitions of fiscal multipliers in the literature and we have briefly discussed these different characterizations of fiscal multipliers in Chap. 3.

---

[2]Greece is the only country in the sample to adopt the euro in 2001. This country is not included in Dabla-Norris et al. (2017).

In the present chapter we use the following definition:

$$Cumulative \quad Fiscal \quad Multiplier = \frac{\Sigma_{j=0}^{k} \Delta Y_{t+j}}{\Sigma_{j=0}^{k} \Delta G_{t+j}} \tag{6.12}$$

Hence, the cumulative multiplier at horizon j is computed as the ratio of the cumulated response of output and the cumulated response of government spending at the selected horizon (see e.g. IMF 2009). An advantage of this measure is that it takes into account the persistence of the shock, thus providing a realistic overall picture of the dynamic effects exerted by changes in government spendings, which is what policymakers are ultimately interested in. In order to measure the spillover effects in Euro-area countries, we use the same definition of the fiscal multiplier, but while the cumulated changes of output refer to domestic output in the country of interest, the cumulated response of government spending refers to fiscal changes in Germany.

Finally, it should be noted that multipliers and spillovers are expressed in euro-to-euro terms, i.e. they can be interpreted as the output effects of an increase in 1 euro in government spending. This also implies that it would not be correct to directly compare our results with others in the literature that are expressed as elasticities.[3] Reviewing alternative definitions of fiscal multipliers adopted in the literature, in Chap. 3 we have stressed that rescaling for the fiscal share, i.e. in this context the ratio between government spending and GDP, may produce unreliable results in the presence of long time series periods and variability over time of the fiscal share. Nevertheless, we wish to reiterate that our investigation is relatively free from these problems, given our focus on the EMU period which covers around 17 years.

6.4.1 German Government Spending Multiplier and Spillovers in the Euro Area

Table 6.1 reports the German fiscal multiplier and the estimated spillovers for the sample period 1999–2016, computed at horizon of one year.[4] As shown in the table, the domestic government spending multiplier in Germany has a median value of 1.45, and is statistically different from one. A fiscal multiplier above unity is in line with the higher estimates obtained for the United States during normal times (see e.g. Blanchard and Perotti 2002 and Mountford and Uhlig 2009). It is worth recalling that economists like Barro (2009), who have criticized the excessive confidence in the ability of fiscal policy to stimulate the economy, maintain that in the US economy, at least in peacetime, the government spending multiplier is near zero and, in any case,

[3]This is the case, among others, in Dabla-Norris et al. (2017).

[4]The effects of the shock die out after one year, therefore we do not report later horizons.

Table 6.1 Output fiscal multipliers and spillovers in response to a 1 percent of GDP increase in government spending in Germany (1999–2016)

Germany	1.45 (1.12,1.73)
France	0.20 (0.09,0.27)
Netherlands	0.33 (0.18,0.45)
Belgium	0.26 (0.14,0.36)
Austria	0.35 (0.20,0.46)
Italy	0.29 (0.13,0.41)
Spain	0.23 (0.09,0.30)
Ireland	0.78 (0.22,1.05)
Finland	0.45 (0.19,0.62)
Portugal	0.26 (0.11,0.34)
Greece	0.53 (0.21,0.73)

well below one. Hence, the results that we obtain for Germany seem to contrast this view, and instead support the Keynesian view of fiscal multipliers.

International spillovers always exhibit a positive sign, i.e. expansionary fiscal policies in Germany cause an increase of output in the other Euro-area countries.

Moreover, spillovers are statistically different from zero, and in most cases are non-negligible. Sizeable spillovers are observed in Germany's largest trade partners. For example, spillovers to Netherlands (0.33) and Austria (0.35) are large. As for Italy and Belgium, two other countries with important trade flows with Germany, the expansionary effects equal 0.29 and 0.26 respectively. The size and economic diversification of the recipient economy also appear to matter. In the case of Finland, whose export base is largely dependent on Germany, the spillover equals 0.45. Similarly, the size of fiscal spillovers is large in Greece (0.53), in which case the main transmission channel is likely through tourism.[5] The spillover is instead smaller in France (0.20), where the economic cycle is probably less dependent upon that in Germany.

Instead, our finding that Ireland has the greatest expansionary effects (0.78) from a positive fiscal shock in Germany deserves some further consideration. Given the small trade flows between the two countries, we are led to conclude that there are other important macroeconomic factors underlying the spillovers from fiscal shocks.

[5]Germany is consistently among the top source markets for tourism in Greece.

In particular, the economic relations between open economies are not restricted to flows of goods and services: financial linkages and flows among economies are equally important and the financial interdependence between Ireland and Germany (as well as other Euro-area countries) is quite strong. Indeed, it is also worth stressing that during the first decade of EMU, i.e. before the financial crisis, Ireland represented an important financial attractor in the Euro Area for foreign companies.

Since the effects of fiscal policy may depend on a number of factors and, consequently, change over time, we also estimated the model over several sub-samples. We observe a tendency for both fiscal multipliers and spillovers to increase in the samples covering the period from 2011 to 2014. This period broadly corresponds with the Euro-area sovereign debt crisis, the launch of the Long-Term Refinancing Operations and of successive rounds of quantitative easing amidst worries that monetary policy was constrained by the zero-lower bound. The estimates are lower in the last two sample windows, and closer to the pre-crisis period, when economic conditions tend to normalize.

These results are indeed fully consistent with some conclusions of the literature concerning the relevance of the state of the economy, with fiscal multipliers larger in recessions, and the importance of an accommodative monetary policy in generating stronger effects of fiscal shocks on output.[6]

6.4.2 *The Domestic and International Transmission of Spending Shocks*

Figure 6.2 reports the domestic fiscal multiplier estimated over different sample periods. This evidence complements the discussion on the domestic fiscal multiplier in the previous section, and allows us to shed some light on the domestic patterns of transmission of the shock.

Government spending jumps on impact and exhibits some persistence increasing for approximately two years, after which it peaks. Domestic output increases in response to the fiscal shock, with a persistence profile similar to the one observed for government spending: as the positive fiscal impulse vanishes, domestic output also converges to its long-term trend.

The conventional wisdom on the effects of a positive government spending shock is that domestic aggregate demand will be stimulated. In turn, the associated increase in GDP will cause the emergence of a trade deficit, via the expansionary effects exerted on imports. In other words, one would expect to observe the socalled twin deficits phenomenon. Our evidence for Germany is consistent with this prediction: the median response is negative and large (the current account falls by more than 2 percent). However, large confidence bands leave room for considerable uncertainty in the sign of the response.

---

[6]We do not report the figures describing the sub-sample analysis in order to avoid an inflation of graphs.

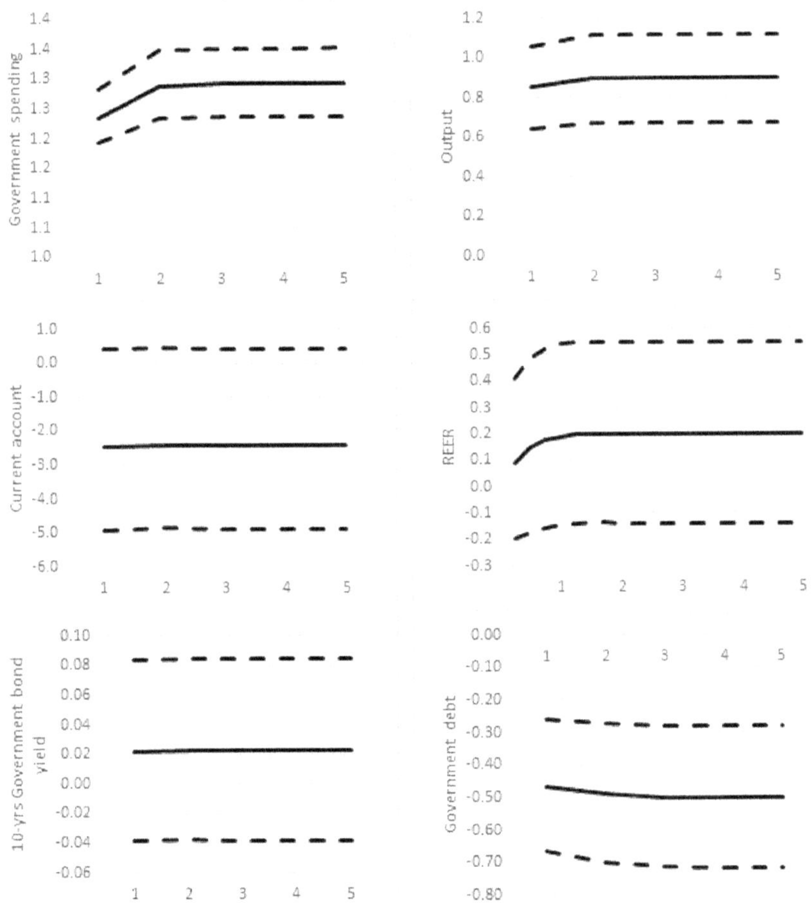

Fig. 6.1 Cumulated impulse response functions to a one percent increase in government spending in Germany. *Note* Dashed bands represent 95 percent confidence bands. The y-axis scale is in percent; the x-axis represents years after the shock

Fig. 6.2 Domestic fiscal multiplier to a government spending shock in Germany estimated over different sample periods. *Note* Dashed bands represent 95 percent confidence bands

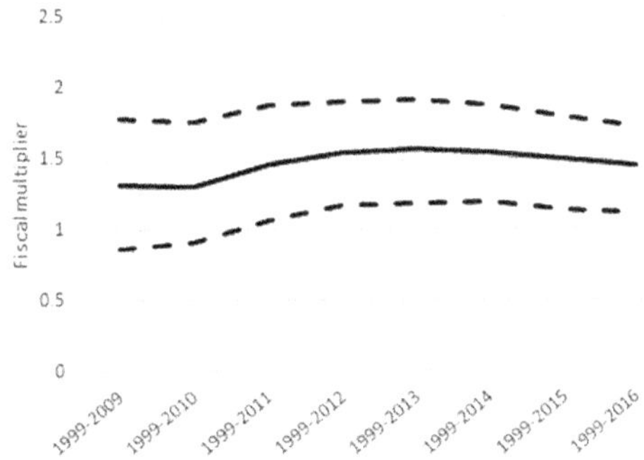

The dynamic response of the real effective exchange rate is consistent with most of the available empirical literature on Euro-area countries, which typically detects a real appreciation. While uncertainty is once again sizeable, the fiscal expansion determines a deterioration of domestic competitiveness.

This can stem from domestic pressures for higher wages, as the economy picks up and labor market conditions tighten; a Euro-area wide trade surplus with the rest of the workd, which is possible despite heterogeneous responses in individual countries; or, lastly, higher interest rates and a nominal appreciation of the Euro if the European Central Bank responds to fiscal policy changes in the largest economy of the Monetary Union. The impulse response also shows that the higher real effective exchange rate takes some time to materialize (Fig. 6.1).

Finally, while the yield on domestic government instruments does not move, government debt falls in response to the shock. Given the estimated bands, the results are statistically significant. The explanation of this result might lie in the large fiscal multiplier detected for the German economy, as well as other factors, including an effective management of the maturity structure, and the ultra-expansionary monetary policy pursued by the ECB in recent years which led to negative interest rates in Germany.

The international effects of a government spending shock in Germany are broadly consistent with the domestic effects. Output abroad increases and, as observed in the previous section where we described fiscal spillovers, the magnitude of the change varies across countries. Figure 6.3 shows the output response in selected countries, i.e. the largest Euro-area economies and those with the strongest trade links with Germany; and Fig. 6.4 shows the impulse responses in the remaining economies.

The spillovers are sizeable in all the six high debt countries considered in previous chapters, but particularly notable in two small open Euro-area economies, respectively, Ireland and Greece which exhibit the larger spillovers from German government spending shocks.

The long-term interest rates outside Germany do not react. Of course, this does not rule out that spending increases at times of strained public finances, or heightened market uncertainty may determine spikes in governments borrowing costs. Given a modest impact of the fiscal shock on domestic competitiveness, it is not surprising that the effects are small also abroad.

The current account has typically been postulated as the single most important series to capture the transmission abroad of fiscal policy shocks. One would expect that the impact of an increase in domestic demand is to expand exports of other economies. However, during the last decade, trade flows, including within the Euro Area, have substantially evolved. Countries have become more integrated through trade, but at the same time a larger share of intermediate inputs in the manufacturing supply chain is sourced from different markets.

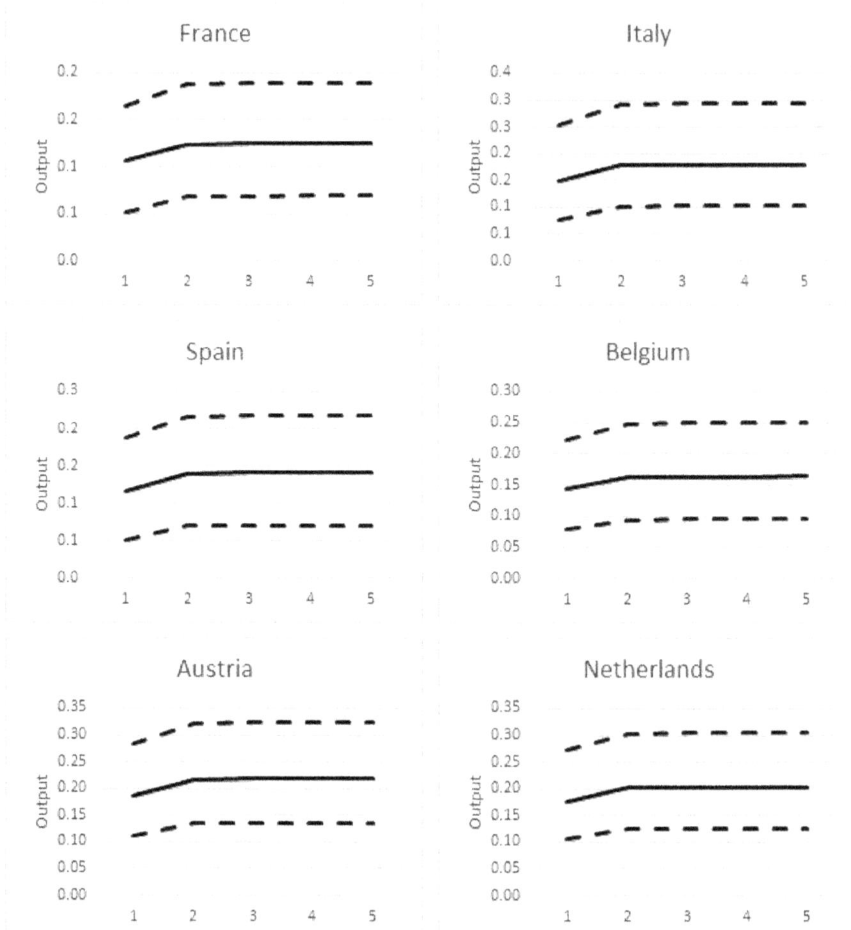

Fig. 6.3 Cumulated impulse response functions of foreign output in selected Euro-area countries, to a one percent increase in government spending in Germany. *Note* Dashed bands represent 95 percent confidence bands. The y-axis scale is in percent; the x-axis represents years after the shock

This contributed to making the effects of fiscal stimulus on a country's current account balance less predictable.

Indeed, in our analysis we do not find evidence in support of large positive effects of an expansionary fiscal impulse in Germany on the current account of other

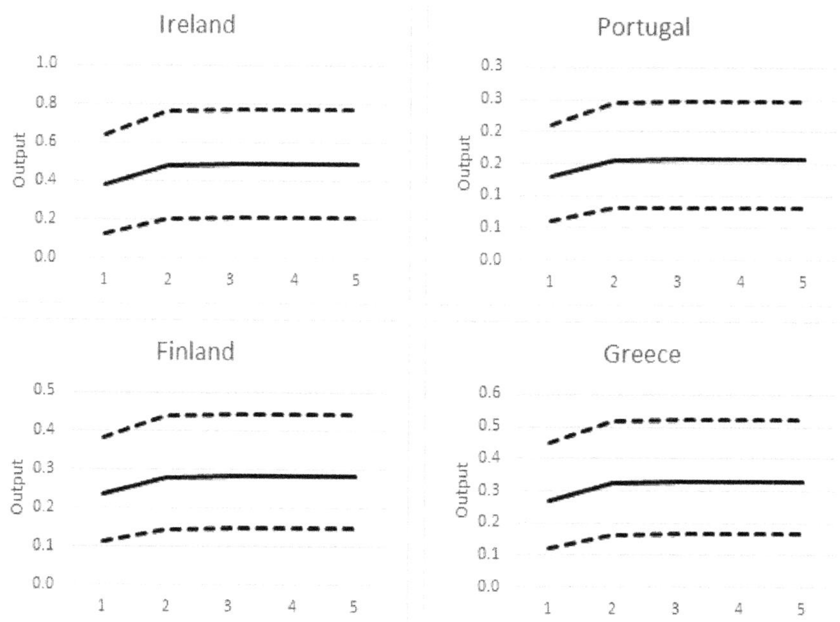

Fig. 6.4 Cumulated impulse response functions of foreign output in selected Euro-area countries, to a one percent increase in government spending in Germany. *Note* Dashed bands represent 95 percent confidence bands. The y-axis scale is in percent; the x-axis represents years after the shock

Euro-area economies. In a number of cases the responses are not statistically different from zero, e.g. France, Italy, Spain and Austria (see Fig. 6.5). In two countries that represent important trade partners for Germany, i.e. Belgium and Netherlands, the response is larger (more than 1 percent), and is negative. Besides changes in the structure of international trade mentioned above, another possible explanation for our results is that our model is capturing not only the contemporaneous effects of the shock, but also the lagged effects and cross-country interdependencies. These complicate the analysis, since spillback effects stemming from higher domestic output and, consequently, imports can undo the initial expansion of the domestic current account.

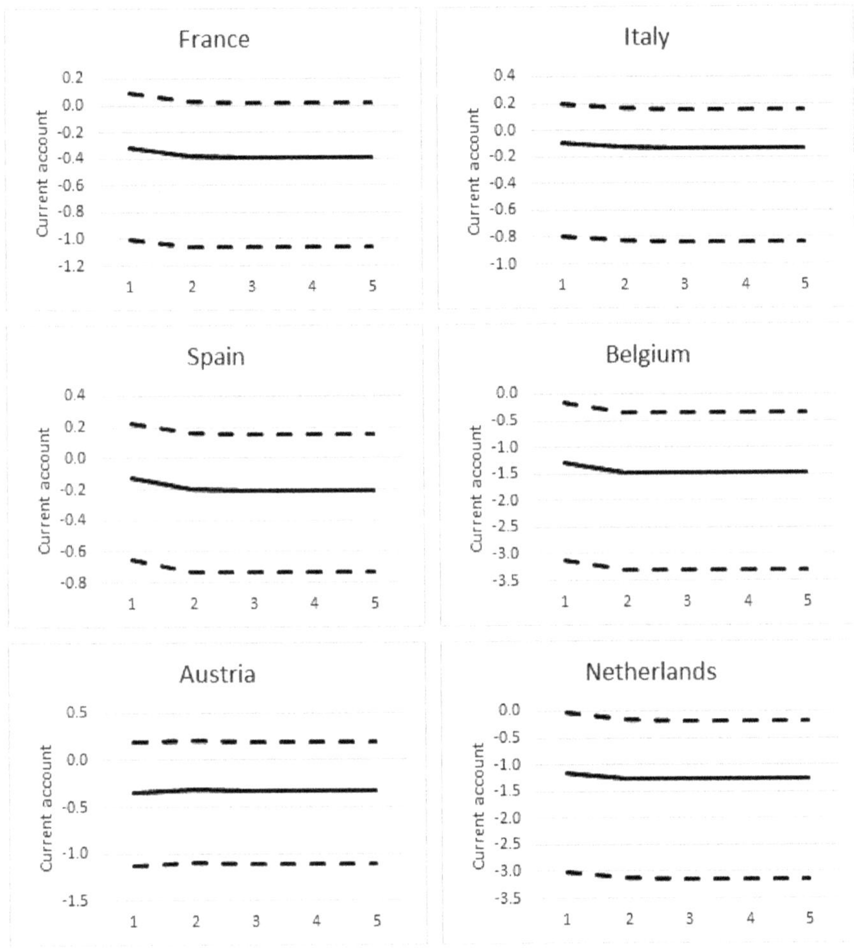

Fig. 6.5 Cumulated impulse response functions of the foreign current account balance in selected Euro-area countries, to a one percent increase in government spending in Germany. *Note* Dashed bands represent 95 percent confidence bands. The y-axis scale is in percent; the x-axis represents years after the shock.

6.5 Conclusions

Measuring the effects of government spending shocks in the national economy and the spillover effects in foreign economies is important for academic economists, given the lack of consensus on the size of fiscal multipliers and spillovers, and also for policymakers. In the Euro Area the matter has been widely debated in recent years.

This chapter has aimed to provide novel empirical evidence for Germany (the national economy in this context) and for a sample of 11 EA countries covering the EMU period. By employing a panel-VAR model, including a wide set of macroeconomic variables, we find that the government spending multiplier has a size of 1.45 in Germany, and that spillovers in the other Euro-area countries are sizeable, especially for trade partners, small and less diversified economies.

The conclusion that the domestic fiscal multiplier is positive and large, while fiscal spillovers are non-negligible is not surprising, given the feature of large open economy exhibited by Germany and the high degree of trade and financial integration between Germany and the Euro-area countries. Moreover, our evidence supports the view that fiscal stimuli adopted by large economies with fiscal space might boost growth in other member countries and, not less important, might help to reduce the macroeconomic imbalances in the Euro Area.

The current account appears to be the main channel of transmission for fiscal shocks both domestically and abroad. However, strong trade integration among countries in the Euro Area, and spillback effects can zero-out the net impact in a sample that covers only the post-euro period. Therefore, we do not find systematic evidence in favor or the twin deficit hypothesis, and in a few cases, we observe a decoupling between the (positive) output dynamics and the (negative) response of the current account.

Beyond trade and financial flows, we do not find strong evidence in support of other possible transmission channels. On the one hand, the real effective exchange rate, which is commonly regarded as a proxy for a country's competitiveness, moves little in response to a government spending shock. This result is not surprising: prices and wages tend to be sticky in the short run, and the common currency and the centralized conduct of monetary policy likely contributed to dampen fluctuations of the nominal exchange rate in response to domestic fiscal innovations. On the other hand, long-term interest rates do not appear to respond systematically to spending innovations.

The sub-samples analysis essentially confirms the results obtained over the whole period. Nevertheless, both a larger domestic multiplier and spillovers between 2011 and 2014 are detected. This is far from surprising since over this period the monetary policy in the Euro Area had an highly expansionary stance. One of the main conclusions of the literature on fiscal shocks, largely confirmed in the various chapters and investigations conducted in the present book, is that the positive effects on aggregate output of fiscal stimuli are magnified in the presence of an accommodative monetary policy.

We started this investigation posing the question: Can Germany do it? In light of the results shown in this chapter the answer is a qualified 'yes'. For, while the macroeconomic adjustment in the Euro Area requires continuous efforts from those countries - in particular Southern countries affected by structural problems of competitiveness, high public debts and still too low flexibility in the various domestic markets - an important role in this adjustment process should be placed on the shoulders of the EMU anchor country: Germany, i.e. the anchor country, has both the economic strength and the fiscal space to sustain aggregate demand at the area-wide level, thus limiting the pain associated with the process of structural (and non-structural) reforms in peripheral Euro-area economies and thus contributing to the rebalance. In other words, empirical results and macroeconomic analysis call for a more symmetric (or less asymmetric) rebalancing in the Euro Area.

References

Auerbach AJ, Gorodnichenko Y (2013) Output spillovers from fiscal policy. Am Econ Rev 103:141–146

Barro RJ (2009) Government spending is no free lunch. Wall Str J, 22 January 2009

Beetsma R, Giuliodori M (2004) What are the spill-overs from fiscal shocks in Europe? An empirical analysis. ECB Working Paper No. 325

Beetsma R, Giuliodori M, Klaassen F (2006) Trade spillovers of fiscal policy in the European Union: a panel analysis. Econ Policy 21(48):641–687

Belke A, Osowski T (2016) Measuring fiscal spillovers in EMU and beyond: a global VAR approach. CEPS Working Paper No. 428

Blanchard OJ, Erceg CJ, Lindé J (2015) Jump starting the Euro Area recovery: would a rise in core fiscal spending help the periphery? NBER Working Papers, No. 21426

Blanchard O, Perotti R (2002) An empirical characterization of the dynamic effects of changes in government spending and taxes on output. Q J Econ 117:1329–1368

Canova F, Ciccarelli M (2013) Panel vector autoregressive models: a survey. ECB Working Paper No. 1507

Canova F, Pappa E (2007) Price differentials in monetary unions: the role of fiscal shocks. Econ J 117:713–737

Christiano L, Eichenbaum M, Rebelo S (2011) When is the government spending multiplier large? J Polit Econ 119:78–121

Clancy D, Jacquinot P, Lozej M (2015) Government expenditure composition and fiscal policy spillovers in a small open economy within a monetary union. ESM Working Paper Series No. 4

Corsetti G, Meier A, Mueller G (2012) What determines government spending multipliers? Econ Policy 27:521–565

Corsetti G, Meier A, Mueller G (2010) Cross-border spillovers from fiscal stimulus. Int J Cent Bank 6:5–37

Cwik T, Wieland V (2010) Keynesian government spending multipliers and spillovers in the Euro Area. ECB Working Paper No. 1267

Dabla-Norris E, Dallari P, Poghosyan T (2017) Fiscal spillovers in the Euro Area: letting the data speak, IMF WP, forthcoming

ECB (2014) Fiscal multipliers and the timing of consolidation. Mon Bulletin, April 2014

Eller M, Feldkirchner M, Huber F (2017) How would a fiscal shock in Germany affect other European Countries? Evidence from a Bayesian GVAR model with sign restrictions. Austrian Central Bank. Focus on European Economic Integration 1:54–57

European Commission (2011) Scoreboard for the surveillance of macroeconomic imbalances: envisaged initial design. Commission Staff Working Paper, 8 November 2011

Gadatsch N, Hauzenberger K, Stähler N (2015) German and the rest of the Euro Area fiscal policy during the crisis. Deutsche Bundesbank Discussion Paper, No, p 05

Galí J, Lopez-Salido JD, Valls J (2007) Understanding the effects of government spending on consumption. J Eur Econ Assoc 5:227–270

Gambetti L, Gallio F (2016) Measuring fiscal policy spillovers in the Euro Area. ADEMU WP 2016/044

Georgiadis G, Hollmayr J (2016) Fiscal spillovers in the Euro Area: Sign, size and determinants. mimeo

Geweke J (2000) Using simulation methods for Bayesian econometric models: Inference, development, and communication. Econom Rev 18:1–73

IMF (2009) Fiscal multipliers: Size, determinants, and use in macroeconomic projections. Technical notes and manuals. No. 09/11

Mountford A, Uhlig H (2009) What are the effects of fiscal policy shocks? J Appl Econ 24:960–992

Pappa E (2009) The effects of fiscal shocks on employment and the real wage. Int Econ Rev 50(1):217–244

Veld J (2013) Fiscal consolidations and spillovers in the Euro Area periphery and core. European Commission Economic Papers, No, p 506
Veld J (2016) Public investment stimulus in surplus countries and their Euro Area spillovers. European Commission Economic Brief, No, p 016

Chapter 7
The Labor Market Outcomes of Austerity. Evidence for Europe

Abstract In this chapter we aim to provide an empirical characterization of the relationship between government spending and labor market variables for a group of Euro-area countries using data since the early nineties. To this end we estimate a panel Bayesian VAR model including fiscal, real and monetary variables. Government spending shocks are identified by imposing sign restrictions on the responses of selected variables. We find that unemployment multipliers are heterogeneous across countries and government spending tools. The unemployment multiplier is large in countries like Spain and Germany and small in Italy. In light of the large public investment projects promoted in Spain and of the structural reforms approved in Germany in the early 2000s, we are led to conclude that a combination of institutional reforms and public infrastructure investment projects can strengthen the link between fiscal policy and jobs.

7.1 Introduction

The last few years have witnessed an unprecedented use of fiscal policy tools in advanced economies. Fiscal measures were taken in an attempt to cushion the severity of the downturn and boost private demand soon after the onset of the 2008 financial crisis, as central banks quickly hit the zero lower bound, responding to the collapse of houses and assets prices, and the credit channel was impaired by a dysfunctional banking sector. According to estimates from the OECD (2009), the United States deployed the largest fiscal package, with an implied cumulated budget impact over the period 2008–2010 of about 5% of domestic output expressed at 2008 prices. In Europe, the size of fiscal interventions was smaller and, for the most part, these were effected through automatic stabilization mechanisms rather than discretionary measures. Nonetheless, the implied adjustment in the volume of revenues and in spending plans represented a sizable portion of domestic output by historical standards in most Member States. Since 2010, stimulus policies were considerably reduced and eventually replaced by fiscal consolidation programs. These were aimed at breaking the negative spiral of skyrocketing government deficits and ballooning public debts that resulted from the fall in tax revenues and the increase in expenditures. Austerity

© Springer International Publishing AG 2018

A. Cavallo et al., *Fiscal Policies in High Debt Euro-Area Countries*,
https://doi.org/10.1007/978-3-319-70269-8_7

measures were therefore activated in several countries, under the close supervision of European partners with sounder public finances and larger trade surpluses, with the twin goals of restoring confidence in the Euro Area and setting its economies back on a long-term growth path.

These events revived attention, both in policy circles and academia, towards the consequences of fiscal policy, its interplay with the state of the economy, the monetary policy stance, the level of debt and credit conditions (see Blanchard and Leigh 2013; Corsetti et al. 2012; Guajardo et al. 2011; Auerbach and Gorodnichenko 2013; Christiano et al. 2011). While most of the research undertaken so far (including the research presented in the first five chapters of this book) investigates the link between fiscal policy and output growth, this chapter focuses on the labor market outcomes of fiscal interventions in Europe.

Labor market variables are among the most important real indicators available to economists and policymakers, and complement the information provided by aggregate output. While output multipliers describe the possible benefits, or costs, for the economy in the aggregate, the response of labor market variables provides an accurate picture of the repercussions that fiscal interventions entail for a country's employment outcomes. In turn, these can have important economic consequences, hardly accounted for by conventional measures of output multipliers. For example, high unemployment and low participation destroy human capital, are more likely to determine tension and turmoil (Voth and Ponticelli 2012), and the associated income shortfalls are strong predictors of household mortgage defaults (Gerardi et al. 2013).

The recent context in Europe is particularly prone to stimulating attention towards the link between fiscal policy and the labor markets: unemployment has been at historic highs in a number of countries - e.g. Greece, Spain and Portugal; measures of discouraged workers, or workers only marginally attached to the labor force, have been growing; and a debate about the sustainability of region-wide recovery plans based on fiscal responsibility and internal devaluation is still ongoing.

Thus, although in this book we have mainly focused on the effects of fiscal shocks on aggregate output in the Euro-area economies, we believe that the investigation presented in this chapter is very useful for completion of the research.

The scope of this chapter is primarily descriptive and its goal is to provide an empirical characterization of the relationship between government spending and various labor market variables for Europe as a whole and for several European countries individually. To this end, we examine a set of Euro-area Member States - Austria, France, Germany, Greece, Italy, Netherlands, Portugal and Spain - and we estimate a panel Bayesian random coefficient VAR model featuring fiscal, real and monetary variables. The panel structure is advantageous as it allows an average response to be computed, which can be broadly seen as Euro-area wide evidence, while retaining information on individual country results.

First, unemployment multipliers are heterogeneous across countries and government spending tools. For example, the unemployment multiplier is four times larger in Spain than in Italy. The response of unemployment to fiscal policy shocks is also large in Germany. These are notable examples since Spain has undertaken large housing and public infrastructure investment projects since the early 2000s, while in

Germany the labor market legislation has been reformed (Hartz plan), and the country's system of industrial relation reorganized as well.[1] This evidence suggests that institutional reforms and dedicated policy actions can strengthen the link between fiscal policy and jobs given a similar macroeconomic outlook, a point also raised in IMF (2014).

Second, the interplay of fiscal contraction and economic slack has had adverse consequences on the participation rate in peripheral Euro-area countries. Using the sample ending in 2007, the participation rate typically increases in response to cuts in government consumption - a dynamic consistent with the negative income effect associated with fiscal tightening. However, if the crisis period is included, the average response becomes negative. In our view, this can be attributed to the discouraged worker effect prevailing over the income effect observed during normal times. The gloomy economic outlook and scarce outside options in place since the onset of the crisis could induce laid-off workers to give up looking for jobs. Interestingly, the reversal is led by the results in Greece, Italy, Portugal and Spain, while no change is observed in core Euro-area countries before and after 2007. The geographical divide is likely attributable to: (i) Peripheral Member States being more severely hit by the crisis; and (ii) The alternative of black markets in southern Europe. The data seem to uphold our reading. By the end of 2013, the number of discouraged workers in Italy represented 13% of the workforce, three times above the European average, while in Germany it stood at just above 1%. The black labor market also ballooned in the Euro-area periphery, reaching an estimated 20% of national income in Italy, Greece and Spain according to Eurostat.

Third, several policy prescriptions stem from our analysis. Labor markets in Europe are still segmented, as shown by the cross-country heterogeneity of unemployment multipliers, and the resilience of unemployment to fiscal shocks is low, since impulse responses display only moderate signs of mean reversion many quarters after the shock. Reducing geographic segmentation would likely lower the adjustment costs to exogenous shocks hitting the common currency block. To prevent higher unemployment levels from having significant hysteresis effects, and to minimize the risk that prolonged unemployment spells turn into long-term unemployment, efforts should be made to foster active labor market policies (ALMP). Even in the context of shrinking government bills, it is advisable that policymakers set aside the resources necessary to cushion the adverse impact of austerity measures on laid-off workers, in order to prevent temporary budget cuts from turning into permanent losses of human capital and productive potential.

The responses of wages and hours worked are small compared to those observed in unemployment and the participation rate. These findings place emphasis on the relatively low degree of flexibility characterizing European labor markets, especially in peripheral countries. Movements in hours worked, if quantitatively relevant, could offer an alternative channel of adjustment to adverse shocks, in addition to the

[1] For Spain, consider the Plan Estatal de Vivienda y Suelo 1999–2001, 2002–2005, 2006–2008, and the Plan de Infrastructuras, Transporte y Vivienda 2012–2024. For Germany see Krebs and Scheffel (2013) and Dustmann et al. (2014).

extensive margin captured by the binary choice of working versus not working. Similarly, wage negotiation could provide a way out for workers' layoffs during periods of weak demand. Therefore, our results reinforce the argument that European countries should undertake efforts to enhance labor hoarding practices, and adopt labor market reforms to reduce downward wage rigidities and increase the flexibility of hours to labor market conditions.

The closest works to ours are Pappa (2009), Brückner and Pappa (2012) and Bermperoglou et al. (2013). These papers adopt a multi-country approach and present stylized facts on the responses of labor market variables to fiscal shocks using VAR methods. Pappa (2009) studies the dynamics of the real wage and employment in the US, both at the federal and at the state level, after either a government consumption, government investment or a government employment shock. Bermperoglou et al. (2013) consider also shocks to government wages in a group of countries including the US, UK, Japan and Canada and find that cuts in the government wage bill may be expansionary and reduce unemployment, while other types of shocks are typically associated with output losses and increases in unemployment. Brückner and Pappa (2012) examine the effects of government spending shocks on labor market variables in a sample of OECD countries and show that fiscal expansions can lead to significant increases in the unemployment rate. In comparison to this literature, we also find that shocks to different government spending tools have qualitatively and quantitatively different effects on unemployment. Cuts to government investment always imply an increase in unemployment. However, in the case of government consumption shocks, we cannot rule out that negative shocks may reduce unemployment.

Other authors adopt VAR methods to identify the determinants of fluctuations in the unemployment rate in individual countries, such as Dolado and Jimeno (1997) for Spain, Gambetti and Pistoresi (2004) for Italy and Alexius and Holmlund (2007) for Sweden. Their focus is broader compared to ours, which is instead specific to fiscal policy. However, an interesting commonality emerges: several of these papers emphasize the hysteretic behavior of the unemployment rate in response to shocks, a finding that is consistent with the persistent dynamics that we observe in our data.

The rest of the chapter is organized as follows. Section 7.2 describes the model and the estimation techniques. Section 7.3 outlines the data used, motivates the choice of the endogenous series included in the model, and describes the identification assumptions for the shock. Section 7.4 presents and discusses the results from the general model, as well as two applications dedicated to sectoral specific results and spending reversals. Sections 7.5 concludes.

7.2 The Methodology

We use a hierarchical panel VAR model along the lines of Jarocinski (2010). Since the time dimension of European data is not long, VAR coefficients can be imprecisely estimated. Also, the countries in our sample are likely to be characterized by considerable cyclical heterogeneity as they include Member States from both the north and the south of Europe: while some notoriously lead the European economic cycle others lag, and their national account figures differ remarkably. While the first argument raises concerns about the opportunity of running single-country VAR models using OLS, the latter indicates that it is not a good idea to estimate a pooled VAR for all countries either.

The distinctive feature of the multi-country random coefficient Bayesian VAR model that we adopt is to efficiently combine unit-specific and cross sectional information by assuming that country-specific dynamic coefficients are realizations from the same underlying data-generating process. In other words, the dynamics of transmission of the shocks are potentially different across countries, but the distribution from which they come has a common mean. The first point allows the model to be estimated without imposing homogeneous dynamics. The second point minimizes the small sample problem by setting an average prior for the individual country results that summarizes cross-country information.

Multi-country random coefficient Bayesian VAR models have been used in Canova (2005), Ciccarelli and Rebucci (2006), Canova and Pappa (2007), Jarocinski (2010).

For each country, the VAR model is:

$$y_{n,t} = B_n' y_{n,t-1} + \Gamma_n' z_t + u_{n,t} \tag{7.1}$$

where $n = 1, 2, \ldots, N$ denotes countries; $t = 1, 2, \ldots, T_n$ time and T_n varies with the country; $y_{n,t}$ is an $M \times 1$ vector of endogenous variables; $z_{n,t}$ collects deterministic components; $u_{n,t}$ are VAR innovations; B_n and Γ_n are matrices containing the slopes and the intercept coefficients. Rewrite (7.1) as:

$$Y_n = X_n B_n + Z_n \Gamma_n + U_n \tag{7.2}$$

where X_n is the matrix obtained by stacking vertically the T_n observations in $y'_{n,t-1}$. Thus Y_n and U_n are $T_n \times M$; X_n is $T_n \times M$; Z_n is $T_n \times Q$; B_n is $K \times M$; Γ_n is $Q \times M$. Let $y_n \equiv vec(Y_n)$, $\beta_n \equiv vec(B_n)$ and $\gamma_n \equiv vec(\Gamma_n)$. We assume that the slope coefficients satisfy:

$$p(\beta_n | \bar{\beta}, O_n) = N(\bar{\beta}, c \times O_n) \tag{7.3}$$

where $\bar{\beta}$ is the common mean and $c \times O_n$ is the dispersion, c being the parameter that controls the general tightness of the restriction. We initially tried to be agnostic about how much the country-specific coefficients differ from the common mean and imposed a diffuse prior on the parameter. However, such a choice resulted in fairly large estimates of c and, in turn, in systematic violations of the stability test for the VAR coefficients $\bar{\beta}$. This may be caused by a lack of sufficient information in our sample to precisely estimate this parameter. Therefore, its value is treated as fixed. Letting σ^2 be the variance of the error in the univariate autoregression of each VAR series, the i-th element of O_n is:

$$O_{n,i} = diag\left(\sigma^2_{n,i} \otimes \frac{1}{\sigma^2_{n,n}}\right), \quad i = 1, \dots m. \tag{7.4}$$

We employ this scaling factor since, with a single variance parameter c, it may be difficult to capture the cross variable variations in the β_n. Adding O_n makes the variance of $\beta_{n,i}$ specific to the variable i.

The VAR innovations are i.i.d. $N(0, \Sigma_n)$ and the prior on their covariance matrix is diffuse, i.e.:

$$p(\Sigma_n) \propto |\Sigma_n|^{-\frac{1}{2}(N+1)} \tag{7.5}$$

The priors for the coefficients on the deterministic variables and for the common mean are also diffuse:

$$p(\gamma_n) \propto 1 \tag{7.6}$$

$$p(\bar{\beta}) \propto 1 \tag{7.7}$$

The posterior densities for the coefficient of interest are computed by combining prior information with the likelihood which, for the stacked vector of countries, is:

$$p(Y|\beta_n, \gamma_n, \Sigma_n) \propto \Pi_n |\Sigma_n|^{-\frac{T_n}{2}} exp\left[-\frac{1}{2}\sum_n (y_n - X_n\beta_n - Z_n\gamma_n)'(\Sigma_n^{-1} \otimes I_{T_n}) (y_n - X_n\beta_n - Z_n\gamma_n)\right] \tag{7.8}$$

Since the priors are conjugate, the conditional posterior densities are analytically available and this enables us to numerically compute the joint posterior distributions with the Gibbs sampler. The joint posterior for the unknowns is:

$$p(\beta_n, \gamma_n, \Sigma_n, \bar{\beta}|Y) \propto p(\beta_n, \gamma_n, \Sigma_n, \bar{\beta})\, p(Y|\beta_n, \gamma_n, \Sigma_n, \bar{\beta}) \tag{7.9}$$

$$\propto \Pi_n |\Sigma_n|^{-\frac{T_n}{2}} exp\left[-\frac{1}{2}\sum_n (y_n - X_n\beta_n - Z_n\gamma_n)'(\Sigma_n^{-1} \otimes I_{T_n}) (y_n - X_n\beta_n - Z_n\gamma_n)\right] \tag{7.10}$$

$$\times |c|^{-\frac{NMK}{2}} exp\left[-\frac{1}{2}\sum_n (\beta_n - \bar{\beta})'(c \times O_n)^{-1}(\beta_n - \bar{\beta})\right] \tag{7.11}$$

$$\times \Pi_n |\Sigma_n|^{-\frac{M+1}{2}} \tag{7.12}$$

Let $\Theta \equiv [\beta_n, \ \gamma_n, \ \Sigma_n, \ \bar{\beta}]$ and denote by Θ/α the vector of Θ excluding the coefficient α.

$$p(\beta_n|Y, \Theta/\beta_n) = N(\tilde{\beta}_n, \tilde{\Delta}_n) \tag{7.13}$$

where

$$\tilde{\Delta}_n = \left(\Sigma_n^{-1} \otimes X_n'X_n + c^{-1}O_n^{-1}\right)^{-1} \tag{7.14}$$

$$\tilde{\beta}_n = \tilde{\Delta}_n \times \left((\Sigma_n^{-1} \otimes X_n')(y_n - Z_n\gamma_n) + c^{-1}O_n^{-1}\bar{\beta}\right) \tag{7.15}$$

The conditional posterior of γ_n is:

$$p(\gamma_n|Y, \Theta/\gamma_n) = N(\tilde{\gamma}_n, \tilde{\Gamma}_n) \tag{7.16}$$

where

$$\tilde{\Gamma}_n = \left(\Sigma_n^{-1} \otimes Z_n'Z_n\right)^{-1} \tag{7.17}$$

and

$$\tilde{\gamma}_n = \tilde{\Gamma}_n \times \left(\Sigma_n^{-1} \otimes Z_n'\right)(y_n - X_n\beta_n) \tag{7.18}$$

The conditional posterior of Σ_n is:

$$p(\Sigma_n|Y, \Theta/\Sigma_n) = iW\left((Y_n - X_nB_n - Z_nC_n)'(Y_n - X_nB_n - Z_nC_n), T_n\right) \tag{7.19}$$

The conditional posterior of $\bar{\beta}$ is:

$$p(\bar{\beta}|Y, \Theta) = N(\bar{\bar{\beta}}, \bar{\Delta}) \tag{7.20}$$

where

$$\bar{\Delta} = \left(\sum_n c^{-1}O_n^{-1}\right)^{-1} \tag{7.21}$$

and

$$\bar{\bar{\beta}} = \bar{\Delta} \times \sum_n c^{-1}O_n^{-1}\beta_n. \tag{7.22}$$

As for the conditional posterior of β_n, by iteratively sampling from (7.13)–(7.20), one obtains a sequence for Θ that can be used for inference. The first 300,000 draws are used for burn-in. Subsequently, 500 draws are used for posterior inference. These represent the last draw of chains counting 500 draws each. This solution, instead of thinning from the same chain, is well suited for parallel computing, a strategy that is adopted here. Convergence and autocorrelation diagnostics are satisfied.

As detailed above, the multi-country VAR model is put into action by adopting a hierarchical structure in which the country-specific coefficients are randomly drawn from a Normal distribution with a common mean. This is typically referred as the first stage of the hierarchy. The second stage consists of prior assumptions about the distributions of the common mean and of the country-specific variances. For the former we employ noninformative priors; the latter are estimated in an Empirical Bayes fashion.

The conditional posterior for β_n has a natural weighted average format where sample and prior information receive weights proportional to their relative precision. Thus, the country model whose coefficients are more tightly estimated receives more weight relative to the prior as compared to the model where the coefficients are imprecisely estimated. The variance of country-specific coefficients depends on how different the estimated country-specific coefficients are and on their precision. If they are different and the uncertainty around the estimates is small, the variance in the second level of the hierarchy will be large, indicating significant heterogeneity. Conversely, if country-specific coefficients are similar, the variance in the second level of the hierarchy will be smaller.

7.3 Data and Model Specification

The sample spans from 1991:Q1 up to 2012:Q4 for all countries except Spain, Portugal and Greece for which we have to start in 1995:Q1 (Spain and Portugal) and 2000:Q1 (Greece). Since our estimation approach does not allow for time-varying coefficients, but breaks and parameter instability are possible with two decades or more of data, we also use fifteen-years-long windows starting in 1991:Q1 and roll from one year to the next keeping the window size constant. This results in a total of seven subsample estimates.[2]

All real variables are expressed in per capita terms at constant 2005 prices and enter the VAR in logs. All variables are in levels, except for the CPI inflation rate which is in first differences. A constant and a linear trend are added to the VAR.

There is little guidance on which data to include in the VAR model. As a general principle, all series relevant for the phenomenon to be described should be considered. This reduces the risk of leaving important information outside of the model. For example, as fiscal and monetary policies operate in tango (Davig and Leeper 2011), VAR aiming at characterizing fiscal policy outcomes but neglecting monetary variables are likely to provide distorted conclusions (Rossi and Zubairy 2011). More generally, research based on factor models (Forni et al. 2014) and large VAR models (Banbura et al. 2010) has shown that there it is of advantage for the econometrician to dispose of a large information set. However, in practice these recommendations often collide with the challenge of producing reliable parameters estimates, or finding sensible identification restrictions when the system is beyond minimal. As a result, the literature has witnessed a fairly large range of VAR specifications to investigate the same phenomenon.

[2]In the case of Greece, the estimation sample remains forcibly fixed at 2000:Q1-2012:Q4 always. For Spain and Portugal, the starting date of the window is kept fixed at 1995:Q1 for the first four runs.

To avoid the arbitrariness of picking one, among several possible sets of variables, and in order to gauge the repercussions on the results from using models of different sizes, for each country in our sample we run a battery of VAR models, from smaller to bigger, estimated by OLS.[3]

The small version features data on government spending, revenues and debt, unemployment, domestic output and the short term interest rate. Government spending is split into investment, consumption and social benefits (or social transfers in kind), which encompass several social safety net programs including unemployment benefits. This system contains the minimal ingredients to study the effects of fiscal shocks on the economy: the fiscal series and output allow fiscal shocks to be meaningfully identified, controlling for the business cycle; the level of debt accounts for the significant country heterogeneity that characterizes our sample in this respect[4]; the short term interest rate proxies the monetary policy instrument; finally, unemployment is the variable of interest.

The intermediate VAR model further includes total wages, hours worked per employee, the participation rate and the inflation rate. Compared to the previous one, this version features a richer set of labor market indicators, which can be useful to control for changes along the intensive (hours) or the extensive (participation) margin, and in the elasticity between earnings and vacancies. It also allows for a trade-off between inflation and unemployment.

The large VAR has a richer description of the real and financial sides of the economy. It includes private consumption and investment in housing from the national account identity, as well as domestic banks credit to non-financial firms and the yield on 10-year government bonds.[5] The last two series have been at the top of the watch list of policymakers and analysts, especially for peripheral countries, since the onset of the financial crisis, when domestic credit conditions deteriorated markedly and

[3] As argued in Sect. 7.2, these VARs are likely to be affected by many shortcomings given our set-up. For this reason, the emphasis here is not on inference, but instead on the insights that can be gained in terms of model specification. The implicit assumption is that, while inference changes depending on the methodology, the dynamic relationships between variables captured by the system of VAR equations remain stable. The additional advantage is to work with a computationally lighter version of the model.

[4] We do not allow for feedback from selected endogenous variables to the debt level. Research based on US data did not find remarkable differences for the dynamics of macroeconomic variables other than the debt itself (Favero and Giavazzi 2007). Using annual data from 1970, Nickel and Tudyka (2013) show that the level of debt matters for the effects of fiscal stimulus policies in a group of European countries. Our sample is, however, much shorter and throughout this period no country experienced large swings in its stock of debt. Also, interest rates have been converging along a downward trend and the monetization of debt through inflation has not been an option during at least half of our sample period as the creation of money was centralized and separated from national government authorities. In this scenario, it is unlikely that the preferences of domestic policymakers were greatly concerned with debt stabilization. Some of these conditions changed from 2008 onward. So, as a robustness exercise, we identify shocks also imposing a mean reverting process on the dynamics of debt: differences are negligible.

[5] Due to the short sample available for Greece, the large VAR runs into stability issues when estimated using OLS. To circumvent this problem, instead of adding a third round of series, we substitute the latter to the set of labor market variables used in the medium sized VAR model.

doubts on the solvency of national governments demanded higher returns for holding their debt. As fiscal policy instruments were heavily called into question, through either automatic stabilizers or discretionary programs of stimulus first and austerity later, their interaction with the former becomes of particular interest in the last portion of the sample.

The VAR specification also features four exogenous variables that are intended to control for developments in the US- and EU-wide business cycle and monetary policy stance: the US and Euro-area output, and the t-bill and Eonia interest rates. The lag length is set to one, which is sufficient to whiten the residuals from autocorrelation.

The visual inspection of the sequence of orthogonalized residuals for government consumption and investment, for each of the countries in our dataset in the three different VAR models that we described above, reveals the following. The innovations for both government consumption and investment appear to be broadly consistent across the three different models. Therefore, it is unlikely that an econometrician running any of these would arrive at antithetical conclusions. However, these preliminary tests indicate that the small VAR may sometimes produce results distant from those obtained from the two alternatives. A rationale for the observed differences may be that the small VAR misses some relevant information for the correct identification of the innovations. As a result, the residuals absorb spurious fluctuations that are, instead, filtered out in the two bigger models.

For this reason we decided to leave the small VAR model aside, and to adopt the intermediate model as our benchmark. In turn, we keep the large VAR for robustness.

Throughout the analysis, the system of equations characterizing our VAR will remain the same. This choice is consistent with the definition of the VAR model as a self-contained system of endogenous equations, whereby dropping one or more series for the purpose of a given exercise actually alters the definition of the stylized economy and impinges on the theoretical foundations for comparability of the results. One may argue that, as far as inference is not affected, these details can be overlooked. However, Fig. 7.1 shows that it is possible to encounter cases confirming our concerns.

The diamond line plots the innovations in the government investment equation obtained from the benchmark VAR model, while the black line shows the same concept constructed from a VAR where the government investment series is tossed, depending on the identified shock. The examples of Portugal and Spain are of particular interest as they show not only that distortions can be large, but also of opposite sign: in one case the shocks are overestimated, in the other underestimated.

7.3.1 *Identification of the Shocks*

The shocks are identified using the sign restrictions approach proposed by Canova and de Nicoló (2002). For each posterior draw k, the method is based upon drawing a random normal matrix with zero mean and unit variance, performing a QR decomposition to obtain the matrix H such that $HH' = I$ and computing $Q(s, j, k)H = R(s, j, k)$, where Q is the impulse response matrix to shock s at horizon j produced by a Cholesky

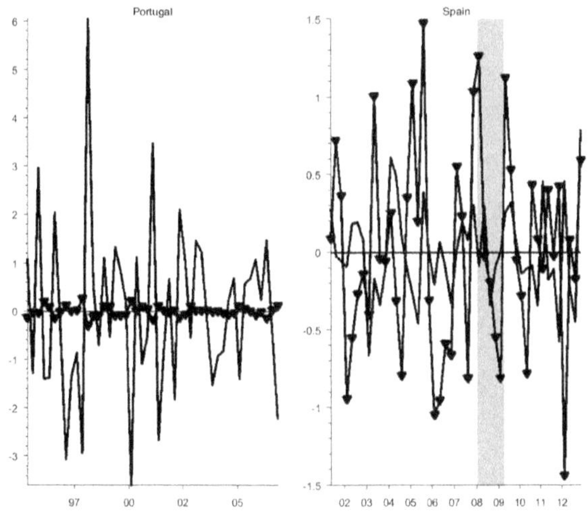

Fig. 7.1 Government innovations in the "full" or "toss" benchmark VAR. model

decomposition of the residuals covariance matrix. If the rotated impulse response matrix R satisfies the theoretical restrictions, the rotation is stored and the routine moves to the posterior draw that follows, otherwise a new rotation is generated according to the steps outlined above. Therefore, the results reflect both parameter and identification uncertainty.

The restrictions imposed to identify government spending shocks are standard and they involve a total of four instantaneous sign restrictions: (i) government consumption, or investment, declines; (ii) government revenues are non-positive; (iii) deficit declines; (iv) output declines. We consider only contemporaneous restrictions since theory typically provides robust restrictions for only a limited number of periods (Canova and Paustian 2011).

When fiscal policy shocks are the object of interest, this approach avoids most of the shortcomings affecting identification schemes based on a triangular decomposition of the covariance matrix. In fact, since all variables are endogenous, there is no need to impose exogeneity of some with respect to others (Blanchard and Perotti 2002). Also, the identification does not rely on time lags between approval and implementation of a policy decision, therefore concerns regarding the predictability of fiscal innovations are ruled out (Ramey 2011).

The output and unemployment multipliers on impact are computed as the change in either one or the other series for a 1% change in government spending. The cumulative multipliers are constructed in a similar way, except that the changes are summed over the impulse response function horizon, which is sixteen quarters.

Table 7.1 Unemployment multipliers

	Impact multiplier		Cumulative multiplier	
	G consumption	G investment	G consumption	G investment
Average	1.20	1.06	1.87	17.82
	(−1.99,3.84)	(0.11,1.99)	(−4.87,9.15)	(4.85,55.78)
Austria	−1.01	0.30	−7.13	2.34
	(−5.28,3.42)	(−0.13,1.06)	(−12.49,9.63)	(0.76,4.39)
France	0.41	0.14	0.01	1.50
	(−4.88,8.43)	(−2.13,3.04)	(−7.54,17.24)	(−3.04,8.83)
Germany	3.85	0.81	7.51	2.71
	(−0.06,7.55)	(−0.02,1.46)	(−0.55,21.46)	(0.75,4.80)
Netherlands	−2.24	0.54	−5.03	3.65
	(−4.26,0.80)	(−0.27,1.19)	(−9.16,1.60)	(1.07,6.69)
Greece	1.17	1.80	1.40	5.67
	(−1.19,2.91)	(−0.22,3.77)	(−3.73,6.38)	(0.86,12.36)
Italy	1.20	0.68	2.82	2.89
	(−0.19,2.51)	(−0.28,1.76)	(−0.77,7.17)	(0.30,6.39)
Portugal	5.26	1.34	7.90	3.53
	(2.94,10.50)	(0.20,2.52)	(2.47,18.77)	(0.99,7.07)
Spain	1.29	5.05	−3.99	8.52
	(−7.52,11.91)	(1.30,10.38)	(−17.42,27.39)	(2.65,20.86)

Note Impact multipliers are constructed as the value at time zero of the unemployment rate impulse response divided by the value at time zero of the government spending shock. Cumulative multipliers are constructed as the sum over time of the value of the unemployment rate impulse response divided by the sum over time of the value of the government spending shock. In parenthesis are 68% posterior credible intervals

7.4 The Results

7.4.1 The Labor Market Outcomes

A discussion of the labor market outcomes of fiscal policy shocks can be organized around a few key results.

First, the unemployment responses are heterogeneous across countries: the response of unemployment can take on different signs and varies substantially in magnitude across countries. As Table 7.1 shows, unemployment falls in Austria in response to a contractionary government consumption shock, and the same is true in Portugal for both government consumption and investment shocks.

While these numbers are not statistically significant on impact, Fig. 7.2 shows that the impulse responses become significant over time. Instead, unemployment increases after negative fiscal shocks in all other cases. The magnitude of the unemployment responses, however, varies substantially from one country to another.

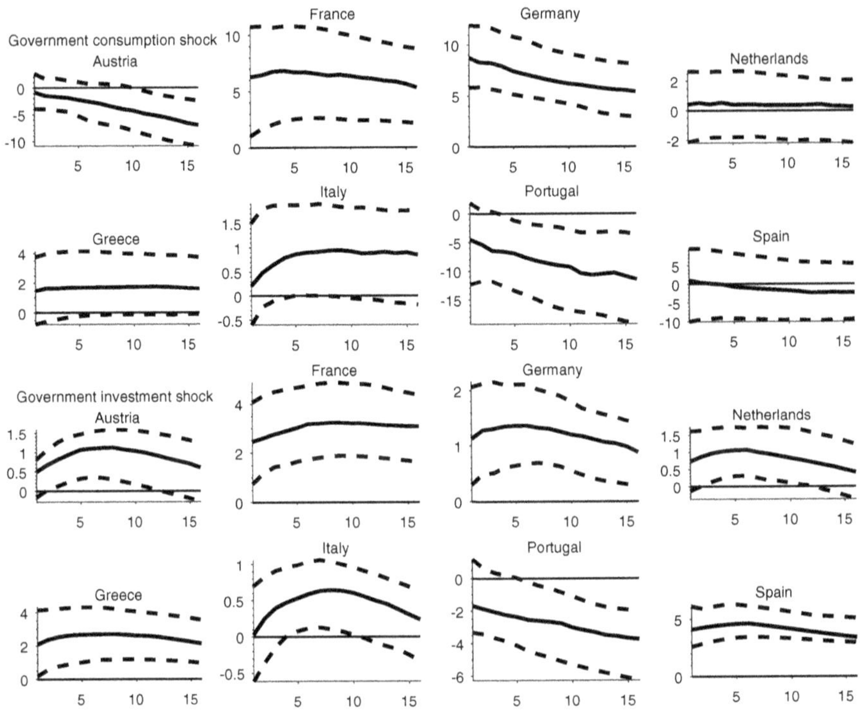

Fig. 7.2 Contractionary government spending shocks: country-specific unemployment. *Note* Dotted line: 68% confidence bands

As cross-country heterogeneity is also observed using a sample that includes the last six years, the different country-specific elasticities of the unemployment rate to fiscal shocks are likely attributable to structural factors of the Euro-area economies, rather than the adverse economic cycle that prevailed recently and affected some countries more than others.

The heterogeneity that we observe does not seem to occur at random. Some cases in particular deserve a few words.

Spain, where ambitious public infrastructure and housing plans have been implemented since the late 1990s, scores the highest unemployment multiplier to government investment shock.[6]

And Germany has the largest unemployment multiplier in response to innovations in government consumption. This evidence squares well with the reform efforts undertaken by German policymakers undertook for more than a decade, and that led to a new system of industrial relations, wage negotiations and legislative framework.[7]

[6]The major ones have been Plan Estatal de Vivienda y Suelo 1999–2001, 2002–2005, 2006–2008, and the Plan de Infrastructuras, Transporte y Vivienda 2012–2024.

[7]See Krebs and Scheffel (2013) and Dustmann et al. (2014) for a discussion.

Therefore, while the link between jobs and growth varies remarkably across countries, a point also raised in IMF (2014), dedicated policy plans and institutional reforms can help to foster the link between fiscal policy and labor markets.

Second comes the evidence on the participation rate, which is usually regarded as an important indicator of labor market conditions. In fact, it is a proxy for the available human capital stock, therefore higher participation rates are usually seen as a positive signal for the long-term growth potential of a country.

Contractionary government spending cuts can affect the participation rate by reducing available income, thus forcing more households to look for jobs. In turn, participation would rise as a consequence of the negative income effect.[8] However, if the probability of finding a job exceeds the effort needed for searching, households may also decide to drop off the labor force, pushing participation down.

Both forces seem to have been at work in the Euro Area. Figure 7.3 compares the average response of the participation rate over the short sample (diamond line) to the response from a sample ending in 2012:Q4 (continuous black line).

Leaving the crisis period out, it is easy to see that the median response of the participation rate is positive. Therefore, our evidence supports the idea that the negative income effect dominates during normal times, pushing more people to join the labor force in response to government spending cuts. This is beneficial since the increase in the participation rate helps to mitigate the negative consequences of higher unemployment on the employment to population ratio.[9]

However, the response of the participation rate to government consumption shocks becomes significantly negative when the sample is extended to include the crisis period. The average result is driven by a reversal in the sign of the responses in peripheral countries - Greece, Italy and Spain - while the evidence for core countries is consistent across subsamples (see Fig. 7.4).

The geographical dichotomy is stark and in our view it can be explained by (i) peripheral Member States being more severely hit by the crisis, and (ii) the role of black markets in southern Europe.

While gauging developments in the grey economy is obviously difficult, labor market conditions in southern Europe clearly deteriorated more severely compared to core countries. In turn, this likely resulted in lower job finding rates that pushed people out of the legal labor force. The data uphold our reading. By the end of 2013, the number of discouraged workers in Italy represented 13% of the workforce, three times above the European average, while in Germany it stood to just above 1%. The black labor market also ballooned in the Euro area periphery, reaching an

[8]On this, see Campolmi et al. (2011). An alternative explanation has to do with expectations of future expansion in activity following adjustments in public spending, see Giavazzi and Pagano (1990).

[9]The employment to population ratio (EP) can be written as one minus the unemployment rate (UR) multiplied by the labor force participation rate (LFPR), that is $EP = (1 - UR) * LFPR$. When we construct a decomposition of the labor market changes by taking differences of logs, we obtain $\Delta log(EP) = -\Delta UR + \Delta log(LFPR)$, making use of the approximation that the log of $(1 - UR)$ is equal to the negative of UR.

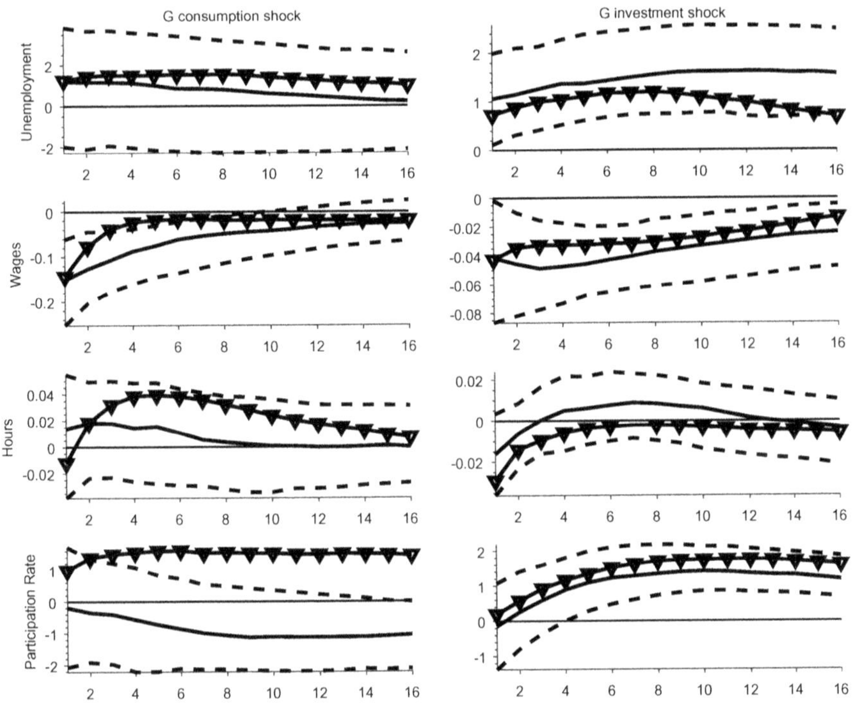

Fig. 7.3 Contractionary government spending shocks: average IRFs across samples

estimated 20% of national income in Italy, Greece and Spain according to estimates from Eurostat.

Various reasons can explain why this phenomenon is not observed in the case of government investment shocks. For example, public investments are directed to sectors with a lower proportion of women, whose incentives to leave the labor market and dedicate to family-care activities are stronger compared to men; sectors that require the acquisition of technical know-how, thereby making it more costly for workers to leave the labor force; or sectors sheltered from business cycle fluctuations, thus less prone to be affected by the discouraged worker phenomenon.

As Fig. 7.3 shows, negative fiscal shocks occurring at times of slack activity are especially adverse not only for the participation rate, but also for unemployment. Leaving the crisis period out, the median jump of unemployment after a government investment shock is about one third less on impact and 70% smaller four years later compared to the baseline.

So far we have discussed aspects pertaining to the extensive margin of adjustment to fiscal shocks, i.e. the repercussions on the number of people willing to work but without a job, and on the share of the population in the labor force.

Reducing the amount of hours worked per employee or lowering wages, while minimizing the number of layoffs, is, in principle, an alternative strategy to respond

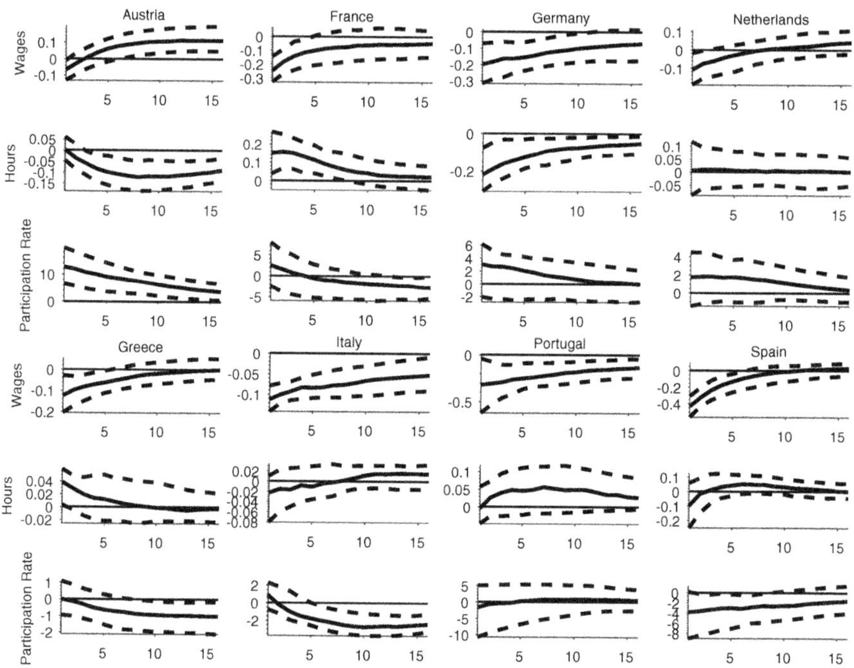

Fig. 7.4 Contractionary government consumption shocks: country-specific labor market variables

to shortages in aggregate demand. Responsiveness of hours and wages to economic conditions is usually regarded as highly desirable: it helps to mitigate the rise in unemployment which in turn allows firms to be ready to expand production quickly when the recovery is established.

According to our evidence, however, these mechanisms do not yet seem to be operative in Euro-area countries, particularly in the periphery.

The median average response of hours worked displayed in Fig. 7.3 is not statistically significant at all horizons and is quantitatively small compared to the change in unemployment. The country responses shown in Fig. 7.4 reveal that hours worked react to government consumption shocks somewhat more noticeably in Austria, France and Germany. Instead, they are never significant in the periphery, where labor markets are less flexible (Fig. 7.5).

Real wages fall in response to both government consumption and investment shocks.[10] The median decline following a government consumption innovation is approximately three times as large as the one observed after an investment shock. This is in part explained by the fact that salaries of public employees enter into government consumption data. In part, there may also be signaling effects, meaning

[10]This finding is consistent with most studies that employ VAR techniques and consumption - instead of product - wages definition.

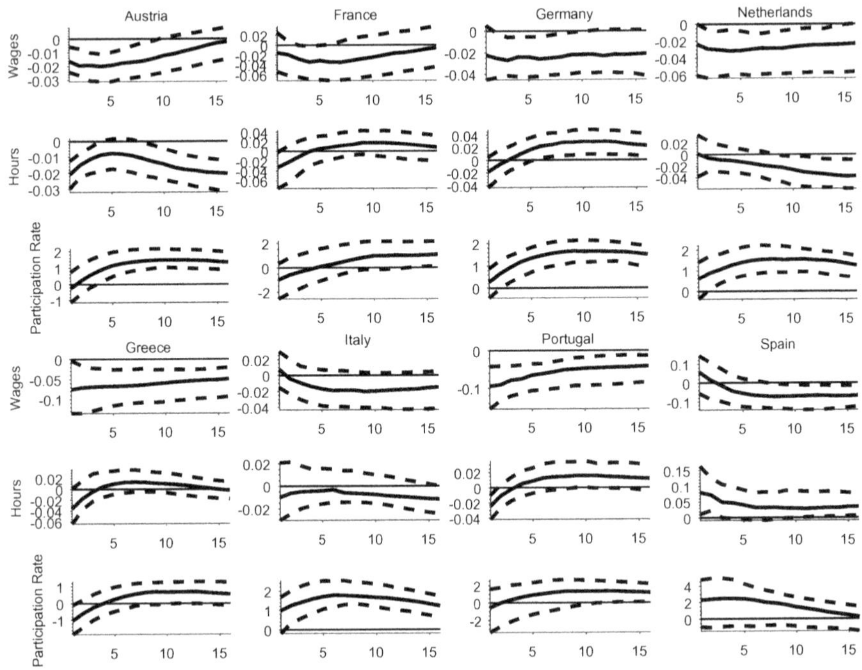

Fig. 7.5 Contractionary government investment shocks: country-specific labor market variables

that when the government reduces public salaries (by wage freezes or cuts) the private sector follows as well.

7.4.2 *Allocative Effects Across Sectors*

The allocation of government spending is usually directed to a few sectors of activity where the government is the largest buyer or the main provider of services. This raises a concern about whether the results described in the previous paragraph are representative of the dynamics across sectors, or else aggregate figures hide remarkable differences.

To shed light in this direction we construct the IRFs of the employment rate by sector of activity in each of the countries in our dataset and compare the latter with the country-specific IRFs obtained from aggregate data. By doing so, we can check how close the sectoral IRFs are compared to the aggregate. The sectors are: (i) agriculture, forestry and fishing; (ii) industry (except construction); (iii) manufacturing; (iv) construction; (v) financial and insurance; (vi) real estate; (vii) public administration.

The focus on employment is motivated by the fact that employment numbers are the only labor market indicators available at the sectoral level for European countries. Employment is not among the observables used to estimate our benchmark VAR models. However, we can use the equivalence $ER = (1 - \frac{UR}{100})LFPR$ to back out the employment rate (ER) from the unemployment rate (UR) and the participation rate ($LFPR$), which are included in our model.

The sectoral IRFs are obtained, first, by estimating a distributed lag model

$$y_t = \alpha_1^s x_t^s + \alpha_2^s x_{t-1}^s + \cdots + \alpha_n^s x_{t-n}^s \tag{7.23}$$

where the dependent variable y_t is the total employment rate and the explanatory variables x^s are the contemporaneous and lagged values of employment rates by sector of activity s. We use a relatively large number of lags, $n = 20$, because employment series are extremely persistent. We take the resulting coefficients as a reduced form representation of the relationship between employment in the aggregate and at the sectoral level. Next, we use the estimated sectoral coefficients to back out the sectoral impulse response function according to the formula

$$irf_t^s = \beta_1 irf_t + \beta_2 irf_{t-1} \tag{7.24}$$

where irf_t^s denotes the sectoral impulse response function of the employment rate at time t, irf_t without the sectoral subscript s identifies the aggregate one and $t = 2, \ldots, 16$ is the chosen length of the impulse response interval. The coefficient β_1 is the average of the α^s for the first ten periods, β^2 for the last ten. We experimented with alternatives, such as the sum or the median and splitting the time unevenly, but the overall conclusions did not change. Finally, in (7.24) we use only one lag to be in line with the formulation of the panel VAR used in estimation.

Tables 7.2 and 7.3 report the results for the government consumption and investment shocks respectively. The top half of the table presents the distance between aggregate and sectoral IRFs on impact; the bottom half shows the cumulative distance which is constructed as the sum of the distance at every t.[11]

Sectoral differences are more common in response to government investment shocks and in core Euro-area countries. Italy is the only one in the pool of peripheral economies to display significant variations in the dynamics across sectors.

Shocks in industry, manufacturing and construction have a similar magnitude on impact, with the sole exceptions of the industry sector in Netherlands and the manufacturing and construction sectors in France.

[11]From the numbers in the tables, one cannot distinguish whether the employment rate IRFs are positive or negative, but can only see if the sectoral IRFs are comparatively bigger or smaller than the aggregate IRFs. Positive numbers mean that the sectoral IRFs react more, either more positively or more negatively. Negative numbers mean that the response of the sectoral IRFs is more muted.

Table 7.2 Government consumption shock, employment rate by sector of activity: distance from aggregate

	Impact distance						
	Agriculture	Industry	Manufacturing	Construction	Financial	Real estate	Public administration
Austria	17.21*	−4.86	−4.51	5.41	25.17*	79.43*	−6.41*
France	1.58	2.55	4.77*	7.54*	10.89*	20.35*	−0.90
Germany	13.15*	−1.22	−1.13	1.68	5.74*	21.01*	−1.37
Netherlands	1.60	−0.99	−0.68	1.08	3.75*	19.30*	−1.16
Greece	0.01	−0.05	−0.04	−0.00	0.75	15.76*	−0.06
Italy	3.87*	0.62	0.67	−0.12	1.82	20.80*	−0.08
Portugal	0.67	0.69	0.68	0.07	3.55	11.72*	−0.67
Spain	2.07	−1.39	−1.16	−0.71	13.92*	33.08*	−1.53
	Cumulative Distance						
Austria	144.17*	−44.12	−40.20	46.52	229.31*	723.13*	−57.22
France	0.78	36.84*	63.05*	48.45*	51.15	197.38*	−16.10
Germany	81.72*	−6.98	−6.52	10.37	38.36*	133.68*	−8.32
Netherlands	30.88*	−4.52	−3.13	12.58	36.48*	185.47*	−11.10
Greece	−1.37	−2.16	−0.92	2.82	43.28*	1190.42*	−6.03
Italy	76.01*	−18.68	−18.02	9.84	81.87*	756.42*	−14.32
Portugal	−2.19	−5.29	−5.00	−0.78	33.32	113.00*	−4.26
Spain	23.94	−14.62	−12.27	−7.50	151.88*	357.72*	−18.63

Note The impact distance is constructed as the difference between the sectoral and the median aggregate employment rate IRFs to a government consumption shock in the first quarter. The cumulative distance is constructed as the sum over sixteen quarters of the difference between the sectoral and the median aggregate employment rate IRFs. Asterisks mean that the difference is significant at 68% level. Agriculture includes also forestry and fishing; industry excludes construction; financial includes insurance

Shocks in manufacturing die out more quickly in France, Germany and Italy; this is also the case for the industry sector in France, Germany, Netherlands and Italy. The dynamics are instead more persistent in the construction sector in Germany and Netherlands. Similar patterns are observed in the public administration sector: while the difference on impact is never significant, sectoral IRFs in Austria, Germany, Netherlands and Italy die out sooner.

The agricultural, real estate and financial sectors are very idiosyncratic. Here, differences with respect to aggregate are quantitatively large; occur both for government consumption and investment shocks; last over all horizons; and are positive, indicating that the shocks take longer to vanish compared to the aggregate case.

However, the tiny employment numbers of these sectors (below 4% of the labor force) make the economic impact of such big differences negligible, and susceptible to measurement and specification error.

Table 7.3 Government investment shock, employment rate by sector of activity: distance from aggregate

	Agriculture	Industry	Manufacturing	Construction	Financial	Real estate	Public administration
	Impact distance						
Austria	2.31*	−0.04	−0.18	0.52	0.13	0.47	−0.23
France	0.77	1.36	2.46*	3.62*	4.89*	8.07*	−0.30
Germany	3.97*	−0.64	−0.58	0.54	0.48	4.89*	−0.50
Netherlands	−1.01*	−1.10*	−0.75	0.30	1.87*	9.92*	−0.60
Greece	−0.15	−0.01	0.07	0.29	0.85*	45.28*	−0.33
Italy	3.44*	−0.85	−0.83	0.36	2.78*	31.92*	−0.56
Portugal	0.53	0.69	0.67	0.08	0.69	2.13	0.23
Spain	0.71	−1.02	−0.84	−0.52	8.11*	20.47*	−0.17
	Cumulative Distance						
Austria	36.97*	−7.11	−7.37	10.49	36.28*	114.85*	−10.33*
France	−2.39	−10.42*	−14.47*	−6.63*	10.85	84.73*	−7.04
Germany	114.52*	−12.87*	−11.87*	14.94*	39.54*	170.74*	−12.68*
Netherlands	18.23*	−11.00*	−7.54	12.14*	41.93*	215.82*	−12.98*
Greece	−1.02	−1.28	−0.44	2.07	26.62*	762.91*	−4.01
Italy	48.21*	−13.46*	−12.94*	7.54	61.79*	516.89*	−10.43*
Portugal	−5.25	−11.04	−10.50	−1.59	55.90*	190.13*	−6.30
Spain	15.60	−7.57	−6.40	−3.90	86.90*	200.09*	−13.42

Note The impact distance is constructed as the difference between the sectoral and the median aggregate employment rate IRFs to a government investment shock in the first quarter. The cumulative distance is constructed as the sum over sixteen quarters of the difference between the sectoral and the median aggregate employment rate IRFs. Asterisks mean that the difference is significant at 68% level. Agriculture includes also forestry and fishing; industry excludes construction; financial includes insurance

7.4.3 Spending Reversals

Fiscal stimulus packages are, by their very nature, temporary. Once the welfare policy objectives have been obtained or the economic fundamentals restored, governments withdraw the spending increases and tax rebates that were initially voted. Sometimes, expansionary fiscal measures are not only in place for a limited amount of time but are also undone at a later stage to meet binding fiscal constraints, like deficit rules and debt ceiling, or to fulfill the political agenda of the ruling party. For example, as discussed in the introduction to this paper, a number of Euro-area countries initially reacted to the crisis by passing stimulus packages, deploying automatic stabilizers and approving further selective discretionary easing. However, most of these initiatives were abandoned when national budgets seemed to go off-the-cliff and governments quickly turned to a conservative fiscal stance.[12]

[12]Spending reversals can apply not only to selected policy initiatives, but more generally to positive government spending innovations. Fitting a VAR model to US data, Corsetti et al. (2012) show that

Fiscal expansions with spending reversals are more cost effective, as the debt overhang is necessarily reduced (OECD 2009). Moreover, a credible commitment to compensate the increase in spending - or the drop in revenues - can help to limit interest rates hikes and thus the cost of borrowing for countries starting from high levels of debt.

If the budgetary implications of spending reversals are fairly straightforward, their real effects are more uncertain. A major concern is whether the beneficial effects of the fiscal stimulus are long-lasting, or else if they vanish as soon as the stimulus is withdrawn and the reversal kicks-in.

To measure the success of spending reversals with respect to the labor market, we choose to track the performance of the unemployment rate conditional upon two alternative spending plans. The baseline scenario involves a permanent increase in government spending for four quarters. The magnitude of the jump is set to one standard deviation and occurs on the last available observation of our sample, which coincides with 2012:Q4 for all countries. The reversal scenario implies that the increase in government spending lasts only for two quarters and is followed by a decrease of identical magnitude. Conditional upon these two alternative cases, we forecast the value of the unemployment rate using the estimated coefficients from the VAR model (Blake and Mumtaz 2012).

The results are reported in Table 7.4. The first column to the left reports the observed value of the unemployment rate on 2012:Q4 in each of the countries in our dataset. The remaining columns show the forecast four quarters ahead under the baseline or the reversal scenario, for both an expansion in government consumption and government investment.

The main point that emerges from the table is that fiscal expansions followed by spending reversals eliminate most of the benefits coming from the initial spending increase. This is especially clear when conditioning on the path of government investment. Take the case of Germany. The forecasted value of the unemployment rate drops by 53% after four quarters of higher government spending. If instead we allow for a reversal after the second quarter, the median forecast at the end of the period is 7.2%, which means 33% higher than the latest available observation. This outcome is also observed in Austria and Netherlands. In France, Italy and Portugal the projected unemployment rate declines under both scenarios, but the difference is nonetheless large.

When conditioning upon a path for government consumption the picture is less clear and blurred by larger uncertainty. The same insight that is observed in the case of government investment shocks applies to Greece, Italy and Spain. Instead, the results for Austria and Netherlands show a deterioration under the baseline and an improvement under the reversal. This is counterintuitive, however consistent with evidence of expansionary fiscal austerity (Brückner and Pappa 2012).

(Footnote 12 continued)
the trajectory of government spending after a shock falls below zero from the twelfth quarter onward and interpret this pattern as evidence of debt-stabilizing spending reversals. We do not observe any undershooting in our VAR, which may suggest that European countries did not systematically react to their debt levels, or that they did not do so sufficiently strongly over the estimation period.

Table 7.4 Conditional forecasts: unemployment rate

	2012:Q4	Government consumption		Government investment	
		Baseline	Reversal	Baseline	Reversal
Austria	4.57	9.31	−9.77	2.76	5.34
		(3.02,16.30)	(−23.96,3.05)	(2.01,3.54)	(3.50,7.35)
France	10.50	5.91	−2.71	3.51	5.59
		(−1.56,13.37)	(−21.15,17.01)	(1.60,6.53)	(−1.77,10.11)
Germany	5.40	−3.20	19.24	2.52	7.20
		(−8.81,2.15)	(7.41,31.93)	(1.59,3.32)	(5.07,9.42)
Netherlands	5.63	10.54	−11.81	1.66	9.13
		(7.09,13.83)	(−20.24,−2.39)	(0.60,2.54)	(6.57,11.74)
Greece	26.10	2.01	12.17	2.30	10.78
		(−1.68,7.08)	(−0.41,20.45)	(−0.03,4.49)	(5.39,17.82)
Italy	11.40	1.91	11.58	2.92	7.18
		(−0.86,4.42)	(4.26,19.38)	(1.73,4.23)	(4.59,10.28)
Portugal	17.03	−6.07	34.78	2.12	10.03
		(−10.95,−2.38)	(23.93,46.87)	(1.05,3.09)	(7.09,13.25)
Spain	26.13	7.20	−1.91	4.74	3.89
		(−14.31,23.15)	(−37.79,50.21)	(−0.91,10.70)	(−13.54,21.02)

Note Forecasts are conditional on an assumed path for government consumption or government investment. Under the baseline scenario government consumption (or investment) grows by one standard deviation and remains fixed at that value for four quarters. Under the reversal scenario, the positive jump during the first two quarters is followed by a reversal during the last two quarters. The table shows the initial value of the unemployment rate observed in 2012:Q4 and the forecast at the end of the fourth quarter for each case

7.5 Conclusions

In this chapter we presented empirical evidence on the link between fiscal policy and the labor markets for a group of Euro-area countries using data since the early nineties. In fact, while output multipliers have received a lot of attention in recent research, this paper shows there's a lot to learn from studying other indicators of real activity.

To start with, the link between growth and jobs may vary considerably across countries. That is, countries with similar output responses to fiscal innovations can experience very different unemployment multipliers.

The relationship between growth and jobs can be influenced by specific public spending plans and institutional reforms. Spain and Germany - one launched ambitious public investment plans in transportation and housing, the other reformed its system of labor relations - are flagship cases. Spain has a four times larger unemployment multiplier to government investment shocks with respect to Italy; and Germany has a large unemployment multiplier to government consumption shocks.

This segmentation in labor markets exposes the common currency block to risks and high adjustment costs, as individual countries respond differently to shocks.

However, our evidence shows that movements in hours worked are small and often not statistically significant, especially in peripheral countries. Wages appear to respond to cuts in government consumption, although restoring price competitiveness through lower salaries has proven politically difficult and painful when implemented.

Overall, our evidence makes a case for (i) the adoption of a coordinated agenda for labor market reforms in order to reduce heterogeneity within the Euro Area; and (ii) efforts to enhance labor hoarding practices, reduce downward wage rigidities and increase the flexibility of hours worked to labor market conditions.

Nonetheless, the large unemployment multiplier found for Spain seems to suggest that a combination of reforms and public infrastructure investment projects can strengthen the link between fiscal policy and jobs. Moreover, expanding government investments may also offer a cushion for the short-run adverse macroeconomic effects often associated with structural reforms in the labor markets.

Our results also show that the interaction of fiscal policy shocks with the state of the economy can deliver perverse effects on unemployment and the participation rate. The mechanism at work in the case of the participation rate is complex and deserves model validation. We argue that during normal times the negative income effect associated with fiscal contractions prevails and forces agents to join the labor force and look for jobs, thus participation goes up. However, since the onset of the 2007 crisis, a discouraged worker effect dominates in peripheral countries, and people quit the labor force in response to austerity in public spending.

Finally, we show that the dynamics described using aggregate data provide a good representation of the likely outcomes of government spending shocks in the public administration, manufacturing, industry and construction sectors.

References

Alexius A, Holmlund B (2007) Monetary policy and Swedish unemployment fluctuations. IZA DP No. 2933

Auerbach AJ, Gorodnichenko Y (2013) Output spillovers from fiscal policy. Am Econ Rev 103:141–146

Banbura M, Giannone D, Reichlin L (2010) Large bayesian vector auto regressions. J Appl Econom 25(1):71–92

Bermperoglou D, Pappa E, Vella E (2013) Spending-based austerity measures and their effects on output and unemployment. Mimeo

Blake A, Mumtaz H (2012) Applied bayesian econometrics for central bankers. Centre for Central Banking Studies Technical Handbook No. 4, Bank of England

Blanchard OJ, Leigh D (2013) Growth forecast errors and fiscal multipliers. Am Econ Rev 103(3):117–120

Blanchard O, Perotti R (2002) An empirical characterization of the dynamic effects of changes in government spending and taxes on output. Q J Econ 117:1329–1368

Brückner M, Pappa E (2012) Fiscal expansions, unemployment and labor force participation: theory and evidence. Int Econ Rev 53:1205–1228

Campolmi A, Faia E, Winkler R (2011) Fiscal calculus and the labor market. J Macroecon 11(1):1–25

Canova F (2005) The transmission of US shocks to latin america. J Appl Econom 20(2):229–251

Canova F, de Nicoló G (2002) Monetary disturbances matter for business fluctuations in the G-7. J Monet Econ 49(6):1131–1159
Canova F, Pappa E (2007) Price differentials in monetary unions: the role of fiscal shocks. Econ J 117:713–737
Canova F, Paustian M (2011) Business cycle measurement with some theory. J Monet Econ 58(4):345–361
Christiano L, Eichenbaum M, Rebelo S (2011) When is the government spending multiplier large? J Polit Econ 119:78–121
Ciccarelli M, Rebucci A (2006) Has the transmission mechanism of European monetary policy changed in the run-up to EMU? Eur Econ Rev 50(3):737–776
Corsetti G, Meier A, Mueller G (2012) What determines government spending multipliers? Econ. Policy 27:521–565
Davig T, Leeper EM (2011) Monetary-fiscal policy interactions and fiscal stimulus. Eur Econ Rev 55(2):211–227
Dolado JJ, Jimeno JF (1997) The causes of Spanish unemployment: a structural VAR approach. Eur Econ Rev 41(7):1281–1307
Dustmann C, Fitzenberger B, Schönberg U, Spitz-Oener A (2014) From sick man of Europe to economic superstar: Germanys resurgent economy. J Econ Perspect 1(28):167–188
Favero C, Giavazzi F (2007) Debt and the effects of fiscal policy. NBER Working Papers No. 12822
Forni M, Gambetti L, Sala L (2014) No news in business cycles. Econ J 124(581):1168–1191
Gambetti L, Pistoresi B (2004) Policy matters. The long run effects of aggregate demand and mark-up shocks on the Italian unemployment rate. Empir Econ 29(2):209–226
Gerardi K, Herkenhoff KF, Ohanian LE, Willen PS (2013) Unemployment, negative equity and strategic default. Federal Reserve Bank of Atlanta Working Paper Series No. 2013-4
Giavazzi F, Pagano M (1990) Can severe fiscal contractions be expansionary? Tales of two small European Countries. NBER Chapters NBER Macroecon Annu 1990:75–122
Guajardo J, Leigh D, Pescatori A (2011) Expansionary austerity: new international evidence. IMF Working Paper No. 11/158
IMF (2014) Fiscal multipliers: Size, determinants, and use in macroeconomic projections. Technical notes and manuals
Jarocinski M (2010) Responses to monetary policy shocks in the east and the west of Europe: a comparison. J Appl Econom 25(5):833–868
Krebs T, Scheffel M (2013) Macroeconomic evaluation of labour market reform in Germany. IMF Economic Review
Nickel C, Tudyka A (2013) Fiscal stimulus in times of high public debt: reconsidering multipliers and twin deficits. VOX, CEPRs Policy Portal
OECD (2009) The effectiveness and scope of fiscal stimulus. Economic Outlook Interim Report
Pappa E (2009) The effects of fiscal shocks on employment and the real wage. Int Econ Rev 50(1):217–244
Ramey VA (2011) Identifying government spending shocks: it's all in the timing. Q J Econ 126:1–50
Rossi B, Zubairy S (2011) What is the importance of monetary and fiscal shocks in explaining US macroeconomic fluctuations? J Money Credit Bank 43(6):1247–1270
Voth J, Ponticelli J (2012) Austerity and anarchy: budget cuts and social unrest in Europe, 1919–2008. UPF Economics Working Papers, No. 1342

Index

© Springer International Publishing AG 2018
A. Cavallo et al., *Fiscal Policies in High Debt Euro-Area Countries*,
https://doi.org/10.1007/978-3-319-70269-8

Printed by Printforce, the Netherlands